WHITTLING AND WOODCARVING

He who works with his hands is a laborer,
He who works with his hands and his head
   is an artisan,
But he who works with his hands, his head,
   and his heart is an artist.

—*Author Unknown*

FIG. 1 (next page) · Whittled white-pine head in relief, appliquéd on black-walnut panel with punched background. See Chaps. XVI, XX, and XXI particularly pages 217 and 240

WHITTLING AND

WOODCARVING

BY

E. J. TANGERMAN

DOVER PUBLICATIONS, INC.

NEW YORK

This Dover edition, first published in 1962, is an
unabridged republication of the work originally
published by Whittlesey House and the McGraw-
Hill Book Company, Inc., in 1936.

Standard Book Number: 486-20965-2

Manufactured in the United States of America
Dover Publications, Inc.
180 Varick Street
New York, N.Y. 10014

FOREWORD

MOST people have the urge to create—to make something worth while with their hands. Whittling and woodcarving satisfy that urge with a minimum of investment in time and materials. To whittle, you need only a pocketknife and the side of a discarded box. To carve, add a few chisels and a carpet-covered board for a worktable. For simple pieces, you won't need elaborate instruction—just a few pointers and suggestions.

This book is intended to supply those suggestions and to give some information usually not readily at hand. In twenty-five years of whittling and carving, I have never yet been at a loss for new things to make—my grandfathers made wooden shoes, burls and peachstone carvings, my father used the knife as a utility tool, the Boy Scouts taught me the rustic pieces of Chapter V, my friends in later years have suggested all sorts of pieces. Descriptions of all of them, and many more, are included in this book.

Don't worry about your lack of skill. You'll find that you have a surprising amount once you get at it, and a little practice will develop more. The wife of a friend, who never before had used a knife outside her kitchen, started whittling. She began with a sailorman. Her first wasn't at all bad, her second was quite creditable—and figure carving is supposed to be hardest! My son at four made practical wooden knives—although his more ambitious pieces sometimes collapsed. His mother makes buttons, linoleum blocks, model ships and so on. A banker friend makes ship models, another makes airplanes, another makes chessmen. None have had instruction—just a pointer here and there. Why not try it? You'll be surprised at the results of a bit of wood and your own imagination.

Dozens of individuals and companies have been unsparing of their time and materials in assisting in preparation of this manual.

FOREWORD

I am particularly indebted to *Popular Mechanics, Popular Science Monthly, Scouting, Everyday Science and Mechanics, Scholastic Magazine,* and *The Home Craftsman* for permission to incorporate in these pages certain portions of my own and others' articles previously published by them. Among major sources of pictures and data are Remington Arms Co., Inc., National Soap Sculpture Committee, Procter & Gamble Co., The Metropolitan Museum of Art, The American Museum of Natural History, Universal School of Handicrafts, *Oil Power,* Pan American Airways, Seamen's Church Institute, German Tourist Information Office, Cunard White Star Line, *The Art News,* H. T. Webster, *Collier's Weekly, The Chicago Tribune,* Albert Wood, Murray Russell, F. Marchello, I. K. Scott, Levi Golden, John Phillip, Annette Navin, Freda Bone, Mrs. Lewis F. Day, Capt. George Sherwood, Edward F. Drake, Robert S. Bartlett, The Grolier Society, Alfred Field & Co., American Type Founders, Inc., Monotype Co., National Geographic Society, M. W. Perinier, G. W. Stewart, Bob Davis, Cobb Shinn, and many others. Their cooperation has permitted the inclusion of many pictures.

E. J. TANGERMAN.

PORT WASHINGTON, NEW YORK,
 September, 1936.

CONTENTS

〚 ix 〛

CONTENTS

WHITTLING AND
WOODCARVING

HISTORY · *Backgrounds*

JESUS of Nazareth was *not* a carpenter; he was a woodcarver. The original Greek word that bibliophiles have interpreted as "carpenter" means "smith," an artisan. Moreover, wood was too scarce in Nazareth to permit its use for anything besides interior decoration and carving.[1]

Whittling and woodcarving have come down to us from the mists of unrecorded time. Man's first tool was probably a crude ax evolved from a sharp-edged war club; his second was the knife. He soon discovered the relative ease of forming wood, for earliest historical records already mention wood casually as the accepted carver's material. And these records are not limited to one people or continent; Asia (except Western), Africa, Australia, America, Europe, even remote islands, all provide examples. A famous one is the "Sheikh-el-Beled," carved during the ancient Egyptian Empire (2980–2475 B.C.), and preserved by Egypt's dry climate.

Four thousand—perhaps five thousand—years ago where Danzig now stands, neolithic men carved pieces of amber into the likeness of animals. In the Woldenburg district of Pomerania a man carved a representation of a horse. About 2300 B.C., a Sumerian in Mesopotamia carved a steer out of bone.

The Bible is replete with references to woodcarving. It is recorded in Genesis[2] that Rachel stole her father's images—probably wood, or she could not have carried them. Again and again there appear references to graven images,[3] to the burning of idols (only wooden ones would burn),[4] to carved images,[5] and

---

[1] William Smith, *Bible Dictionary*, 1872. Many other references are from Robert Folkestone Williams, *Historical Sketch of the Art of Sculpture in Wood*, London, 1835. [2] Gen. xxxi-19. [3] Lev. xxvi-1. Isa. xl-20, xliv-13 to 17. Jer. li-47. [4] II Kings x-26. II Chron. xv-16. [5] I Kings vi-18. II Chron. xxxiii-7, 22, xxxiv-3.

〖 3 〗

Fig. 2 · *Staircase from Cassiobury Park, Hertfordshire, a seventeenth century masterpiece by Grinling Gibbons. (Owned by Metropolitan Museum of Art. Photograph courtesy The Art News.) (See page 222.)*

to workers in wood and timber.[6] Images were of chittim wood (a cedar or boxwood),[7] cedar, oak, ebony, fir, and cypress.

The Lord told Moses that Bezaleel knew how to carve timber,[8] so Moses chose him to supervise construction of his tabernacle. Nebuchadnezzar had a mulberry coffin in ancient Babylon.

Later Solomon built a temple, "And the cedar of the house within was carved with knops and open flowers . . . and he carved all the walls of the house round about with carved figures of cherubims and palm trees and open flowers within and without. . . ."[9] The "almug" which Solomon imported for pillars in his own house and for musical instruments is really algum or fragrant sandalwood.[10]

Ebony had a particularly colorful history in biblical times. It was brought to Tyre before 1000 B.C.[11] It was also used by the ancient kings of India for scepters, images, and drinking cups (the latter because it was believed proof against poison).[12] The Ethiopians sent a tribute of 200 logs every three years to Persia.[13] Pliny called it equally durable with cypress and cedar.[14] The ancients believed the tree produced neither leaves nor fruit and was never found exposed to the sun.[15]

In Greece, woodcarving was the earliest form of archaic sculpture. Phidias and other great Greek artists made woodcarvings. Pausanias, Lucian, Livy, and Arrian wrote that the most celebrated Grecian sculptors, particularly during the Age of Pericles (480–400 B.C.) worked in ivory, gold, cedar, and ebony. Phidias' statue of Jupiter at Olympia was wood, as were many statues in Rome, Pompeii, Athens, and Corinth.

At the time when Jesus was a boy in Nazareth, a woodcarver had these tools: rule, measuring line, compasses, plane or other smoothing instrument, saw, hatchet, knife, awl, hone, drill, mallet, chisels. Fifteen hundred years earlier in Egypt a woodcarver's chest of tools (unearthed recently) contained chisels with wooden handles, a saw, drill bow and spindle, rasp, plummet (our

[6] Exod. xxxi–1 to 5, xxxii. I Chron. xxii–15. II Chron. ii–14. [7] Gen. x–4. I Chron. i–7. Ezra xxvii–6. [8] Exod. xxxi–1 to 5. [9] I Kings vi–18, 29. [10] I Kings x–12. II Chron. ix–10. [11] Exod. xxvii–15. [12] Solinus, *Polyhistory*, Paris 1621. [13] Herodotus, iii–97. [14] *Natural History*, xii–9, xvi–79. [15] Southey, *Thalaba*, i–22.

plumb bob), an oilstone, and a horn for carrying oil for the stone. And that was 3,400 years ago, and more!

Woodcarving flourished for a century or two after Christ, producing such works as the wooden doors of the Santa Sabina at Rome, then went into a slow decline from which it did not emerge for several centuries. But by the ninth century, Scandinavian carvers were doing excellent work, using flat, interlaced scroll and similar patterns suitable to soft wood. In the meantime India, China, Persia, and Asia Minor had kept right on carving. Savages throughout the world were already doing chip carving of the same sort that Captain Cook found on his visits to the South Seas a hundred years ago.

All through Northern Europe, the art gradually revived. By the eleventh century, woodcarving again was becoming common. First it appeared in churches, then in homes. Germany in particular encouraged carvers; in fact, to such an extent that during the fifteenth and sixteenth centuries wood sculpture influenced stone sculpture, sculptors in stone attempting to imitate the wonderful intricacy and delicacy that woodcarvers of that day were obtaining. All through Königsberg, Cologne, Munich, Vienna, Mannheim, Berlin, Nuremberg,

[[5]]

Fig. 3 (Top) · Casket in pear, holly, or box. Flemish, late sixteenth century. Fig. 4 · Coat of Arms of Geo. I by Gibbons. Fig. 5 (Bottom) · Arms of Viscount Scudamore, probably by Gibbons. (These photos courtesy Metropolitan Museum of Art)

Gotha, Dresden, and the other ancient cities, woodcarvings (in oak and chestnut principally) figured prominently in decoration.

Among the early German artists, Tilmann Riemenschneider (1460–1531) was one of the greatest. Born in the Harz Mountains, he went to Würzburg in 1483. Hence most of his works are in the valley of the Tauber, although later ones were sold to the far corners of Europe. From a definite Gothic style, he passed under Italian and French influence, then back into a distinctive Renaissance all his own. Among his most famous preserved works is the "Blood Altar" in Jacob's church, Rothenburg.

Other famous German wood sculptors of this period were Wohlgemuth, Veit Stoss, Pacher, Multscher, Brüggemann, and Borman. Albrecht Dürer, preeminent German artist, gained his fame from his woodcarvings.

England learned woodcarving from Germany, in fact, imported her earliest carvings from there. Also in Holland and Belgium the art flourished. Flemish oak carvings were known throughout Europe. The first statue of Erasmus, erected in Rotterdam in 1540, was wood. In St. Mark's, Venice, Albert Brugle, a Fleming, sculpt walnut bas-reliefs of the life of St. Benedict in 1633.

⟦6⟧

FIG. 6 (TOP) · *The Blood Altar in Jacob's Church, Rothenburg, Germany, by Tilmann Riemenschneider.* FIG. 7 (BOTTOM) · *A detail of the middle section of the altar.* (Photographs courtesy German Tourist Information Office, N. Y.)

In England the Collegiate Church of St. Stephen, West-minster, the Henry VII Chapel of Westminster Abbey, the cathedrals of Durham, Exeter, Gloucester, Canterbury, and York were all decorated with wood sculptures. English carving was already of fine quality in the time of Richard II (1377–1399), though it reached its zenith during the reign of Elizabeth.

Probably the greatest of all woodcarvers was Grinling Gibbons. Born in 1648, he was of part English and part Dutch descent. Charles II employed him to carve decorations for public buildings, and he also had many private commissions. He worked for Sir Christopher Wren, the great English architect, and also did carvings in Canterbury Cathedral, Windsor Castle, and Cambridge University. He excelled particularly in flowers and foliage, achieving astonishing delicacy with great spirit and verve. Horace Walpole said of him, "There is no instance of a man before Gibbons who gave to wood the loose and airy lightness of flowers, and chained together the various productions of the elements with a free disorder, natural to each species." John Evelyn and Samuel Pepys were among Gibbons's close friends.

As a young man, Gibbons carved over a doorway a pot of flowers which was so delicate that its elements shook when coaches passed in the street. He also made the archbishop's throne at Canterbury and pieces in St. Paul's, St. James's, All-hallows, Kensington, etc. So famous did he become that George I made him master carver in 1714, and he found it necessary to employ many woodcarvers to carry out his designs. Most wonderful of his human figures was a copy of Tintoretto's great picture "The Crucifixion" at Venice, in which there were over 100 figures. He died in 1721.

There were also many famous French and Italian woodcarvers. Among great French woodcarvings were those in Les Célestins, Paris, the carved walnut gates of the Cathedral at Aix, the decorations of the interior of the Sainte-Chapelle de Vincennes, and the choir of the Abbaye de Royamont. Houses in Rouen had particularly elaborate carvings, especially chimneypieces.

Spain and Portugal also produced some good work, at first Moorish, then French, then Italian in influence. In Italy real perfection in carving was attained, largely through the aid of the Church of Rome. Brunelleschi made a splendid choir for the Campanello del Duomo early in the fifteenth century (it was replaced by a much inferior piece in 1547). Benedetto da Majano was another celebrated woodcarver of the time.

Michelangelo himself was a woodcarver as well as a sculptor and muralist. He made a wooden crucifix for the Monastery of San Spirito about 1493, a cornice for the Farnese Palace, and many other pieces in wood. Donatello sculpt a Crucifixion in wood for the chapel of the Church of Santa Croce, Florence, also. Other famous Italians include Jacopo Tatti (1514), Francesco of Volterra, Domenico Tibaldi (mid-sixteenth), Giovanni Fiammingo.

At the time America was settled, woodcarving was already fighting against machine production. Most woodcarving here was done by visiting artists or artisans. Some of the earlier mansions, however, had elaborate work done, some of it shown later in this book.

For the past one or two hundred years, woodcarving has survived principally in flat carving and furniture decoration, the training and skill being passed down from father to son, or taught in isolated schools. In 1835, some 2,000 families in Bavaria were woodcarvers. Oberammergau, Bavaria, still has over 1,000 wood sculptors, and an extensive school. Outside of isolated schools and craftsmen, however, it was not until recently that wood-carving received much notice. The art is so old, has been so generally accepted, that even two hundred years ago it was considered an artisan's work, not an artist's. Most sculptors even today feel that they must use stone to express the value of their work and to obtain permanence, though certain things are much better done in wood.

The modern desire to sell things by the yard has produced woodworking machines which can imitate carving. True wood-carving is slow work and, judged by modern standards, expensive. Only appreciation of the individuality of handwork, the beauty of original design, and the sheer joy of creation have kept it alive.

Paradoxically, however, furniture making has been one of the factors that has kept woodcarving (and woodcarvers) alive. The high-relief caryatids and acanthus leaves of the Italian Renaissance (1450–1585) were mirrored in the elaborate cupboard and armoire carving of the French (1483–1589), the Spanish, and the English. Gradually, exuberant carving of the Elizabethan Age was tamed during the Jacobean, and baroque carving and inlay came in. From 1660 to 1685, baroque was clear and incisive. The French rococo of the time of Louis XV was modified in England by Thomas Chippendale, then still further modified by Robert Adam, Thomas Sheraton, and George Hepplewhite, all neoclassic English carvers who also abandoned Chippendale's deeper, heavier carving. Meanwhile in America there was Duncan Phyfe, a follower of the simple Directoire style of France which appeared between Louis XVI and the Empire period with its elaborate ormolu (brass decoration on mahogany). Phyfe it was who paid ship captains a premium to bring him fine mahogany logs, which they brought back to America as ballast.

Caricatures in wood, which many people believe fairly modern, are really centuries old. Savages have caricatured their chiefs in dolls, early woodcarvers carved cartoons *under* the seats of pews in Worcester and Ely cathedrals and the Priory Church of St. Malvern in England, as well as formal carvings on top. Historians explain that the obscene caricatures were the political cartoons of their day, executed by woodcarvers for various sects or religious orders to depict rival orders in obscene activities, an outgrowth of the intense rivalry of the times.

Fig. 8 · *A French sixteenth-century Renaissance door panel. (Photograph courtesy Metropolitan Museum of Art)*

[9]

Whittling, as such, has practically no written history. It is a natural outgrowth of man's desire to ornament everything he handles, from the Polynesian savage's paddle to the American Indian's fishhook. A child instinctively begins to whittle patterns on bark; a savage anywhere in the world whittles out a crude image of what he believes his gods look like. Knives were of course used by earliest woodcarvers and still are used today, although some woodcarvers feel it is a weakness to mention it. The knife is a universal tool probably more flexible in cutting abilities than any other, although it meets limitations in hard-to-get-at places and in certain kinds of flat work. Yet use of the knife is a practical art and a logical step toward use of more specialized tools.

The term "whittling" early came to mean that particular branch of carving with a knife that deals with such stunts as the fan, the ball-in-a-cage, and the chain. Sailors, woodsmen, and farmers, habitual knife carriers, learned the versatility of the knife and adapted it to whole groups of specialized pieces, shown in the first chapters of this book. The Boy and Girl Scouts and similar groups have picked up and carried on this tradition, particularly in rustic work. Combined, they are helping whittling, or "knife-craft," to live down the bad name it received from those of its exponents who elected the front of the village store for their activities, particularly those exponents who merely whittled pieces of the box they were sitting on and produced only tall stories and shavings. The decline of the village store, increasing use of cardboard cartons, and the modern belief that a man can sit down without giving the appearance of doing anything have also helped to eliminate shaving makers.

Whittling has had its famous exponents too, although they are not celebrated in history for that trait. Abraham Lincoln was a whittler, Calvin Coolidge was a whittler, Will Rogers was a whittler—so was many another. And their grandsons and granddaughters are learning that the person who handles a knife well can handle other tools better and can appreciate true art and craftsmanship in whatever guise it appears.

So you see, even if you are a beginner at woodcarving and whittling, you have nothing to be ashamed of. You have a proud tradition of which to prove worthy, generation after generation of artists and craftsmen each contributing his part to the beautiful things of the world. Try to do nearly as well as they.

Remember, when you cut a piece of wood, that you can make from it only what you can see in it. If you have no clear-cut mental picture of what you are making, you will almost certainly be disappointed in your results.

Remember also that the piece you are cutting has probably lived longer than will anything you can make of it; hence treat it with respect. The pine you whittle is 20 to 30 years old, fir 80 to 100, teak 200 or 300, English oak 400, redwood possibly a thousand years old or more. Try always to make your carving worthy of the wood. Then, if you fail, you can at least have the satisfaction of having tried—and of having had a lot of fun.

Fig. 9 · *In the State Carving School at Oberammergau, Germany. This Bavarian town is famous for carvings, particularly of religious subjects. (Courtesy German Tourist Information Office, N. Y.)*

FIG. 10 · *Locust tree and wood. (Courtesy American Museum of Natural History)*

CHAPTER I

WOODS · *Which and Where*

"STOUT as oak," "solid to the core," "wooden ships and iron men," "black as ebony"—all everyday phrases, all based on that universal material—wood. So common it is, in fact, that we fail to realize how necessary it is to our daily lives. Few of us realize its potentialities, fewer still its infinite variety. But the whittler and the woodcarver must realize both, lest they work in vain, for wrong wood, poor or improper in structure or appearance, can ruin more carving than lack of skill.

Selection of the proper wood for carving involves no problem for the beginner. White pine among softwoods, basswood, black walnut and mahogany among hardwoods, are commonly available in good widths at reasonable prices. They cut easily, are straight-grained, are free from knots, and finish well. At a lumberyard, ask for "northern white pine," which is a better, less resinous, slower growing wood than southern pine.

The advanced carver must consider these factors: type of design, woods available, place and character of use, "style" of design.

Is the piece or design simple or complicated? Does it require "figure" (grain pattern) to decorate flat surfaces? Is it a delicate, intricate piece, or is it large, bold, and rugged? A simple and large piece calls for a fairly open-grained wood such as walnut, oak, mahogany, chestnut, or basswood. None of these is likely to split along a sharp-cut edge, and all accentuate ruggedness. A delicate piece with complicated parts requires a close-grained wood that supports detail better, such as ebony, box, lime, or apple. For figure, walnut, chestnut, quarter-sawed oak, or one of the rare woods available as lumber is required. ("Quarter-sawed" or "comb-grained" is used to describe hardwoods sawed so the annual rings run at 45 degrees or more with the wide faces. In softwoods, the terms are "edge-grained" or "rift-sawed." Usually lumber is "flat grain" or "plain-sawed.")

If your selection of woods is limited by your location or your pocketbook, the second factor becomes important. In ancient Egypt you would have used sycamore or cedar, in Hindustan sandalwood, in Switzerland satinwood, because in those countries those woods were most readily available. If you have a rare-wood or woodcarver's supply company near by, or the address of a reliable one (national popular mechanical, scientific, and homecraft magazines carry their advertising), you are fortunate, for then the factor of availability enters only in whether or not the wood you prefer to use is available in the sizes you require.

Place and character of use introduce these questions: Is the carving to be handled or used, or is it purely decorative? If it is to be handled, must it be flexed or bent? Is it indoors or outdoors, and how is it to be finished? The table at the end of this chapter will give you many of the answers offhand. Oak is the standard material to withstand weathering and decay, but many other woods will stand up also with proper protection—check the *Durability* column in the table. If the piece is to be flexed or bent, you must consider the data in the column on *Elasticity*. Hard-

⟦ 13 ⟧

FIG. 11 · *"Believe it or knot"*— *an unusual knot in a Pondosa pine board sawed by Potlach (Idaho) Lumber Co.*

ness is an important element of wear resistance; another major element is finish. If the piece is to be painted, wear resistance is not so important.

"Style" of design I use for want of a better term. This fact enters if you are planning a woodcarving to suit a particular period of design, or if you are copying an old master. The Greeks and Romans used cedar; almost all Gothic carving was in oak; Renaissance in walnut; and Duncan Phyfe, Chippendale, Sheraton, and Heppelwhite in mahogany. Grinling Gibbons used lime or pear. If your copy is to be authentic, it should be of an equivalent wood.

In any case, select sound wood, free of knots (unless you want a burl or figure), straight-grained, close-textured, proper in color, dry, well-seasoned, and as durable and easy to cut as possible under the circumstances. Many of these things the wood seller will watch for you, if you explain that the wood is for carving. Straightness of grain is indicated by long, parallel grain lines running the length of the piece and parallel with its edges, or you can take a shaving off a corner of the piece and see how the wood splits. Close texture shows up in a smooth, unpitted appearance. Sound wood will be true and clear in color, resist penetration by a knife blade; and small pieces should ring or snap sharply when struck. Beware of a dull thud. Usually stocks of selected and rare woods are carefully chosen pieces, so the woods should be in proper condition.

Color should be clear and even over the wood surface except at the edges of wide boards, which usually include sapwood. Avoid board ends and attendant splitting and checking. If you want a figure in oak and chestnut, get the quarter-sawed variety, which in addition is not so likely to check or split.

Order wood planed on all sides (unless for in-the-round carving) but *not sanded*. A sanded piece will inevitably retain some silica dust, which takes the edge off a cutting tool just as quickly as would any other stone. Order the piece slightly oversize—you can always cut away an edge later, but it is hard to add wood to a board that is too small. Cypress, basswood, cottonwood, and

yellow poplar are all available in wide, knot-free boards.

This all assumes that you are buying the wood. If you are getting your own, I recommend careful study of the table, comparison of available varieties, and some drying and storage place. My grandfather always had several lengths of hickory seasoning out in the barn so one would be in proper condition when an ax was to be helved. I keep several boxes filled with odd bits of wood from which to make a selection to fit a particular job. The main points are dry storage, thoroughly seasoned wood, straight grain, and freedom from knots. If you hunt for your wood, do not fear down trees. Unless decayed or checked, their wood is as sound as that of a standing tree.

Now to specialized data on woods: Wood is commercially classified as hardwood or softwood, not necessarily based on relative hardness (see the table). Commercial American hardwoods are oak, sycamore, willow, ash, elm, gum, chestnut, alder, aspen, basswood, beech, birch, buckeye, butternut, cherry, hackberry, locust, magnolia, hickory, maple, and poplar; commercial softwoods are the pines, junipers, cypress, redwood, tamarack, yew, hemlocks, spruces, larch, the firs, and the cedars. Any wood has heartwood and sapwood. The first is from the core of the tree, is usually darker in color than the sapwood (the outer part), more resistant to decay, and usually heavier. Hence heartwood is preferable for whittling and woodcarving.

Suitable soft woods (now meaning relative hardness) generally available include white pine (called "yellow pine" in England) and basswood (or "bee tree," kindred to lime and linden in Europe). Yellow pine, 30 per cent of our annual lumber production, is knotty, resinous, and splinters easily, hence is very, very hard on tools and unsuited for carving. Basswood is soft and easy

WHITTLING

to cut with sharp tools, is not brittle, and is fairly durable. It is almost white (light tan or yellow tinge), close-grained, and smooth. White pine is similar but slightly harder, contains more resin, and shows tints of pink and yellow. Most early American architectural woodcarving was done in white pine.

Cypress and butternut are likewise soft and easy to carve, but are not very resistant to wear. Red cedar has an agreeable odor and attractive wine-red color but can be bought only in more or less knotty, narrow pieces. It cuts cleanly, thus is particularly good for chip carving. Sweet gum or American satinwood, brownish in color, is more durable and uniform in texture. Redwood (sequoia) is very soft and has an attractive dull-red color.

Beech, holly, and sycamore are all slightly harder woods, light in color, and good for shallow cutting.

Among hard woods (again based on hardness) the standard architectural wood is oak. Almost all early English carving was done in English oak, a hard, close-grained white wood that ages to a beautiful dull yellow. It ranges in hardness between American red and white oaks and is very durable. Austrian oak is also used in Europe, and is somewhat coarser in texture than English.

American oaks fall in two great classes, the reds and the whites, the former softer, darker, and with a greater tendency to splinter. Seasoned white oak is very durable but so hard that it offers much difficulty in carving, even with sharpest tools. It is light tan in color. All oaks resist wear, hence are good for exterior carvings and also for much-used furniture, particularly if massive and rugged in design.

Mahogany, either red or brown in color, close and even in grain, fairly hard and very easy to work, is the great indoor carving material. Most period furniture is of mahogany. It is imported wood, coming from the West Indies, Mexico, Central America, Spain, and Africa. Best types are Honduras (now almost unavailable, except from mission buildings, etc.), Cuban (hardest and best in color), and Spanish (close-grained, from Santo Domingo, and difficult to get now). The Honduras variety cuts much like walnut. Mexican mahogany is usually poor, and the so-called "Philippine mahogany" still poorer, coarse in grain, and off-color.

Mahogany is so rich in color that it must be handled carefully, although many great period-furniture makers used it in very large pieces. Raleigh took it to England in 1597 as repair timbers in one of his ships, but it was not available commercially for another 150 years.

Walnut is the other great furniture material. It is dark brown (sapwood is light yellow), with a more pronounced grain or figure than mahogany. It is also harder and closer in grain. The American black walnut was once so common that it was used in buildings, the so-called "Lincoln Courthouse" in Henry Ford's Greenfield Village being made entirely of it. Such use has made it scarce and difficult to get in wide boards. (I have gotten most of mine from old cabinet and drawer fronts). Its firm grain, even texture, and ability to take a high polish have made it highly suitable for furniture and interior decoration.

English walnut usually has too much "figure" for carving. Italian has a fine, even texture and close grain and cuts about like English oak. Very little of it is available in America, and that must be picked carefully to avoid wide-grained or sapwood pieces. Burl walnut, with a very elaborate figure, is used for inlay.

Chestnut, light brown in color, fairly soft, and coarse-grained, with an attractive figure, has a tendency to warp, splits easily, and has alternate layers of hard and soft wood—so watch it! If your chisel or knife sticks in a hard layer (the summer wood), a part of the hard layer may lift or split away from the softer spring wood beneath. Try to select pieces with the figure most prominent in flat uncarved sections and less prominent where you carve. Use it preferably for large, undetailed work.

Maple is another great furniture wood, partly because it was so readily available throughout the Middle West. It is hard, fairly long-wearing, has an attractive figure and is generally available. Bird's-eye maple and curly maple have more prominent figures, hence make beautiful flat surfaces, but be very careful in working them—I ruined one of my best boyhood penknives on bird's-eye!

Cherry, light creamy or pinkish in color, is also a favorite. It wears well, takes sharp cuts, but is hard to work and available only in small pieces. It has often been used to imitate mahogany, for when well stained and finished only an expert can distinguish it. Apple and pear (favorites with German carvers) also work out well but are available only in small pieces. All woods from fruit and flowering trees are liable to have rot and worms.

Lignum vitae (African favorite), ebony (favorite in Japan), lancewood, sandalwood, briar, pear, and box (Swiss and German favorite) are all extremely hard, hence should be avoided ordinarily, although they do produce beautiful small, special pieces. Teak, brown with darker streaks, is fine wood, but expensive. It resembles coarse mahogany. Indian teak is more dense than the African. Ironwood is a common substitute for it.

Some varieties of wood have such elaborate figure that they can be used in combination to make a portrait or landscape in colors. I've seen them thus used in inlaid trays, drawer fronts, and medallions. Many of them are available only as $\frac{1}{28}$ to $\frac{1}{16}$ in. veneer; others can be gotten as lumber.[1]

Avodire, straw to light yellow in color, is an African wood with a decided figure. Its texture is fine and its grain close. A quarter-striped piece looks like moiré silk. It is used for inlay, sometimes with zebrawood or rosewood. Zebrawood, also African, gets its name from its prominent brown stripes on a yellow or gold background. It is close-textured and used for overlays, diamond inlays, borders, etc. (see Chap. XXII). Lacewood, an Australian

[1] Philip Myers in "The Home Craftsman," September-October, 1935.

flesh pink or reddish-brown wood, is often called "silky oak." When quarter-sawed, its figure is small with high-lighted satiny spots close together. It is used for overlays with walnut and mahogany.

Rosewood, "the aristocrat of woods," ranges in color from light red to deep purple with streaks of yellow and black. It is close-grained, very hard, and beautifully figured. That coming from Brazil is more uniform in color and darker, but East Indian is more commonly used because of its deep browns, purples, blacks, and yellows. It is used in borders and inlays with avodire, maple, primavera, and satin-wood. It is also used for marquetry.

Satinwood is golden yellow, close-grained, and can be purchased straight-grained, striped, or mottled. The East Indian wood is wider and has a more pronounced figure than the Brazilian. It can be had as lumber or veneer. For inlays and overlays, the "fire" or lively figure of the mottled makes it preferable. For banding and borders, use the striped. On large surfaces, straight-grained is better and may be relieved with ebony.

Ebony comes from Africa, India, Ceylon, and the Dutch East Indies. The Gaboon or Gabun variety, from Africa, is a dead black; Macassar (Dutch East Indies) and Calamander

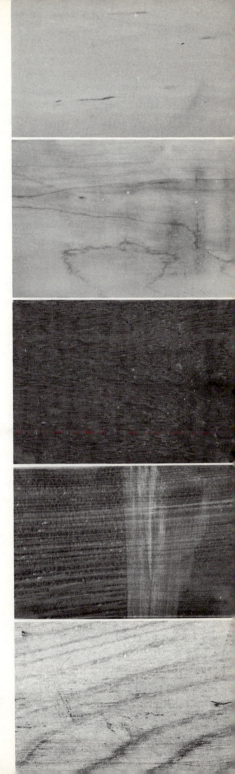

Fig. 14 (Top) · *Cherry.* Fig. 15 · *Maple.* Fig. 16 · *Cuban mahogany.* Fig. 17 · *Red cedar.* Fig. 18 (Bottom) · *Red-wood (sequoia), a very soft wood but durable, with dull red color*

(Ceylon) are brown with a black stripe, the former coffee-colored and the latter hazel brown. Sapwood in all varieties is white. The black is usually used as lumber with other woods, the brown for borders and aprons on tables.

Holly, native Southern wood, is chalky white, close-grained and even-textured. It is used with oak for inlays, marquetry, and borders, and with ebony for small overlays, etc.

Harewood, or English sycamore, is a veneer with plenty of cross-fire figure in a fiddle pattern. The wood itself is really white, but silver-gray dye brings out its figure. It is available as veneer and in thicknesses up to ½ in., and can be used for delicate furniture trimmed with ebony.

Tamo, or Japanese ash, is cream or straw colored with overlapping curly figures. Grain is open, but the high figure makes it very suitable for overlays on commoner domestic woods.

Many common woods have very elaborate figures in their burls or crotches, so these are usually available commercially. Cypress crotch is light cream in color and highly figured. Madrone burl is deep pinkish and figured with an overlapping knot. Thuya burl, native to North Africa, is a rich red brown, very hard, has a tendency to be brittle, but finishes very

[[20]]

Fig. 19 (Top) · *Satinwood.*
Fig. 20 · *Zebrawood.* Fig. 21 ·
Lacewood. Fig. 22 · *Rosewood.*
Fig. 23 · *Snakewood.* Fig. 24 ·
Macassar Ebony. Six of the best-known rare woods. Photographs courtesy "The Home Craftsman" magazine

well. Myrtle burl is pale gold in color, very curly, and used in inlays and overlays. English ash burls are dark greenish yellow with a lively brown figure. They are hard, resemble olivewood, and take a beautiful polish.

Any of these woods can be used with native woods such as mahogany, walnut, maple, birch, and gum.

Now for a few notes, before we examine the table. First as to hardness. Dense woods are usually harder than more open woods. Wide rings in oak and narrow ones in pine indicate great hardness. Heartwood is harder than sapwood, and dry wood generally harder than green. Frost increases hardness. Very soft woods are balsa, basswood, white pine, sugar pine, redwood, and willow. Soft woods include chestnut, tulip tree, sweet gum, Douglas fir, yellow pine, larch, horse chestnut, hemlock, cottonwood, and spruce. Medium woods are ash, oak, elm, beech, cherry, mulberry, birch, sour gum, and longleaf pine. Hard woods are hickory, dogwood, sugar maple, sycamore, locust, hornbeam, and persimmon. One scale of hardness frequently used is: hickory (shellbark) 100, pignut hickory 96, white oak 84, white ash 77, dogwood 75, scrub oak 73, white hazel 72, apple 70, red oak 69, white beech 65, black walnut 65, black birch 62, yellow oak 60, hard maple 56, white elm 58, red cedar 56, wild cherry 55, yellow pine 54, chestnut 52, yellow poplar 51, butternut 43, white birch 43, white pine 30.

Cleavability indicates ease of splitting. Hard to split are black gum, elm, sycamore, dogwood, beech, holly, maple, birch, and hornbeam. Medium in splitting are oak, ash, larch, cottonwood, linden, yellow poplar, and hickory. Easy to split are chestnut, pine, spruce, fir, and cedar.

Weathering is of importance only with soft woods. The major danger is from decay. Woods liable to decay and thus short-lived include red oak, red gum, beech, elm, spruce, shortleaf pine, and hemlock. Medium-lived are white oak, slippery elm, black walnut, hickory, longleaf pine, tamarack, and Douglas fir. Long-lived are cypress, redwood, red cedar, white cedar, Osage orange, and catalpa.

If you carve bowls, dishes or cutlery of wood, remember that some woods impart their odor and taste to foods, particularly to butter. If we rate ash, which imparts least odor and taste, as 100, soft maple is 84, hackberry 83, sycamore 80, beech 73, yellow poplar 71, soft elm 68, black gum 64, cottonwood and red gum 58.

If you are worrying about the shavings or your ruined efforts at the "masterpiece of the ages," here are the relative values of woods as fuels: best—hickory, beech, hornbeam, locust, and heart pine; good—oak, ash, birch, and maple; moderate—spruce, fir, chestnut, hemlock, and sap pine; poor—white pine, alder, linden, and cottonwood.

Now to the table. It gives accurate data from the best available sources by which 182 different woods may be compared for any purpose. Explanations of the factors are given at the end.

WOODS AND THEIR CHARACTERISTICS

Common Name of Species	Weight	Shrinkage	Bending Strength	Stiffness	Elasticity	Hardness	Durability	Ability to Stay in Place	Ease of Gluing	Splitting Value	Workability	Remarks
Alder, red	28	123	76	139	11	48	...	..	1	...	1	Pale pinkish brown
Apple, wild	47	170	85	139	9	118	M	..	..	...	..	Checks. Very close grain
Arbor vitae	23	75	50	94	6	35	H	..	2	L	3	
Ash, black	34	144	77	126	11	64	M	1	3	M	1	Dark grayish brown. Withes
Ash, blue	40	113	109	139	10	119	M	1	3	M	1	Close grain
Ash, green	40	122	107	157	12	107	M	1	3	M	1	Good withes from all ashes
Ash, Oregon	38	129	88	143	10	94	M	1	3	M	1	Grayish brown. Red tinge
Ash, pumpkin	36	113	86	118	10	103	M	1	3	M	1	
Ash, white	41	126	110	161	12	108	H	1	3	M	1	Grayish brown. Red tinge
Ash, white, Biltmore	38	121	107	156	12	104	H	1	3	M	1	
Ash, white, commercial	41	126	110	161	15	108	H	..	3	M		
Aspen	27	111	63	107	9	31	...	2	2	..	2	Checks. Close grain. Lt. brown
Aspen, large tooth	27	116	66	130	9	38	...	2	2	...	2	Close grain
Balsa	8	...	L	L	VL	VL	L	1	1	M	1	
Basswood	26	158	61	126	9	31	L	2	1	M	1	Close grain. Creamy
Beech	45	162	102	169	16	96	L	3	5	H	2	Checks. Close grain
Beech, blue	48	184	76	114	8	116	L	2	5	H	..	Checks. Close grain
Birch, Alaska white	38	166	89	161	12	61	L	2	5	L	..	Checks. Close grain
Birch, gray	35	147	61	85	8	54	L	2	5	H	..	Checks. Close grain
Birch, paper	39	158	78	137	10	58	L	2	5	H	2	Checks. Very close grain
Birch, sweet	46	154	117	207	16	104	L	2	3	H	2	Checks. Close grain
Birch, yellow	43	166	106	174	16	86	L	2	3	...	2	Checks. Close grain. Withes
Blackwood	58	157	123	185	..	185						
Buckeye, yellow	25	118	58	112	8	31	...	..	2	H	1	Close grain
Buckthorn, cascara	36	77	71	93	6	86	...	..	..	...	4	
Butternut	27	100	64	115	8	40	M	1	2	...	1	
Buttonwood	50	144	89	159	12	122						
Catalpa	29	73	63	110	9	43	H	..	..	...	1	
Cedar, Alaska	31	91	80	136	12	53	H	2	2	L	1	(S) Very close grain
Cedar, incense	26	81	70	97	10	47	H	2	2	L	1	(S) Very close grain
Cedar, Port Orford	29	106	82	168	12	48	H	2	2	L	1	(S) Very close grain
Cedar, red, eastern	33	78	67	80	6	81	H	2	2	L	1	(S) Very close grain

WOODS AND THEIR CHARACTERISTICS

Common Name of Species	Weight	Shrinkage	Bending Strength	Stiffness	Elasticity	Hardness	Durability	Ability to Stay in Place	Ease of Gluing	Splitting Value	Workability	Remarks
Cedar, red, western.....	23	76	60	108	10	38	H	2	2	215	1	(S) Very close grain
Cedar, white, northern..	22	69	50	78	8	30	H	2	2	L	1	(S) Very close grain
Cedar, white, southern..	23	83	53	93	8	35	H	2	2	L	1	(S) Very close grain
Cherry, black.........	35	113	93	150	10	72	H	2	2	H	3	Very close grain
Cherry, pin..........	28	129	62	117	9	41	H	2	2	H	3	Very close grain
Chestnut.............	30	111	68	112	10	50	H	1	1	431	1	Checks. Grayish brown
Chinquapin, western....	32	128	83	125	9	62	...	...	...	...	4	
Cottonwood, black.....	24	123	60	119	9	29	L	4	1	M	2	Close grain
Cottonwood, eastern....	28	138	62	123	9	36	L	4	1	M	2	Close grain
Cypress, southern.....	32	104	79	136	12	52	H	2	2	286	2	(S) Close grain. Lt. br.
Dogwood, flowering....	51	194	100	124	11	154	...	1	5	H	3	Checks. Close grain. Hoops
Dogwood, Pacific.......	45	168	86	142	10	116	..	..		H	..	Checks. Close grain. Hoops
Douglas fir, Coast type..	34	121	90	181	16	59	M	2	1	272	2	(S) Hard, yellowish
Douglas fir, inland type..	31	112	80	159	10	58	M	2	1	356	2	(S) Hard, yellowish
Douglas fir, mountain type	30	103	75	142	12	52	M	2	1	310	2	(S) Hard, yellowish
Ebony, Indian.........	61	...	78	...	13	VH	H					
Ebony, E. African.....	48	...	55	...	10	VH	H					
Elder, box............	36	149	72	115	10	68	L	2	1	H	3	Close grain
Elm, American........	36	145	85	130	12	66	L	4	1	H	..	Very close grain. Lt. br.
Elm, rock.............	44	137	106	148	13	104	L	4	1	H	..	Very close grain. Lt. br.
Elm, slippery.........	37	138	92	140	12	72	M	4	1	H	..	Very close grain. Dk. br.
Eucalyptus, Karri, W. Australia.............	52	...	121	...	20	H	H	..	..	...	..	Baskets in sprg. & sumr. Brittle
Eucalyptus, N. S. Wales mahogany...........	66	...	115	...	17	H	H	..	..	...	..	Brittle
Eucalyptus, W. Australian mahogany........	49	...	105	...	15	H	H	..	..	...	..	Brittle
Fig, golden...........	31	...	61	67								(S)
Fir, alpine...........	23	92	51	94	9	33	...	4	2	..	3	(S)
Fir, balsam..........	26	103	59	118	10	31	...	4	2	L	3	(S) Nearly white
Fir, cork bark........	21	90	51	104	10	27	...	..	2	..	..	(S)
Fir, noble...........	26	126	74	150	12	39	...	4	2	267	2	(S)
Fir, red, California.....	27	114	78	134	11	52	...	..	2	L	..	(S)
Fir, silver...........	27	142	70	147	11	37	...	..	2	267	..	(S)
Fir, white...........	26	95	72	127	11	42	L	4	2	267	2	(S) White. Reddish tinge
Fir, white, commercial...	26	110	72	141	11	41	...	..	2	267	..	(S) White. Reddish tinge
Fir, white, lowland.....	28	105	72	156	12	43	...	..	2	267	..	(S) White. Reddish tinge
Greenheart (British Guiana).............	70	...	...	...	..	VH						
Gum, black...........	35	133	83	118	12	78	...	4	2	H	3	Checks. Brownish gray
Gum, blue............	52	226	134	223	17	132	L	4	2	H	..	Checks
Gum, red............	34	150	86	134	12	60	L	3	1	H	2	Checks. Reddish brown
Gum, tupelo..........	35	122	82	127	12	78	L	3	2	H	..	Checks. Brownish gray
Gumbo-limbo.........	22	77	39	66	5	30						
Hackberry...........	37	138	76	108	9	74	L	..	2	L	3	Light greenish gray
Haw, pear...........	48	...	95	107	9	127						
Hemlock, eastern.....	28	98	72	121	11	51	L	4	2	230	3	(S) Pale buff
Hemlock, mountain.....	33	114	81	131	9	64	L	4	2	M	3	(S) Pale buff
Hemlock, western.....	29	120	74	144	14	50	L	2	1	283	2	(S) Pale buff
Hickory, bigleaf, shagbark	48	195	126	165	14	H	M	2	4	M	3	Very close grain. Withes
Hickory, bitternut......	46	180	127	170	16	H	M	2	4	M	3	Close grain. Withes
Hickory, mockernut.....	51	182	135	185	16	H	M	2	4	M	3	Very close grain
Hickory, nutmeg.......	42	180	111	147	17	H	M	2	4	M	3	Close grain. Red brown
Hickory, pignut.......	53	182	144	198	17	H	M	2	4	M	3	Close grain. Red brown
Hickory, shagbark.....	51	170	133	185	16	H	M	2	4	M	3	Warps. Close grain
Holly...............	40	155	76	102	8	86	...	..	5	H	..	Very close grain
Hornbeam, hop.......	50	183	101	150	13	126	M	..	5	H	4	Checks. Very close grain
Inkwood............	56	184	124	182	16	181						
Ironwood, black.......	80	125	157	254	22	H	M	1	2	M	2	Very close grain
Jacaranda, Brazilian rosewood..........	53											
Juniper..............	36	73	63	60	4	107	M	..	..	....	..	(S)
Larch, western........	36	129	89	153	13	64	M	4	2	267	2	(S) Reddish brown
Laurel, mountain......	48	144	97	110	9	143	H	..	5	...	3	Close grain
Lignum vitae.........	80	L	H	VH	VH	VH	H	1	5	H	4	Hardest. Heaviest. Closest grain

WOODS AND THEIR CHARACTERISTICS

Common Name of Species	Weight	Shrinkage	Bending Strength	Stiffness	Elasticity	Hardness	Durability	Ability to Stay in Place	Ease of Gluing	Splitting Value	Workability	Remarks
Locust, black or yellow..	48	103	157	220	15	161	H	..	..	L	..	Checks. Close grain. Lt. br.
Locust, honey..........	44	107	112	153	12	155	H	1	5	H	3	Cherry red
Madroña..............	46	173	86	117	9	114	...	3	5	...	4	
Magnolia, cucumber....	34	137	90	175	13	57	H	1	1	...	2	Close grain. Yel.-br.
Magnolia, evergreen....	35	122	81	136	11	80	H	1	1	...	2	Light yellow-brown
Magnolia, mountain.....	31	126	76	142	11	51	H	1	1	...	2	Light yellow-brown
Mahogany, W. Africa...	42	...	123	...	12	...	M	2	1	M	2	Dark red-brown
Mahogany, E. India.....	34	...	69	...	9	...	M	2	1	M	..	Dark red-brown
Mangrove..............	67	123	176	270	24	251						
Maple, bigleaf.........	34	113	83	132	11	73	M	2	5	H	2	Close grain. Lt. red-brown
Maple, black..........	40	140	93	149	16	97	M	2	3	H	2	Close grain. Lt. red-br.
Maple, red...........	38	128	93	158	14	79	M	2	5	H	2	Close grain. Lt. red-br.
Maple, silver.........	33	114	69	106	9	65	L	2	3	H	2	Close grain. Lt. red-br.
Maple, striped........	32	121	78	135	11	59	L	2	3	H	2	Close grain
Maple, sugar.........	44	147	114	178	16	115	M	2	3	857	2	Close grain. Lt. red-br.
Mastic...............	65	123	112	183	15	208	...	..	..	M		
Myrtle...............	39	116	72	89	6	106	...	..	..	M		
Mulberry.............	..	...	...	...	...	...	M	..	..	M		
Oak, black...........	43	142	98	146	12	102	L	4	..	M	3	Checks. Close grain
Oak, black, California...	40	115	69	95	6	99	L	4	5	M	3	Checks. Close grain
Oak, bur.............	45	129	82	104	8	112	M	3	..	739	2	Checks. Close grain
Oak, chestnut.........	46	162	102	166	12	90	M	3	..	739	2	Checks. Close grain
Oak, chestnut, swamp...	47	180	100	171	13	103	L	4	..	739	2	Checks. Close grain
Oak, laurel...........	44	173	94	169	13	99	L	4	..	...	2	Checks. Close grain
Oak, live.............	62	152	142	228	15	240	M	2	..	M	3	Checks. Close grain
Oak, live, canyon......	54	158	110	159	12	181	M	2	..	M	2	Checks. Close grain
Oak, pin.............	44	143	96	167	13	111	L	4	..	M	2	Checks. Close grain
Oak, post............	47	159	99	143	11	122	M	2	..	739	2	Checks. Close grain
Oak, red.............	44	131	99	164	13	103	M	3	3	M	2	Checks. Close grain
Oak, red, southern.....	41	153	83	153	12	86	L	4	..	M	2	Checks. Close grain
Oak, red, swamp......	48	163	131	215	15	123	L	4	..	M	2	Checks. Close grain
Oak, scarlet..........	47	140	155	181	14	120	M	2	..	M	2	Checks. Close grain
Oak, water...........	44	154	110	196	14	101	M	2	..	M	2	Checks. Close grain
Oak, white...........	48	153	102	152	13	108	M	2	1	739	2	Checks. Close grain
Oak, white, Oregon....	51	133	86	107	8	153	M	..	..	M	2	Checks. Close grain. Withes
Oak, white, Rocky Mt..	51	121	70	78	5	137	M	..	..	M	2	Checks. Close grain. Withes
Oak, white, swamp.....	50	172	122	184	15	122	M	..	..	739	2	Checks. Close grain. Withes
Oak, willow..........	49	175	96	167	13	106	M	..	..	M	2	Checks. Close grain
Osage orange.........	53	89	92	158	13	200	H	..	..	...	..	Very close grain
Palmetto.............	27	250	40	55	3	21						
Paradise Tree.........	24	82	42	86	6	32						
Pecan...............	47	137	110	162	14	142	...	..	..	...	..	Close grain
Persimmon...........	52	183	122	172	15	162	...	1	4	...	2	Very close grain
Pigeon plum..........	55	145	108	184	14	189						
Pine, jack...........	30	102	64	111	9	48	...	2	2	L	3	(S)
Pine, Jeffrey.........	28	103	68	116	9	44	L	2	..	L	..	(S)
Pine, limber.........	28	80	69	107	9	39	L	2	..	L	..	(S)
Pine, loblolly........	38	127	93	166	14	62	L	2	2	359	..	(S)
Pine, lodgepole.......	29	114	67	128	10	41	L	2	2	L	3	(S) Lt. red-brown
Pine, longleaf........	41	124	106	189	15	76	M	2	2	359	..	(S)
Pine, mountain.......	37	107	91	151	13	64	L	2	2	L	..	(S)
Pine, Norway, or red...	34	116	85	163	12	46	...	2	2	L	3	(S) Orange to lt. red-brown
Pine, pitch..........	34	110	80	146	10	56	M	2	2	359	3	(S) Very resinous
Pine, pond..........	38	115	89	154	11	64	L	2	..	359	..	(S)
Pine, sand..........	34	104	86	135	10	63	L	2	..	L	..	(S)
Pine, slash..........	48	131	116	195	15	93	M	2	..	359	..	(S)
Pine, sugar..........	25	79	64	112	10	38	L	1	1	298	1	(S) Lt. creamy brown
Pine, shortleaf.......	38	128	97	170	14	68	L	2	2	359	..	(S) Resinous. Close grain
Pine, white, northern...	25	83	63	119	10	35	L	1	1	265	1	(S) Very close grain
Pine, white, western...	27	118	69	137	10	35	L	2	1	1	1	(S) Close grain
Pine, yellow, southern...	28	100	67	125	16	50	L	2	2	359	2	(S) Orange to lt. red-br
Pine, yellow, western...	28	97	65	112	10	41	L	1	1	327	1	(S)
Piñon................	37	99	60	108	10	73	...	..	..	L	..	(S)
Poison wood..........	37	115	69	99	7	62						
Poplar, balsam........	23	104	48	95	7	25	L	..	..	...	..	Close grain

WOODS AND THEIR CHARACTERISTICS

Common Name of Species	Weight	Shrinkage	Bending Strength	Stiffness	Elasticity	Hardness	Durability	Ability to Stay in Place	Ease of Gluing	Splitting Value	Workability	Remarks
Poplar, yellow	28	119	71	135	11	40	M	2	1	447	1	Close grain
Redwood	30	65	90	134	12	59	H	2	1	...	1	Cherry to deep red-br.
Rhododendron	40	158	85	100	7	104						
Sassafras	32	103	71	103	9	60	M	..	..	....	..	Checks
Satinwood (Ceylon)	64	...	97	...	12							
Serviceberry	52	183	121	181	14	131	L	..	..	....	..	Close grain
Silverbell	32	122	74	133	12	53	...	..	..	....	..	Close grain
Sourwood	38	152	94	169	12	83	...	..	..		H	
Spruce, black	28	112	68	143	12	40	L	2	2	L	2	(S) Resinous. Close grain
Spruce, Engleman	23	102	55	100	8	32	L	2	2	L	2	(S) Resinous. Close grain
Spruce, red	28	117	72	138	12	41	L	2	1	268	2	(S) Resinous. Close grain
Spruce, Sitka	28	116	72	144	12	44	L	2	1	268	2	(S) Resinous. Close grain
Spruce, white	28	134	68	123	12	37	L	2	1	268	2	(S) Resinous. Close grain
Stopper, red	61	140	145	197	15	...	...	..	..	....	H	
Sugarberry	36	126	74	103	8	83	...	..	..	....	..	Yellowish or greenish gray
Sumac	33	...	74	94	8	64	...	..	..	....	..	Pithy. Good withes
Sycamore	35	136	74	129	12	64	L	4	2	H	3	Checks. Very close grain
Tamarack	37	128	84	147	13	53	M	..	2	306	3	(S) Russet brown
Teak (India)	36	Low	90	...	13	...	M	1	1	H	2	
Walnut, black	39	116	111	167	13	88	M	1	1	M	2	Checks. Choc. br.
Walnut, little	40	101	91	118	10	...	M	1	2	M	2	Chocolate brown
Willow, black	26	126	45	70	5	35	...	1	2	...	2	Good withes, whistles
Willow, black, western	31	132	67	127	12	50	...	1	2	...	2	Good withes, whistles
Witch-hazel	43	188	108	129	11	107	...	..	..	....	..	Very flexible. Good withes
Yew	44	128	84	147	11	53	...	..	..	....	..	Very close grain (S)

Notes

Weight—Given in pounds per cubic foot.

Shrinkage—Purely comparative figures are given, higher figures denoting greater shrinkage. This is *volumetric*, a composite index of tangential (with grain around tree) and radial (across grain). Low shrinkage also indicates relative freedom from checking because of the narrow range of variation in moisture content when properly seasoned.

Bending Strength—Purely comparative figures are given, higher figures indicating higher bending strength. Derived from fiber stress at elastic limit (static and impact) and modulus of rupture.

Stiffness—Purely comparative figures derived from modulus of elasticity (static, impact, and compression parallel to grain).

Elasticity—Purely comparative figures. If five zeros are added, the figure becomes modulus of elasticity in pounds per square inch.

Hardness—Purely comparative figures, worked out from fiber stress at elastic limit with compression perpendicular to grain, and end, radial, and tangential hardness.

Durability—L is low, M medium, and H high. Indicates relative resistance to rotting from wetting, weathering, or submersion in soil.

Ability to Stay in Place—Woods which do not warp readily are classified as 1, woods which warp badly as 4, with 2 and 3 in order between. Only approximate, but based on research, observation, experience, and estimation.

Ease of Gluing—1 indicates woods used commercially in glued construction, 2 indicates woods about which little is known but which should not be difficult to glue, 3 indicates woods that require care in gluing, 4 woods that present real difficulties in gluing, and 5 woods about which little is known but which are believed to be hard to glue.

Splitting Value—Two types of index, depending upon source of data. L means low, M medium, and H high, H being woods hardest to split. The numbers are composite values based on tension and cleavage data, higher numbers indicating increased resistance to splitting.

Workability—Graduated from 1 to 4 in ease of working, 1 indicating woods easiest to work and 4 being those presenting difficulties in working.

Remarks—"Checks" indicates danger of checking when drying, an important factor that may be avoided by using properly seasoned wood. See *Shrinkage*. "(S)" indicates softwood, as commercially classified. Colors under this heading indicate approximate color of seasoned heartwood. Good woods for withes are shown.

Data from many sources, but principally from U.S. Forest Products Laboratory and U.S. Forest Service bulletins and circulars. Other major sources include Marks' *Mechanical Engineer's Handbook* and the *Handbook of Chemistry and Physics*, twentieth edition.

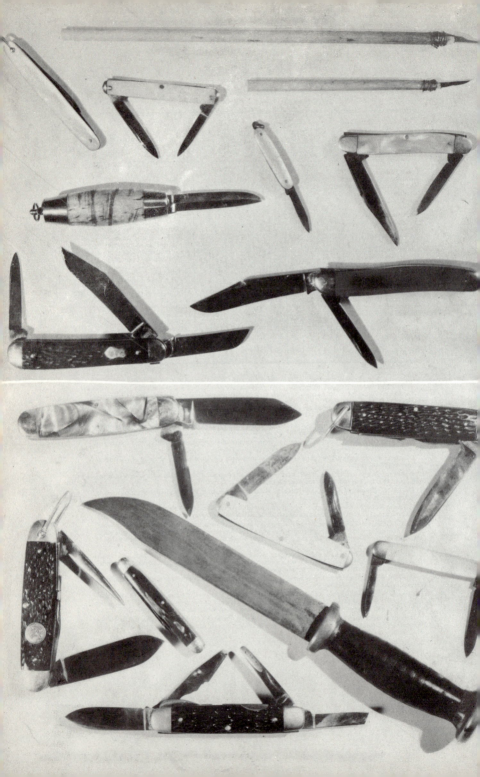

CHAPTER II

KNIVES · *Selection and Care*

W HAT type of knife shall I need?" Commonest of beginning whittler's questions, it is almost impossible to answer unless you decide first what sort of whittling you plan to do. A knife, just as any other tool, must be selected for its job. A penknife is useless for cutting off limbs, as useless as a jacknife is for making a matchstick chain.

First, as to blades: There are dozens of pocket-knife blade shapes—one manufacturer alone makes thirty-five—but only about two dozen are of use to whittlers. Twenty shapes are illustrated in Figs. 27 and 28. Commonest among whittling blade shapes is the *pen* blade, usually a thin, wafer blade in small knives, exactly the sort of thing you need for hard-to-get-at and small work. Its flexibility will help you smooth a surface. A modification, the *cut-off pen*, provides a sharp point at the end of a straight cutting edge, thus is good for finishing corners, chip carving, and roughing down a background. The *punch* blade is similar to a round-nose chisel sharpened on the side and is useful principally in cutting holes in leather or rounding out small holes in wood. It often will make trouble by biting into the grain, and is somewhat hard to sharpen. A modification, the *reaming* blade, is ground oval on the back, thus does not bite in when rounding curves or drilling wood.

Another very common blade shape in knives from the smallest to the largest, is the *clip*, providing a rounded cutting edge together with a sharp long point. This blade is very useful because its long point will get into difficult places and its rounded cutting edge is not so likely to catch at the tip in smoothing surfaces. The *cutback clip* is shorter-tipped, giving a keen point at the

Fig. 25 (Top) · *Razor cutting edges, penknives, a barrel, and two jackknives.* Fig. 26 · *Several utility knives, a homemade hunting knife, and three more penknives*

proper cutting angle, yet is sturdy. The clip itself has several modifications, the *B* clip, the *A* clip, the *Turkish* clip, and the *Texas Tickler* clip, the last two being very long and usually only on large knives. For normal work, I prefer the *B* clip, because the cutting edge is more nearly in line with the handle. The cutback is good for close work and chipping.

A grown-up edition of the pen blade is the *spear*, strong-backed, sturdy, and with the tip centered at its end. This blade is convenient for heavy cutting and roughing out. If the "back-bone," the thickest part of the blade, is in the middle, the blade is called a *sabre spear*. This blade will hold its edge better because the blade thickens more rapidly behind the cutting edge and is very stiff, an advantage in heavy rustic cutting. The same treatment on a clip blade produces the *sabre clip*, again gaining stiffness. Both sabre-type blades are good for hard woods, but are heavy and cause the piece to split ahead of the cutting edge—which spells disaster in making a fan.

Another common type is the *sheep-foot*, somewhat similar to the cut-off pen, but larger and with a rounded hump back of the point. This blade is stiff and gives a good point for chip carving and point work, but the point will dig in when you try to smooth a surface with it. Modifications are the *long sheep-foot* and the

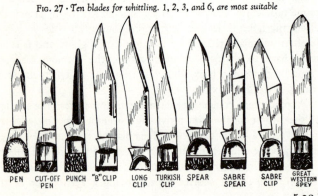

FIG. 27 · *Ten blades for whittling. 1, 2, 3, and 6, are most suitable*

PEN   CUT-OFF PEN   PUNCH   "B" CLIP   LONG CLIP   TURKISH CLIP   SPEAR   SABRE SPEAR   SABRE CLIP   GREAT WESTERN SPEY

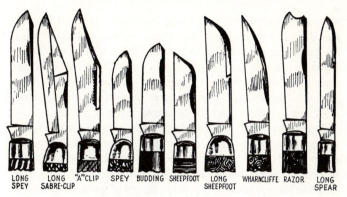

LONG SPEY | LONG SABRE-CLIP | "A" CLIP | SPEY | BUDDING | SHEEPFOOT | LONG SHEEPFOOT | WHARNCLIFFE | RAZOR | LONG SPEAR

FIG. 28 · *Ten more blades. 4, 6, and 8 are usually best*

Wharncliffe, the latter with a very long point and both giving a longer cutting edge. A pruning knife is also a modification in which the point is carried out in front of the line of the handle, making a concave or hooked-end cutting edge.

Last of the important types is the *spey*, direct opposite of the sheep-foot in that the cutting edge is convex-curved. This blade is good for smoothing up a background after it has been sunk and for cutting round-bottomed grooves. The budding blade is exactly like it, but longer. The *razor* blade also is similar, but larger and with a differently shaped end.

One special whittling knife also has a *chisel* blade carrying a cutting edge at its end, really a gouge put into a clasp-knife handle. Another has a blade with diagonal chisel end and a sharpened side for scraping. Then there are screw drivers, bottle openers, can openers, manicure and file blades, scissors, and dozens of other specialized gadgets, all useful for their particular work, but of no value to the whittler.

As to knife types: In the general group called clasp knives, and meaning knives in which the blade or blades close into the handle, there are three general classes based on size; the smallest being penknives (up to 3 in. long when closed, light in construction and with thin blades); the next being jackknives (3½ to 5 in. long closed, with heavier blades and sturdy frame); and last, folding hunting or clasp knives (up to 8 in. long or so, with heavy blades). Penknives usually have two blades, a pen and a B clip, although some have two pens, one small and one large. Others have specialty blades added. Handle covers are usually pearl, a plastic, solid metal, or some similarly decorative material.

Jackknives usually have one large blade, either a slip or a spear, and one or more small ones, an assortment of pen, cut-off pen, and sheep-foot. Handles are usually staghorn, wood, a plastic material, or bone. Hunting knives are similar, but larger, and often have only one blade, a spear or clip, and a handle of special shape, sometimes with a guard.

Then there are straight-handle or fixed-handle knives, including everything from paring knives to special woodcarving or sheath knives. Blades are usually clip, but may be spear, sabre-spear, or sheep-foot shape. Similar is the Swedish sloyd-bladed barrel knife, shown at the center of Fig. 25, which has a round or barrel-shaped handle into which the blade is inserted. It is necessary to pull out the entire lining to open or close the blade but a blade is *held* open. Some specialized knives, such as the snap-button, spring-opened type also have blade locks. Snapping shut is a danger with the ordinary blade, particularly if you are boring or cutting with the tip. If the tip sticks, the blade may snap shut— then woe betide any fingers in the way! I have nicked myself once or twice this way but have not had any serious trouble. It is a matter of learning how—just as closing a clasp knife is. Learn to do the latter by holding the handle in the tips of the fingers and closing the blade with the palm of the other hand or with the finger tips well back from the cutting edge. And never have two blades open at once—unless you are playing mumblety-peg (bad for a good knife).

My personal preference is for penknives, since most of my whittling is in miniature. Rustic whittling, however, will make good use of a jackknife. Heavy carving calls for the hunting type.

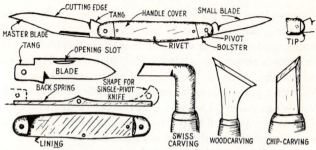

FIG. 29 · *Knife parts with their names, and three special blades*

I believe the well-rounded whittler's kit should contain at least three knives, one a penknife with a pen and a B clip, the latter the larger and both long and thin, the second a small jackknife with a heavy clip blade and a smaller spearblade, and the third a large jackknife with a heavy spear or clip blade and a smaller spear, clip, or spey. The smaller jackknife may well have three blades, the third being a cut-off pen or sheep-foot. I prefer thin handles with sturdy bolsters (the end caps; small ones that do not cover blade pivots are called "tips"), long blades, and if the knife is to be used for whittling principally, no specialty blades or gadgets. Their place is in knives for camping and rustic work. Handle material will make little difference, except in looks and cost.

Select a knife that feels well in your hand and that will do the type of work you want it to do. If you decide the blade shape isn't exactly what you want, it can be modified somewhat by grinding. (When the blade tip breaks, you will have to modify the shape anyway.) The main thing is to get a well-built, sturdy knife with good steel in the blades. The only way to test the steel is to cut with it for a while and see how long the blade holds its edge. Usually a knife bought from any reputable manufacturer will have good steel in it, but it will cost you $1.50 to $2.50. It will be worth every cent of that, though, in saved sharpening time.

After you have bought a knife, keep it in good condition. Don't let it stay wet. Wipe off the blades and oil them and the hinges when you have finished the day's shaving production. Don't stick it in the ground, or use it to cut paper, cardboard, fingernails, pencils, sanded wood, or wire. All these things dull blades. Don't cut knots or resinous woods (pitch pine, etc.), and drill holes with extreme care, otherwise you'll break off the tip or break out pieces. And don't put sidewise pressure on the blade; it isn't built for that. When you grind out a nick on a wheel, be sure to keep the blade cool, or you will burn it and thus take out the temper, just as you may if you use the knife as a poker in a fire.

Above all, keep blades sharp. Otherwise you will be constantly troubled with poor cutting, scuffed-up cuts instead of smooth ones, splitting instead of cutting. I honestly think more good whittling has been ruined by dull blades than by lack of skill.

Some parents feel that dull blades are safer on a child's knife. Quite the opposite is true, providing the child is old enough to have a knife at all, because a dull blade forces excessive pressure behind it, thus causing slipping, splitting, snapping shut, and their attendant hurts. A good clean cut can be handled with a dose of iodine, a bit of a bandage, and forgetfulness. My four-year-old's favorite expression is "I didn't cut myself *berry* badly"—and it was mine too at his age. I remember once I did a very complete job of paring an index finger but didn't tell a soul about it for fear I'd have the knife taken away for a while. I had a boat to finish first.

Incidentally, as you go in for ships in bottles (Chap. XII), or making pliers and scissors (Chap. X), you will need special knives like those at the top of Fig. 25. Make them by breaking off the cutting edge of a razor blade with a pair of pliers and binding it in the split end of a piece of dowel rod. Use pliers, not your fingers. You may have to break several blades before one will break right.

The general rule, "Whittle away from yourself," is sound, proved so by the times when you won't be able to. If you must cut toward yourself, try to keep the holding hand behind the cutting edge (Fig. 30), and don't cut with the piece against your knee or stomach. You aren't a surgeon. Chapter III will give you pointers.

Above everything else, *keep your knife sharp.*

〖 32 〗

FIG. 30 (*On opposite page*) · *Fifteen-year-old Arthur Dayton won a whittling contest in Bridgeport, Conn., with the deer he is whittling here. (Courtesy Remington Arms Co., Inc.)*

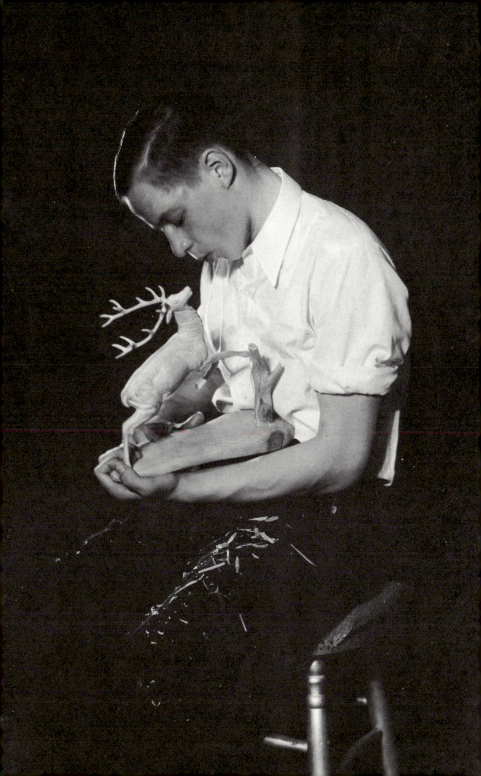

FIG. 31 · *Walnut-shell "whimsies" are simple to whittle*

CHAPTER III

SIMPLE · *To Whittle*

THE old Indian philosophy on learning to hunt also applies to learning to whittle—the way to learn to whittle is to whittle. All I can do is to make the road a little easier.

I use four general types of grips, each for its particular kind of stroke, but I often change off to rest my hand or just for variety. The common cut is the one every country-store manufacturer of shavings uses, the straight cut away from yourself, with the knife gripped as you would a hammer, Fig. 32*a*. It removes waste wood but is hard to control. You get less power but better steering results when you extend your thumb along the back of the blade, as in Fig. 32*b*. Figure 32*c* is just like *a* as to grip but reversed in direction, while *f* shows the forefinger extended along the back of the blade for marking or outlining. On small pieces, you will find it easier to guide the cut with your thumb, Fig. 38, or more accurate to push against the blade with your *left* thumb also.

My list shows eight types of strokes when classified by cutting effect. First there is the *straight cut*, simply removing waste wood. Next is the *sweep* cut, diagrammed in Fig. 32*h*, in which the knife is swung about the cutting edge of the blade as it moves forward, thus giving a curved cut with smooth outline. When you learn to control it, you'll probably use this cut more than any other. Next is the *stop* or *outline cut* which you'll use all through whittling, woodcarving and wood sculpture, made by pulling the knife blade along a line, thus cutting into the wood along the line and pre-venting later cuts from splitting past the outline. The index finger does careful guiding, as at *f*, Fig. 32.

Next is the *chisel cut*, in which you cut with the outer end of the blade and force it through the wood without any sawing action. (Some knives, in fact, actually have chisel blades.) Such a cut is of use in cutting through a hole (as in the ball-in-a-cage or chain), smoothing up, coming close to a line, or similar close work. *Scraping cuts*, safe only for scraping off bark, are usually hard on the cutting edge, and often only roughen a finished piece.

You'll do a lot of cutting with the *tip* of the blade, as in cutting a hole, finishing around an outline, putting in details, and so on. The main thing to remember is to watch the grain, for, when you are cutting with the knife almost perpendicular to the piece, you may forget and try to back the knife out. Instead, the blade tip

FIG. 32 · *Pointers in handling a knife, and some typical cuts*

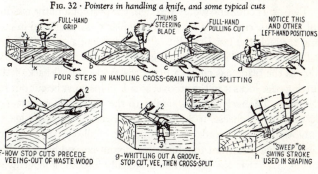

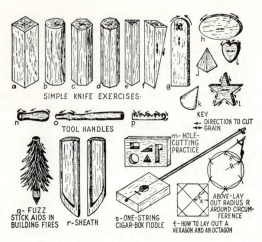

SIMPLE KNIFE EXERCISES·

TOOL HANDLES

KEY
DIRECTION TO CUT
GRAIN

m- HOLE-
CUTTING
PRACTICE

q- FUZZ
STICK AIDS IN
BUILDING FIRES

r-SHEATH

s-ONE-STRING
CIGAR-BOX FIDDLE

ABOVE-LAY
OUT RADIUS R
AROUND CIRCUM-
FERENCE

†- HOW TO LAY OUT A
HEXAGON AND AN OCTAGON

Fig. 33 · *Exercises for the beginning whittler*

sticks in the wood and the blade snaps shut. That's hard on your fingers—you won't let it happen more than once or twice. (Some knives won't close that way—woodcarver's, sloyd, hunting, and the special whittling knives with a spring-locked blade.) Another point to watch is the danger of the tip breaking in hard or tough wood when you change direction. Work the tip loose and around carefully and you will have no trouble.

Two other cuts, and we are through, the saw cut and the rocking cut. The *saw cut* is simply a motion similar to sawing used in cutting through the last little bit of wood holding a chain link or a ball-in-a-cage, and is of little use except for that sort of work. As soon as the blade has cut in a little, the thicker metal back of the cutting edge locks it in the groove, so side chips must be cut out for clearance. The *rocking cut* is similar to the one that a storekeeper uses in cutting cheese, rocking the blade over the cutting edge.

Now for a few words on that bugaboo of all whittlers—grain. Let's assume you want to whittle the double-curved block outline in Fig. 32a; that the grain runs diagonally instead of lengthwise

of the block; and that the wood has a tendency to split. That means that cutting from the rear top edge of the block to the lower front corner would cause the blade to run in to the wood and split off the hump at X. Instead you begin cutting at the outer tip Y, cutting back until you reach Z, the last grain line outside the hump. A cut further back will split off the hump.

Now start on the curve at the rear end of the block, Fig. 32b. First make a stop cut by rocking the blade in perpendicular to the block just at the point where the first grain line from the back of the block crosses the outline of the shape you are cutting, as at b 1. Then cut over to the crossing stop cut, until the block looks like c. Now you must cut toward yourself (yes, you *will* have to cut toward yourself to do certain things, but be careful), shaping upward along the hump. You will run into no danger of splitting the block now— any splitting that occurs will follow the grain line away from the outline. Keep at it as at d 1 until you have rounded off the hump, then shape the lower end as at d 2, again working so that the tendency of the knife to follow the grain leads it *away* from the outline you are trying to save.

Perhaps sketch e will make all this clearer. The full-line arrows show cuts that are safe to make without splitting

〚 37 〛

FIG. 34 (TOP) · Peach-stone Indian head and monkey. FIG. 35 · Apricot-pit turtle and basket. FIG. 36 · Peanut walking duck and parrot. FIG. 37 · Coconut half-shell twine holders, whittled then painted and trimmed. FIG. 38. Close control of cut by guiding with the right thumb on work

away anything but waste wood, while the dotted-line cuts show what happens if you cut *into* the grain line toward the outline. *Cut across, with, or diagonally out of the grain (away from the outline), but diagonally into the grain of the waste wood.*

Now that we have that all settled, let's get on with our whittling. First, try some of the simple exercises in Fig. 33. Take a round block and square it up, as at *a*, then round it to match *b*, then make it hexagonal like *c*, then round up and make the octagon at *d*, the triangle at *e*. These all seem foolish, but they do two vital things: they develop skill with the knife, and they train your sense of proportion, so you will avoid ruining your first real piece.

In case you had trouble laying out the hexagon or octagon of *c* and *d*, *t* shows how it is done. For the hexagon, lay out the largest circle you can get on the block end, then leave the compass at the same radius, *R*, and scribe a series of arcs all around the circle circumference. You'll get almost exactly six. Connect them, and there is your hexagon. For the octagon, draw diagonal lines across corners of a square block end, then measure from the crossing to the center of one side, as at *X*. Mark this distance out on each diagonal, as at *X'*, and draw a perpendicular to the diagonal—that is our octagon.

[[38]]

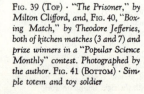

Fig. 39 (Top) · *"The Prisoner,"* by Milton Clifford, and, Fig. 40, *"Boxing Match,"* by Theodore Jefferies, both of kitchen matches (3 and 7) and prize winners in a *"Popular Science Monthly"* contest. Photographed by the author. Fig. 41 (Bottom) · *Simple totem and toy soldier*

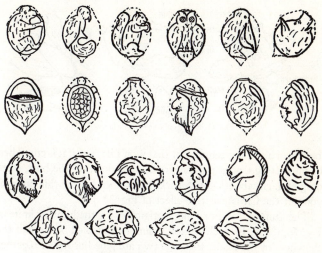

FIG. 42 · *Twenty-two patterns for peach-stone carving*

Next try the wedge at *f*, the plant tag at *g*, and the miscellaneous shapes *h* to *l*, noticing in each case the little single-headed arrow to show what direction to cut in, and the double-headed arrow showing grain. You will find that the star *l* requires cutting in two directions to make the outer faces of its lower points. Work *outward* in accordance with the rules until you come near the tip. Then cut *inward* contrary to rule for the last little bit to avoid snapping the tips off. In this case you violate the rule, but only to save the star tips.

The tool handles *n*, *o*, and *p* will give you good practice, particularly if you make them in hickory or ash, and *m* will develop your skill in cutting odd-shaped holes. The fuzz stick, familiar to both Boy and Girl Scouts as an aid to building a fire when no twigs are available, is a good practice piece for making long shavings and stopping them where you want to. Start with a 1-in. round piece of soft wood about a foot long. Leave a good gripping space at the upper end, and rest the lower against a stump, the floor, a work-

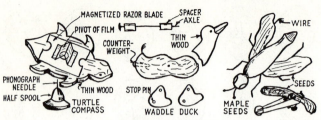

FIG. 43 · *Details of some nut "whimsies"*

bench, or anything convenient that won't be hurt if it is cut. Then begin cutting longer and longer shavings down to the butt, stopping each cut about an inch back from the end. Keep this up until you get the Christmas tree effect of Fig. 33 *q*.

The knife sheath in *r* I made originally for the hunting knife of Fig. 26, Chap. II. Each section is simply hollowed out to half the thickness of the blade, then the two are glued or nailed together and fitted inside a fringed buckskin or chamois covering sewed in place.

As a youngster I had a lot of fun with the one-string or Chinese fiddle made of a cigar box and a broomstick. Whittle out a hole just large enough to fit the broomstick at each end of the box and a larger hole in the bottom. Put the broomstick through until about an inch sticks out of the base, then wedge it in place and nail the box top shut. Drill a hole through the upper end of the broomstick for a key and a slot at right angles to it for the string. Then make a little triangle (see *e*) for the bridge just back of the large hole in the cigar box, whittle out a key (*h* on top of a tapered *b*), run your string from the base up around the key, adjust the bridge and tune up. The cats will leave.

Matchstick carving, originally developed in Europe, is a lot of fun, requiring only imagination and a little patience. Figures 39 and 40 show two prize-winning pieces so made. Curves and angles are produced by cutting, bending, and breaking the matchstick as necessary, holding the break in each case with a spot of glue. Before close splitting (such as separating legs), dampen the wood but do not soak it lest the match head come off. Both human beings and animals can be so whittled, thin animals like the deer being particularly graceful. Pose the figure running, jumping, or in other vigorous action. For dancing figures, use the proportions of the "fashion figure" from Chap. XXI. Make up groups by pasting on cardboard or wood, and preserve with paint or shellac.

All the seed and shell "whimsies" of Fig. 31 are easy. The ostrich, flamingo, and chicken are simply walnut-shell halves glued over shaped pipe cleaners or a central, thin-wood silhouette. The dodo, center background, has a half walnut shell for a head, with lentils glued on for eyes and a bill shaped of thin wood. Neck and legs are $\frac{1}{8}$-in. dowel rod, glued into U-slots cut at the line of joining of the shells. Spider and boat have thin-wood accessories, and the sailboat a paper sail and a half-spool base.

The turtle compass, left, Fig. 31, is explained in Fig. 43. Break the ends off a Gillette-type razor blade at the outer holes, then magnetize it by stroking it with a permanent magnet. Glue it over a cut-out turtle body and legs, and drill a hole in the body to line up with that in the blade. Over the hole glue a little "tent" of shaped photograph film to act as a socket for the pivot. The pivot is a phonograph needle stuck point outward into a dowel-rod, the base a half spool. Balance the turtle on it by adding bits of wood or lead to front or back as needed, then glue on the half shell that forms his back. Figure 43 also shows an airplane and an insect made of maple seeds glued to bits of shaped wood.

Whole peanuts form the parrot and walking duck of Fig. 36. The parrot's feathers are painted paper, its perch a half spool with

Fig. 44 · Industry, as represented by tiny whittled buildings, made realistic by careful painting. Such models can be used in many ways, from decoration to advertising and demonstration

dowel-rod shaft and phonograph needle on top. Details of the duck are in Fig. 43. A thin-wood head is glued on one end and a bit of feather on the other. The legs are little segments of arcs cut from thin wood. They are joined by a common pin passing through the body a little above the center, as shown by the dot, Fig. 43, and held away from the body by thin-wood washers. This axle must turn *in the body*, not in the legs, and the legs must also be joined by a stop pin in back so that they move together. The body is balanced by adding at the tail a nail of proper weight.

Put the duck on an incline of about 25 degrees. It will walk down thus: It tends to slide down, rolling forward upon its feet. As they roll, the stop pin joining them in back comes up and strikes the body, tipping it forward sharply and causing the duck to skid forward a bit on its chest; this relieves the legs and they slide forward again, putting the duck back in its first position.

The coconut-shell faces of Fig. 37 are commonly used as twine holders. A ball of twine is put inside, then the head is hung on the wall with the twine coming out of the mouth. Make them by whittling the "eyes" out of the end of a shell. Half shells can also be made into lampshades and cups, or carved on the surface.

Peach-stone whittling is a good old-fashioned country trick that my grandad taught me. Figure 34 shows an Indian head and a monkey watch charm thus made, and Fig. 35 shows an apricot-pit turtle and basket. The fruit pits should be scrubbed and dried before use. Use a sharp, short, stiff knife blade, and take only short strokes. All pits are harder than wood, apricot, plum and cherry pits particularly. They are also very brittle. Pits are thicker at the butt; so at that end do deep cutting such as the monkey's head. The rib running up the weaker side of a peach pit forms the monkey's tail, horse's mane, or back of an Indian headdress.

Work the natural markings of the pit into the design, as has been done in Edward Drake's excellent pieces in Fig. 46, heading the next chapter. The very exact monkeys, in order of size, are made from peach, damson plum, plum, and cherry pits. The Indian head above them is an apricot pit, and the larger one a peach stone.

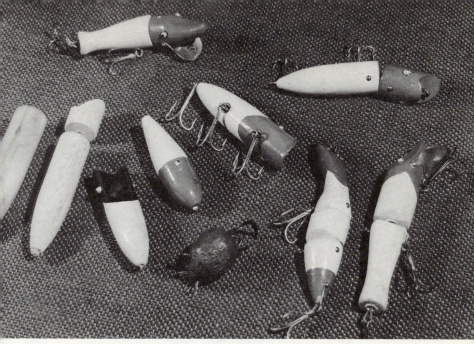

FIG. 45 · *A group of baits, simple and inexpensive, made by John Phillip*

The turtle, basket, and elephants are also peach stones. The crane pendant is a half stone which uses the grain particularly well.

Very simple whittled shapes can be made into realistic model plants or villages by careful painting, Fig. 44. Notice how the artist created the illusion of windows, etc. The smokestacks are matchsticks, the train a bit of thin stick (see Chap. XI).

The "plug" baits in Fig. 45 are mostly red cedar, which is less likely to split than other soft woods. The plug at upper center is hickory—note how it split. Any shape a fish can get into his mouth is likely to catch him—witness the cork mouse with rubber legs and single hook at lower center. Gang hooks on other baits are held by small brass hooks bent to shape. They are used instead of screw-eyes because they have longer shanks. Bushings around eye holes are shoe eyelets fitted into drilled holes; eyes are beads held by cut-off pins. Jointed plugs can be made with thin steel or swivels, and thin steel fins put on. Finish by enameling or lacquering.

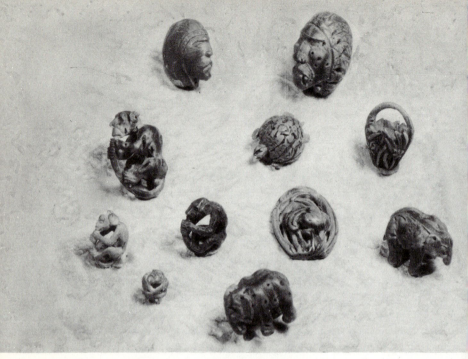

FIG. 46 · *Rustic artistry in fruit pits by Edward F. Drake. See Chap. III*

CHAPTER IV

RUSTIC · *Field and Camp*

FIRST on the list of camping, sporting, and outing essentials is a good, stout pocketknife, for even the greenest camper knows that shanties, camp beds, and camp cookery, to say nothing of fires, depend on it.

But for real use of the knife in the field or in camp, the first re-quirement is a knowledge of local woods; particularly those that cut easily, such as the soft pines; those that are flexible, such as witch-hazel, elm, poplar, willow, hickory, sumac, and basswood; and those that are springy, such as white oak, ash, spruce, locust, hornbeam, and hickory. From the flexible group you will make *withes*, which are simply long, thin, new-growth, green boughs free from knots or branches, and which may be twisted and knotted around bunches of twigs as binders, or woven into baskets, chair seats, and so on.

But first let's discuss that old favorite—the whistle. I was making them in Spring as soon as I could cut down a willow wand, and you can too. You need only a green willow, poplar, basswood, or sycamore branch about ½ in. in diameter and 4 or 5 in. long (substitute any other smooth-bark tree). Cut through the bark down to solid wood an inch or two from one end, then wet and pound all over the rest of the bark with the back of an old knife or a convenient stick (lower right, Fig. 47). After a little pounding, take hold of one end of the stick with each hand, and twist and pull the stick right out of the bark.

As soon as you have it loose, put it back in, and cut the tapering end and notch shown at upper left in Fig. 47. Then pull the stick out again, cut the end off at the base of the notch, slice a thin sliver off the top of the plug for an air passage, and slip this little piece back into place. Then whittle off another piece for a plug at the other end of the whistle, fit it in tightly, and go ahead and blow! If instead of the one-tone whistle, you want one that plays tunes, whittle the outer end piece into a plunger that can be slid back and forth in the barrel, as at Fig. 47 b. A pea in the barrel will put a

FIG. 47 · *It is easy to make a whistle, if you know how to get the bark off in one piece, without cracking. A little pounding does it. Spring wood works best. If you have no green wood, drill a piece of dowel rod, then shape the mouthpiece, notch, and fit the air-passage plug*

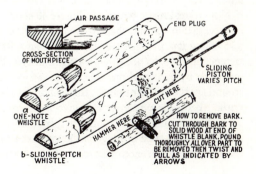

AIR PASSAGE

END PLUG

CROSS-SECTION OF MOUTHPIECE

SLIDING PISTON VARIES PITCH

CUT HERE

a
ONE-NOTE WHISTLE

HAMMER HERE

HOW TO REMOVE BARK. CUT THROUGH BARK TO SOLID WOOD AT END OF WHISTLE BLANK. POUND THOROUGHLY ALL OVER PART TO BE REMOVED THEN TWIST AND PULL AS INDICATED BY ARROWS

b-SLIDING-PITCH WHISTLE

c

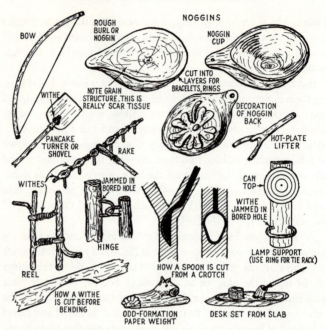

Fig. 48 · *Some of the tricks in working with wood with the bark on*

warble in the whistle, several holes along the barrel will make it a flute. Treat it carefully, and keep it wet when out of use.

Now to real rustic whittling. Figure 48 shows at upper left the bow, varied in size and shape to fit a fire drill or some arrows, and just below it a pancake turner, made from a flat shingle or chip fastened into a split bough with a withe or two. Farther below is a reel made by paring off one side of a two-fork branch, twisting it around another similar branch, then binding the end down with a withe. (Bend the withe slowly; give its fibers a chance to flex.) This reel has handles; one without them is shown at lower right in Fig. 49. One type of hinge is shown next to the sketch of the reel; another much more elaborate one and a proper latch for a cabin door are shown at upper left in Fig. 55. Figure 48 also shows a rake, with sharpened twigs stuck through a branch withed to a handle and with withes holding the twigs in place.

It is possible to fix a twig into a branch quite tightly by boring a small hole or making a deep pyramidal cut into the larger branch, then jamming and driving a pointed end of the twig into the hole. The only requirements are a deep hole and a good fit with the pointed twig end. The rake carries this principle on to splitting the branch to let the twig through, then binding it with a withe, while the lamp support, far right in Fig. 48, has a withe jammed in at both ends to form the circular support. Such a ring may also be used for a hanger or tie rack.

There are often boughs and twigs so shaped that they will save whittling or help to avoid splitting. For example, an ordinary crotch in a branch serves excellently for a shaped spoon or fork because the fibers are so intertwined at the joint that they prevent splitting off of the spoon bowl from its handle. Figure 48 shows how to do it, and Fig. 52 (p. 48), shows it done. Similarly, a very fine cup, bracelet, neckerchief slide, or napkin ring can be made from a noggin (cup) or burl, just a fancy name for what trees do to cover scars on their trunks. They build up a bump

[47]

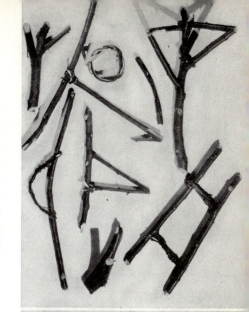

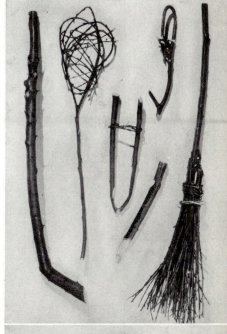

Fig. 49 (Top) · *Rustic coat-hangers, shelf brackets, hooks, door handle, cleat, ring, and reel.* Fig. 50 · *Hockey stick or cane, steak broiler, fire tongs, pot hook, tent peg, and withe broom.* Fig. 51 (Bottom) · *Scale model of Fort Dearborn, Chicago, made by Roy Olsen. Home Work-shop Silver Medal in 1935.* (Courtesy *Popular Science Monthly*)

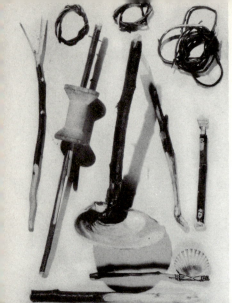

formation that has circular grain structure so may be hollowed out to make a cup, as at upper right, Fig. 48, or sliced into layers for bracelets or rings. It may even be carved and polished. Queer branch formations will make paper weights like that at bottom, Fig. 48, or can be carved into fantastic shapes for heads on walking sticks or handles on paper knives.

Figure 49 shows at upper left a double fork that can be nailed to a cabin wall for use as a hook, and just below it two rustic coat-hangers, one with withe handle, the other with a forked hook thinned at its lower end and twisted about the hanger proper. At upper right is a corner bracket for a shelf, made from a double fork by thinning and bending back for withing to the main branch. Between the coat hangers is a similarly made wall bracket, and at top center a napkin ring woven of split willow and a cleat made from a bent branch. At bottom center is a door handle.

Figure 50 shows a hockey stick or cane (depending on which end is up), a steak broiler (or toaster), fire tongs, pot hook, tent peg, and withe broom, all simple to make. Corner joints are shown at lower right, Fig. 55.

At left top, Fig. 52, is a simple fork, then two napkin rings or neckerchief slides of withes, with a scratch

FIG. 52 (TOP) · More rustic pieces, including fork, spoons, salt and pepper carrier, candle sconce, paper knife, and scratch gauge. FIG. 53 · A coconut wren house, showing assembly. FIG. 54 (BOTTOM) · The wren house ready to hang

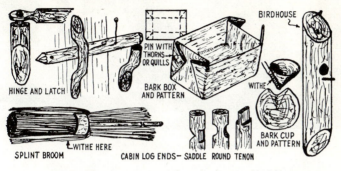

FIG. 55 · *More rustic pieces, including splint broom and bark box*

gauge between them made of a spool, a branch, and a wedge. (Leave out the nail and wedge, notch the spool rims all around, and wind on a piece of string to make a Hallowe'en buzzer for neighbors' windows. Or mount a thin strip of wood so that it snaps over the notches to make a New Year's noise maker.) Over at right is a candle holder. Below it is a salt spoon made from a forked branch, and next to it and below it are a soup ladle and spoon made from split branches wired onto shells. Below is the simple paper knife— select pieces of wood that can be carved into figures, grotesque or otherwise. And at right center is a combined salt and pepper shaker of bamboo or hollow twig. Shaker holes are drilled near each end, then a long plug is fitted into the end. If a flat spot is whittled on each plug, it becomes a rotating valve.

Figures 53 and 54 show a wren house made from a coconut, (⅞-in. hole). Another birdhouse, this time from a hollowed branch, is at right, Fig. 55. Split the log for easy hollowing.

Figure 55 shows at lower left the famous splint broom of our great-grandmothers, made from a 3-in. birch log by peeling it back from one end for a foot, then splitting this section into fine long shavings. The bark is left on in a 2-in. band, and above that re-moved again, this time for 15 in. This section is likewise split down into long shavings, bent back down, and withed in place.

FIG. 56 · *Four types of silhouettes for four purposes*

CHAPTER V

SILHOUETTES · *Flat Toys and Windmills*

O NE of my earliest recollections is a moving picture called
"The Jack-knife Man," in which the hero, a white-haired
old shanty boatman, delighted the town children with toys whittled of thin pine. Queer and grotesque shapes he got too, but they
were dear to the kids for all that, and they had one great virtue—
no two were ever alike!

Start whittling on any piece of ¼- or ⅜-in. soft wood, and some
queer animal will suggest itself almost automatically. An outline
and a few whittled grooves to show eyes, ears, nose, mouth, and
limb positions, and there you are. Man, animal, bird, fish, or
flower—you can bet it will be funny.

For angular, awkward appearance, try the square-cut animals of
Fig. 58. Simply lay out a checkerboard of lines ¼ in. apart on some
¼-in. white pine, then copy in the outline, square for square, of
any animal that intrigues you. Whittle out the outline, cut V-
grooves for the interior lines, and you can call the piece done. If
you keep a sharp knife blade and remember what is said in Chap.

〖 50 〗

III about grain, you should have little trouble. If you want to elaborate a little, cut away the surface ⅛ in. or so of the blacked-in portions of the drawing, or color them dark and leave the rest light. Make eyes by sticking in the tip of a sabre-shaped blade at the four sides of a square diagonally toward the center, thus cutting out a little pyramid.

If the sizes I have shown do not appeal to you or do not fit your plans, lay out your own checkerboard with ⅛-in. squares (thus making the piece slightly larger than it is in the illustration), or use ½-in. squares (thus making the piece about four times as big as its picture here). Or vary square size either way or in-between to suit your needs. If none of these animals appeals to you, draw suitable squares over any picture that does, then transfer the lines, square by square, to a similar checkerboard on your wood, and go to it. You can find suitable pictures in children's story books, grown-up magazines, photographs, and drawings; or you can de-vise new animals by modifying the drawings here reproduced. The fox can be made a dog, wolf, or mouse, the owl a crow or raven, the moose a reindeer or an elk—just by changing details. Try a Noah's Ark of such animals, or use them for a frieze around the nursery wall or for a screen or a transparent shade.

Slightly more elaborate are the rounded figures of Fig. 59. The soldier *a* has movable arms, if you want to make them separately and pin them on. Do this by drilling a ⅛-in. hole in each arm and in his body in the right place, then gluing in a bit of ⅛-in. dowel rod so that it is tight in the arms but rotates in the hole in the body. Sailor *b* is a gawky, scrawny figure that can be changed in costume to represent any other individual you prefer. The negro mammy *c* makes a good place card or mantel knickknack or she or the others can be used for screens, lampshades, or garden ornaments, in colors, of course, the brighter the better.

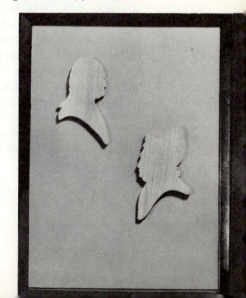

Fig. 57 · *The simple silhouette. These are the familiar George and Martha Washington, shown mounted in* Fig. 64

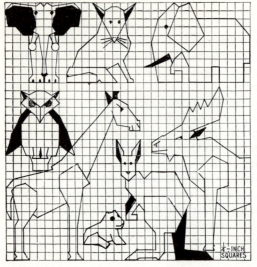

FIG. 58 · *Flat toys,
eight of them, all
capable of variations.
Blacked-in areas can
be cut below the
surface. Changing
square size will give
you any desired size
of finished animal*

Flat toys can be made to do stunts, too. Familiar types are the
rooster and hen pecking at the pan between them, the tumbling
clown, the trapeze artist, and the boxing twins. The tumbling
clown, Fig. 59 *f*, is made of ¼-in. or thicker wood, with his hands
positioned so that the dowel hole is at his center of gravity—in
other words so that his feet weigh as much as his head. When you
get the rough shape cut out, drive a small finishing nail through
about where you think his center of gravity should be, then see if
he will spin evenly along two parallel bars. If he is much too
heavy, move the nail; if only a little too heavy, shave off some of
his cap or his trousers until he balances. Then drill a hole through
the proper nailhole for a dowel about 2 in. long, make a pair of
miniature parallel bars for him of dowel or smoothly whittled
sticks set about 1¼ in. apart, and let him spin at his ease. Paints
help his complexion.

Whittle the hen and rooster, Fig. 59 *e*, out of ⅛-in. soft wood,
each with a bar ¼-in. wide by ¾-in. or 1 in. long extending down

e also ⅛-in. wood, ¼ in. wide and
having the pan silhouette cut in
r with small brads or cut-off pins,
hickens stand straight up when the
pper. All that is necessary to make
lower bar back and forth endwise.
ome Swiss and German whittlers
case, do not whittle out posts be-
ave pads for nailing beneath them.
o that the head end of the chicken
fasten them to the top bar. Then
chicken's tail to a common weight
n, and be sure your hinge joints are
ʋung like a pendulum parallel with
: in turn.

the jointed acrobat of Fig. 59 g, so
t drawn him to scale. Full size, he is
he is a side silhouette, use the sol-
hat his leg should be jointed at knee
at elbow as well as shoulder. (Re-
or the lap joint in each case.) Make
ut him together with bits of wire or
brads formed into an eye just outside each joint. Joints should be
quite loose, and the outer part of each limb should be *away* from
the body. Only in this way will the acrobat "flop" as he should.

The supporting bars are ¼- by ½-in. pieces about 10 in. long,
with a crossbar between them 2 in. long and 2 in. up from the
bottom. Drill twin holes side by side in the top of each supporting
bar, large enough for a heavy thread or light cord, and drill two
holes in each of the acrobat's hands also, *but put them one above the
other*—in other words, one nearer the wrist than the other. Thread
the cord through the holes so that it forms a loop when the acrobat's arms are at right angles to the supporting bars, pull it fairly
tightly, and tie it.

Loosen the crossbar at the bottom so that the newly-laced

thread at the top allows the acrobat to sag. Now if the lower ends of the "H" are pressed sharply together, the acrobat should jump briskly upward with arms and legs flying. If he doesn't, tighten the cord at the top a little. To add to the show, flip the acrobat over and over a couple of times, so that when you press the "H" bottom together the string untwists and flips him back again.

Last of the action toys is the pair of boxers at h. These lads are jointed, as is the acrobat, and are similarly made except that their bodies may be ¼-in. material. From the eye at each side of their arm joints extend a bow-shaped flexible wire that holds them together just in good swinging range. Fasten a cord to the center of each wire bow, take one in each hand, and pull them fairly taut. Now if you jounce the boxers up and down over any surface, they will go through quite a convincing exhibition, except that they may kick in clinches!

Dancers, clowns, or acrobats may be substituted for the boxers or the whole thing may be made up of clothespins. A clothespin figure, incidentally, is made by cutting off the legs at the base of the fork, then cutting each leg in half. Half becomes an arm, the other half a leg, while what is left of the pin becomes the body and head. Drill the pieces and pin them together as before and paint your clothespin figures in as gaudy colors as you wish.

So to silhouettes proper. Figure 56 shows several types. George and Martha Washington, shown in Fig. 57, and properly mounted and in detail in Fig. 64, are the conventional type. They are simply copies of the old favorites, made by tracing an outline on transparent paper, then transferring it to ⅛-in. white pine by retracing the outline over carbon paper on the wood. A sharp knife will follow the outline quite easily. Then sand, oil, and wax, and the pieces are ready for mounting. If you prefer other figures, simply trace side views. You can even make silhouettes of your friends if you have side portraits, and can vary the size from the photograph by using the checkerboard system explained earlier in the chapter. Such miniatures are quite attractive mounted on panels of contrasting color—I used walnut. A similar result can be obtained by cutting the silhouette through only the top veneer of a piece of plywood that has contrasting color inside. I understand a special plywood is available for this.

Directly the reverse is the inverted silhouette of the traffic cop at the left, Fig. 56. Here the silhouette is cut away to leave the background. This particular one, of ⅛-in. white pine, forms a hot-dish pad. If you make him, watch these two things: Do not grip the blank too tightly, or you will split it, and do not force the knife through the grain, or the same thing will happen. The same idea is used in the transparent silhouette of Fig. 63 *f*. A silhouette

FIG. 59 · *More flat toys, four action toys and four windmill-driven toys. The sign at d is a simple silhouette*

whittled out of wood is backed with parchment and fastened to a base carrying a lamp. The light shines through the parchment, putting the silhouette in high relief.

This idea is the basis of the stencil, which can be made of wood just as well as of any other material—for example the block E of Fig. 63 e. Cut out a design this way and use it for a stencil, or mount it on a contrasting background. The left-hand E in Fig. 63 d is the simple silhouette again, except that it is cut on the top of a block and thus forms a woodblock letter suitable for printing. More data on woodblock carving appear in Chap. XVIII.

Common and inverted silhouettes are combined in the clown at center, Fig. 56. His outline is a silhouette, and the spots in his suit are holes, as are parts of the lines indicating his arms and his drum. Whittled out of maple or other hard wood that gives smooth edges, he would make an attractive desk or mantel ornament. A more elaborate piece, with a little decoration in addition to the cutting through is the pattern on the box face in Fig. 62. This is really pierced work, treated in more detail in Chap. XX.

Another desk or mantel ornament is the photograph mounted on silhouette background, just ahead of the clown. This means close whittling around the head, to keep from changing the appearance of the man.

Another interesting stunt is the building up of a scene with silhouette sections, just exactly as it is done on the stage. The

Fig. 60 · *Close-ups of two of the silhouettes in* Fig. 56, *showing the original sketches from which they were designed. Any magazine, book, or newspaper will suggest others*

racehorses at right, Fig. 56, are a simple example to show the principle. Window decorators use the same idea to impart depth or distance to their show windows, to create wave or cloud effects, and so on. Or take thin sections and mount them one atop the other to build up contours or designs. I have decorated boxes with designs built up of flat pieces, and have also made birds and animals for ornaments on the same principle.

Silhouettes have almost endless applications. A common commercial one is sketched in Fig. 59 *d*—the silhouette signboard. Still others are the windmills of Fig. 59 *l*, *m*, *k*, *j*, and *i*. Any windmill involves a rotor that rotates on a shaft. Instead of that, fasten the rotor to the shaft as a farmer does, and put a kink in the shaft for a crank. There you have a means of driving any number of queer things. One of the commonest is the wood sawyer, Fig. 59 *i*. This crude figure of a man is cut out of ¼ or ½-in. wood, with a jointed right arm holding a saw cutting into a block of wood. A wire link from the windmill crank pulls the arm back and forth whenever the wind blows, and your man saws wood. He may be mounted at the base of a miniature tower holding the rotor, or may be quite close to it, as indicated. He will work uncomplainingly until a heavy wind comes along—then you may find him strewn around the yard. One of my friends was a little too realistic-minded, so put a little toothed metal saw in his sawyer's hand. He awoke one morning after a night-long windstorm to find the block sawed through.

If you prefer the cobbler of Fig. 59 *j*, connect your crank at his hand. The donkey at *k* has his forelegs hinged and carries the crank in his hindquarters. Make a little negro like *m* as part of the donkey and fastened to his heels, or separately as in *l* and *m*. The goat at *l* carries the crank just ahead of his ear, so he has a rotary motion that is decidedly menacing toward the pickaninny. (All these figures should be worked out with squares about 1 in. apart instead of the ½ in. of earlier pieces.)

How about the windmill or rotor to drive the figure? We are getting to that, but first let us make the simpler water wheel of

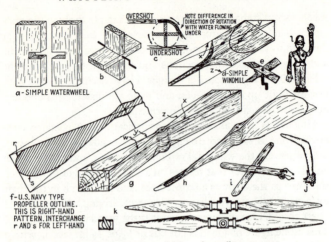

Fɪɢ. 61 · *Water wheels, windmills, and propellers are easy*

Fig. 61 b. Simply take two pieces ½ by 3 by 8 in. and cut a ½-in. notch 1½ in. deep, as at *a*. Then put them together, put an axle through the center or a nail in from each side, balance the wheel by shaving off the heavier blade, and the water wheel is done. If you have a fairly swift stream available, mount it as an undershot wheel, Fig. 51 *c*, letting the water current rotate it. If instead of current you can get a little head of water with a dam, lead the water over the wheel through a flume, as in the overshot type. In either case, of course, the axle can be extended to drive a simple figure or do whatever else you want it to.

The simplest windmill is the type sketched in Fig. 61 *d*. Take any soft wood piece that approximates the shape of the block in *d*. A good size is ½ by 1 by 3 in., if you have to make one. On one 1-in. face draw the diagonals, and where they intersect drill a ⅛-in. hole through. This is the center, or hub. Draw a diagonal across each end also, in each case from lower left to upper right. Begin to cut away the wood at *y*, about even with the center, cutting away the entire corner until the outer end is cut down almost to the end diagonal. Now from the diagonally opposite corners (z is one of them) cut in the same way until the blades are shaped and thin. Then put a ⅛-in. dowel in the hole and see if the propeller balances. If it doesn't, cut a little off the heavy end until it does. Then replace the dowel with a heavy nail through the hole, then through a small spool or thick washer, and into a stick, and see if your propeller will spin.

If you prefer a four-bladed one, begin the shaping farther out from center—¾ in. or so on blocks of the size given above—then make a cross of the two with a joint like that on the waterwheel in *a* and *b*, except that it is made across the wide face of the blocks instead of the narrow one, and will look like *e*. Put in a tight-fitting crank, and there's a wind-power plant.

So to the simple "U.S. Navy" propeller of Fig. 61 *h*. Use a block 10 in. long, ⅞ in. thick, and 1¼ in. wide, or 8 in. long, 11⁄16 in. thick, and 1⅜ in. wide, of any soft wood. (Regular balsa propeller blocks and propeller blanks are available in any model store, the blank looking like *g*.) First study the pattern *f*. Then begin work on your block by drawing diagonals to locate the center on the wide face, and where they intersect sketch in the hub. Cut out the blank until it looks like *g*. Sketch in the dotted lines from lower left to upper right-hand corner on each end, making them curved as indicated so that the upper surface will be concave (hollow) and the lower convex. Now work just as you did on the simple wind-mill, beginning by cutting wood away at *x* and *y* in *g*, then at the diagonally opposite corners, leaving edges *w* and *z* untouched. Work carefully to get the upper surface concave and the lower convex. Shape the ends as indicated in *r* and *s* in *f*, and thin and shape both blades and hub. Drill a 1⁄32-in. hole through the hub, then put a pin through and balance the propeller by taking thin shavings off or sanding the heavier blade on the convex side.

Fig. 62 · *A silhouette design with some extra outlining, a simple pierced design of the type taken up more in detail in Chap. XX. (Courtesy Remington Arms Co., Inc.)*

This is a right-hand propeller, which means that it should be driven clockwise (looking at it from the rear) on a model airplane, and that the wind blowing on it will turn it *counterclockwise*. If you decide to whittle out double-propellered flying models, you may want both left-hand and right-hand ones. Use the same blank as in g, but put the end diagonals from lower right to upper left, and start cutting at *w* and *z*, leaving *x* and *y* intact. The blade-end shape is reversed, *r* and *s* being interchanged. The hub is thinned at the *top* instead of the bottom, also.

The blade shape on the new hollow metal propellers is shown in Fig. 61 *k*. You may want to whittle out one of this type for a show model. Other propeller shapes, as well as the many shapes for ship propellers, can be got from photographs, drawings, or plans.

Remember the whirling-armed policeman that once adorned many radiator caps? He is sketched at Fig. 61 *l*. Make a funny armless figure of a policeman, and drill a hole for an axle through his shoulders (⅛ or ¼ in.). Then make two single-bladed propellers with a hand shaped at the end instead of simple rounding off. Glue one at each end of a dowel rod pushed through the shoulder hole (one up and one down), paint him, and there you are! In the dog of Fig. 63 *a*, the beagle's legs and ears are whittled from separate pieces and nailed or glued in place, thus emphasizing them. Separate, higher planes also emphasize the bird's wings. Such built-up silhouettes are also useful in giving a flat figure motion, a common one being the simple lever and long neck of the chicken in Fig. 63 *c*, by which the chicken lifts its head when its tail is pushed down. The same arrangement can be used to make a

FIG. 63 · *Built-up figures, transparency, and block letters—all silhouette problems*

FIG. 64 · George and Martha Washington in white pine on walnut, oiled and waxed. The silhouettes themselves are of ⅛-in. wood

dog bark, a man lift his hat, an animal open a drawer (around the handle of which his jaws are clamped), and so on.

Figure 63 *b* shows silhouette letters formed into a box handle. Monograms, simple words, or letter groups can be run together to make attractive small handles for cigarette boxes, stamp cases, paper knives, desk blotters, etc. "Blocky" letters must be used.

Kin to the propeller is the boomerang, that Australian weapon that comes back to its thrower if he misses. A common type is sketched at Fig. 61 *j*. Such a boomerang would be about 2½ ft. long and 2½ in. wide at its hump, with an angle at the hump of 90 to 180 degrees or so. The side toward you in the sketch is made flat, the opposite side convex, or humped, and the hump is thinned down to a fairly sharp edge. Also the handle end is made somewhat longer than the outer end. The trick is to keep on shaping and balancing until the boomerang *floats* or *planes* as soon as it begins to lose speed. It is thrown as sketched, with a straight swing as if it were a hammer. It is supposed to hit what it is aimed at as it flies outward, for then it flies in a straight line. As it loses speed, it acts like a glider, coming back toward its thrower in a circle.

Another adaptation of the boomerang is the cross in Fig. 61 *i*. This is simply two thin wide pieces fastened together at their centers, and whittled so that the side up is convex, while the bottom side is flat. This piece flies like the rotor of an autogyro, circling to return toward its thrower.

Fig. 65 · *A group of block puzzles.* (Courtesy "Oil Power," Socony-Vacuum Oil Co.)

CHAPTER VI

PUZZLES · *Simple and Difficult*

MANY whittlers consider the chain, fan, ball-in-a-cage, and hinge joint as puzzles, just as well as those shown in this chapter. Each of those four whittling stunts has so many variations, however, that each has been given a chapter. Here are described some eighteen puzzles and tricks, from the simple Eskimo *gazinta* and the yoke to the complicated dropping ball and Oriental blocks.

Simplest among the puzzles that I know is the yoke, or lapel tag, a standard Boy Scout stunt but one that never fails to mystify. I once helped put on 300 yokes at the entrance to a Father-and-Son banquet hall, and very few fathers listened to the speeches that night—at least until they got *their* yoke puzzle off. Even the speakers fingered theirs absentmindedly.

For the yoke, take a flat bit of wood about ⅛ in. or less thick, ½ in. wide, and 4 in. long. Round both ends and bore or drill a hole near one end, as in Fig. 67 d. Through the hole pass a piece of cord and knot it into a loop just a *little too short* to pass over the opposite end. That is the yoke complete.

The yoke is applied to any convenient buttonhole, and that is where the trick comes in. Spread the loop over the cloth around the buttonhole, then pull buttonhole and adjacent cloth through, as in Fig. 67 *e*, until the undrilled end of the wooden tag can be slipped through the buttonhole. Draw it through, pulling the cord after it, and you will have the loop through the buttonhole as at *f*. To anyone who does not know the trick, it looks as though the loop were simply passed through the buttonhole and the tag then put through the loop, so he tries to take the yoke off by reversing the procedure. But the loop is too short! When you are ready to end his agony, pull the buttonhole back through the loop until the tag can be passed back out, drilled end first.

Similar in shape to the yoke, but without drilled hole or cord is the "buzzer," which sounds like an airplane propeller when thrown properly. Whittle out a flat piece 1 in. wide by 9 in. long of ⅛- or ¼-in. wood. Round the ends. Grasp the ⅛-in. sides of the buzzer at the middle between the thumb and the tips of the fingers so that one flat side is outward. Then simply throw it as hard as you can, just as though you were going to throw a base-ball. If you have thrown it properly, it will fly through the air for a short distance, buzzing like a propeller meanwhile.

Also similar in shape are the bones which Southern negroes use for castanets. Use hardwood for these—maple, walnut, or ebony —and make them 1 or 1¼ in. wide, ¼ in. thick, and 9 in. long. Round the corners and the edges and smooth up all over. You will need two bones, one held loosely between the thumb and first finger close to the base of the finger, the other held loosely between first and second fingers, also close in. About 3 or 4 in. of each bone should extend outside the hand, and the third and fourth fingers should be used to guide and stop the lower bone. Simply twist your hand sharply from side to side, and the bones will set up quite a clatter. A little practice, and you will be able to keep simple or syn-copated time.

The diagonal dovetail of Fig. 67 *b* has made many a cabinetmaker swear—

FIG. 66 · *Another block puzzle and the parts that make it. A little study will show you how to make it. (Courtesy "Oil Power," Socony-Vacuum Oil Co.)*

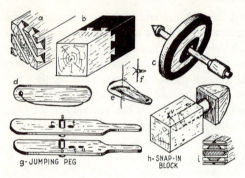

FIG. 67 · These five puzzles are the bases for eight easy ones—the diagonal dovetail, the arrow and target, the yoke, buzzer and bones, the jumping peg and flipping spatula, and the snap-in block

g- JUMPING PEG

h- SNAP-IN BLOCK

at least, that it can not be done (just as he will that the T of Fig. 70 can't be taken apart). If you have ever made a dovetail joint, a little study will convince you that the joint in Fig. 67 b could never be made, let alone separated. But you automatically assume, just as everyone else does, that the dovetail runs square with the sides. It does not; it is cut diagonally, as at a, and can be put together and separated quite easily. Use contrasting colors of wood to make yours, say white pine and mahogany. Each block should be about 1 in. square by an inch or two long. Lay out the dovetail on one piece, whittle it out, then make the mating half. They must mate closely at the surface, or your secret will be out.

If you have trouble with this one, make a standard dovetail squarely across the end face, as at i, then whittle down the edges until an edge comes at the center of each former side.

The arrow-and-target puzzle takes advantage of the habit wood has of swelling when wet. Make the target of white pine about $\frac{3}{8}$ in. thick by 3 in. in diameter, with a $\frac{1}{2}$-in. hole in the center. Next, whittle out a round arrow about 5 in. long, with the pointed head just too large at its base to pass through the hole, and the round section representing the feathers even larger. Soak the target for an hour or two in warm water and it will swell, actually enlarging the center hole and becoming almost doughy and difficult to split in the process. Drive the arrow through the hole carefully, shaving it a bit smaller if absolutely necessary. Dry the assembly, and the target will shrink back to its proper size. The arrow stays in from then on.

The jumping peg, Fig. 67 g, or "magic cricket bat," as it is called in England, is made of ⅛-in. white pine or basswood ½ in. wide and 6 in. long. Narrow down 1 in. of one end to form a handle about ³⁄₁₆ in. wide. Drill two holes ¼ in. apart at the middle, as at s and t Fig. 67 g, and one hole *almost* through from each side, as at r and u, at opposite ends of s and t. Blacken the bottoms of these two holes so that they look as if they have been drilled through. Fit a short peg into the center hole. The idea is to make it jump from the middle hole to the end one and back. Here the hand must be quicker than the eye. Put the peg in hole s and hold the spatula by its handle between your thumb and index finger. Now make a few magic passes over the spatula, and as you make the last, flip the spatula over by rotating the handle between the tips of your fingers. With a little practice, you can make it flip exactly a half turn, so that to the eye, the peg appears to have jumped from one hole to the next. If an observer questions your trick, take the peg out and try it in the other drilled-through hole.

A variation of this trick is a simple undrilled "flipping spatula" with two stars, moons, or other designs on one side and three on the other. By flipping you can add or subtract a moon or a star. But practice long enough to get a fast flip!

The snap-in block, Fig. 67 h, is simplicity itself, but it kept me guessing for several minutes when I first saw it. All there is to it is a block ¾ by ¾ by 2-in. with a ¼-in. hole drilled part-way through from one end. Into this hole slides a pin with a squared and tapered head, as shown. The exhibitor holds the block in one hand and the plug in the other. Carefully he inserts the end of the plug in the hole. Suddenly it snaps out of his fingers into the block. First I thought it was a vacuum created in the little cylinder, then I thought it was a concealed rubber band, but both times I was wrong. Then I noticed the little drilled hole at v, and tried it with the hole held shut. But still it wouldn't work for me. Suddenly I noticed that the tapered plug was worn very smooth at the back. The answer is simplicity itself—the exhibitor goes through a lot of motions, but what he actually does is hold the plug between thumb and index finger, and when the time comes for the snap-in, he simply increases the pressure between his fingers until the tapered plug snaps out between them.

Ancestor of all jigsaw puzzles is the "Seven Ingenious Plan" of ancient China, or "Tanagrams" as we know it today, Fig. 68 a. Take a thin (⅛ in. or less) 3-in. square of wood and cut it with a sharp knife, as at a, into seven pieces. These may then be arranged into hundreds of little patterns, men, beasts, fish, or whatever you will. The only rules are that only one set of Tanagrams be used for a figure and that no pieces overlap. Five simple figures shown in Fig. 68 b I learned from *The Book of Knowledge*.

Once an ancient and wise king offered half his kingdom to a man who could make a plug to fit the three simple geometric shapes of holes, the square, the triangle and the circle. Many men tried it and failed, then his jester whittled out the plug at lower right, Fig. 68 c. It is simply a piece of dowel rod of the same length as its diameter, with two sides tapered to a knife-edge at the top.

Another very old puzzle is the "Jacob's ladder," Fig. 68 d. It is made of any convenient number of pieces of wood, all exactly the same size, and when one end is picked up, another piece seems to fall end over end down the ladder and hang suspended at the bottom. When the bottom piece is held and the ladder inverted, the block falls end over end back to the other end.

Use any convenient wood for the pieces; cigar box is ideal if you have enough. Any number of pieces can be included, but a good number is ten. Make each piece about 2 in. wide by 3½ in. long, and round and smooth up the ends, as shown in Fig. 68 d. Now take ordinary white or black tape about ⅜ or ½ in. wide and cut a number of lengths about 5 in. long. Then study Fig. 68 d until you see the arrangement. Each tape should be long enough to pass the full length of a block and leave enough end for gluing at top and bottom. There are one center tape and two side tapes on each piece, and the arrangement is exactly the same all the way down, no matter how many pieces you use. Center tape *a* on board *A* is fastened to the far side of board *B* at *b*. Side tapes *c* and *d* on *A* are fastened to the other side of *B* at *c'* and *d'*. Middle tape *e* at the top of *B* passes down the back of *B* and fastens to *C* at *f*. Side tapes *g* and *h* on *C* fasten to *B* at *g'* and *h'*, and side tapes *i'* and *j'* run down with *k* to fasten to the next piece in the same way. Use the ladder, as at Fig. 68 *e*, holding *A*, and *B* will appear to drop (from "The Book of Knowledge").

Another old-timer is the Indian six-stick or cane-end puzzle, made from ½-in. wood—maple, mahogany, white pine, basswood, or any other. I learned it from an Indian who used it to decorate the head of a cane or walking stick, but it may also be made with six equal-length pieces as a hand puzzle. Whittle a piece of the wood you select 10 in. long and ½ in. square, then cut it in five 2-in. pieces. Be sure the sides are square and smooth. Notch all five, as in Fig. 69 *a*1, cutting one notch each side of the center from one edge down to the two adjacent ones. Each notch should be right-angled so that one of the other pieces will fit it closely, the bottom of each notch should go squarely across the piece,

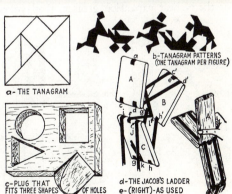

Fig. 68 · *Three more simple puzzles—Tanagrams, ancestor of the jigsaw; the plug that fits three different holes; and the Jacob's ladder. Tanagrams and Jacob's ladder are reprinted by permission of the Grolier Society, Inc., publishers of The Book of Knowledge*

a- THE TANAGRAM

b-TANAGRAM PATTERNS (ONE TANAGRAM PER FIGURE)

c-PLUG THAT FITS THREE SHAPES OF HOLES

d-THE JACOB'S LADDER
e-(RIGHT)-AS USED

and the inner ends of the notches should just meet at the top.

Now notch two of the pieces with a third notch, as at Fig. 69 *a* 4 and 5, from one adjacent edge and exactly between the other two. Take the top of your walking stick or cane and whittle a section 2 in. long exactly square, as in *a*6.

Put 1 and 2 together to form a cross as at *b*, 2 fitting into the lower notch of 1 with its two notches turned up. Now fit 3 against 1 and around 2, as in *c* so that the upper notches in 1 and 3 form a square hole. Lay pieces 4 and 5 each side of 1 and 3 with center notch up. The two notches in 4 and 5 will fit closely against 1 and 3, and they will in turn fit into the notches in 2. Now simply push 6 into the square hole that is left, as in *d*, parallel to 2, and the cane end is finished. If you wish, use different colors of wood.

The T dovetail, Fig. 70 *a*, also assumes that the solver knows about dovetails and realizes that the upright can't be pulled down or pulled out. But actually it can be pulled down, as shown at *b*. The dovetail is tapered back, so that the bottom back is as wide as the widest part of the dovetail top. Use ⅜-in. pieces of contrasting-color woods 2 in. long, and whittle them to the shapes shown in *b*. Keep the joint tight!

There are always friends who believe their lungs are larger, or their chest expansion greater, than yours. The lung tester,

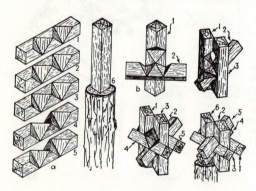

FIG. 69 · The six-stick, or Indian cane, basis of many interlocking block puzzles. It is simply six sticks of the same size with right-angle notches

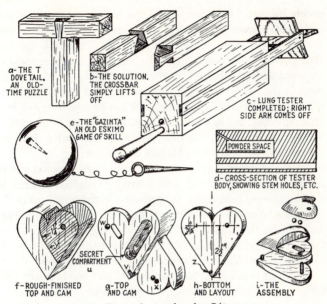

a- THE T
DOVETAIL,
AN OLD-
TIME PUZZLE

b- THE SOLUTION.
THE CROSSBAR
SIMPLY LIFTS
OFF

c- LUNG TESTER
COMPLETED; RIGHT
SIDE ARM COMES OFF

e- THE "GAZINTA"
AN OLD ESKIMO
GAME OF SKILL

POWDER SPACE

d- CROSS-SECTION OF TESTER
BODY, SHOWING STEM HOLES, ETC.

SECRET
COMPARTMENT
u

f- ROUGH-FINISHED
TOP AND CAM

g- TOP
AND CAM

h- BOTTOM
AND LAYOUT

i- THE
ASSEMBLY

Fig. 70 · Two puzzles, a trick, and an Eskimo game

Fig. 70 c, will help to deflate them. When you blow on it, the little paddle-wheel whirls merrily, but when they blow a mighty blast, powder blows back into their faces through the tiny holes near the top!

The block is 1 in. square by $2\frac{1}{2}$ in. long, of any soft wood, with arms recessed in its sides $\frac{1}{8}$ in. or less thick, $\frac{5}{16}$ in. wide, and $3\frac{1}{2}$ in. long, so they extend out to the front 1 in. The little paddle wheel is just wide enough to fit between them, with paddles about $\frac{1}{16}$ in. thick and put together like the water wheel of Fig. 61, Chap. V. It whirls at the ends of the arms on pivots formed of cut-off pins. The mouthpiece can be a bit of sumac with the pith out, or formed of paper or sheet metal.

Cross-section d shows the secret. The lower hole for the mouth-piece is drilled through the block, but the upper one is drilled in only halfway. Under one of the arms, hollow out (with a wafer pen blade) a space for powder, and connect it by cutting down inside into the inner end of the upper hole. Then drill the four little powder holes down diagonally into the powder space. Fill the space with powder and put the arm in tightly. Put the mouth-piece in the *lower* hole. Find the windy friend and demonstrate the tester by blowing a lusty blast. When he asks to try it, be a little unwilling, and as you take it from your mouth, brush against the mouthpiece so it falls out. Apologize and put it back in, *but put it in the upper hole*. He will do the rest.

Eskimo children play with a toy we call the *gazinta*, simply a large wooden or bone ball with a string or rawhide fastened to it and a tapered hole drilled in opposite. On the other end of the string is a tapered pin, as shown in Fig. 70 *e*. The trick is to hold the pin with the ball hanging at the end of the string, then swing the ball up into the air and catch the pin in the hole. It sounds easy, but try it! You will nurse several banged knuckles.

The heart puzzle, Fig. 70 *g*, is a variation of an old secret lock. Let's assume you have two $\frac{1}{4}$-in. ball bearings handy. Take a piece of $\frac{1}{4}$-in. wood and make the bottom, as at *h*, making the lobes $1\frac{1}{2}$-in. (diameter) half circles extended down to the point $2\frac{1}{2}$ in. below. Drill a $\frac{1}{4}$-in. hole at the center of the right lobe and put a stubby $\frac{1}{8}$-in. pin up about $\frac{1}{4}$-in. from the tip and just to the left of the center, as at *z*. Now take a piece of $\frac{1}{2}$-in. wood 3 in. wide by $3\frac{1}{4}$ in. long, lay out the heart on it, and cut out a piece shaped like *f*. From the center of the right-hand lobe, draw the arc of a $1\frac{1}{4}$-in. circle, and extend it downward in a straight line parallel to the left-hand edge as shown. Measure up $\frac{1}{4}$ in. from the back of the piece and draw in line *y*, then whittle out the entire crosshatched section. Make a cam to fit it like the one shown in *h*, and drill both cam and upper heart section with $\frac{1}{4}$-in. holes, so that they fit together neatly, as at *f*.

Drill a $\frac{1}{4}$-in. hole in about $\frac{1}{4}$ in. on the back of the cam, as shown at *x* in *g*, as close as possible to the through hole and a little above and inside it. Turn the heart-shaped top over, and whittle the secret compartment *u* in *g*. Also drill hole *w* clear through the thin part of the heart as close as possible to the pivot hole and in line with it. Now extend the pivot hole *in this piece only* downward parallel to the side for ½ in., so that the two ball bearings will drop in smoothly and still leave room for a pivot at the center of the lobe. Cut the little slot *v* to fit the ⅛-in. pin in the bottom. Careful positioning of this pin and slot is the key to the proper operation of the whole puzzle.

Assemble as at *i*. Put a piece of ¼-in. dowel rod in the bottom 1 in. long. Drop the top over the bottom and see that they fit together snugly, then put in the two ball bearings. Test to be sure that the top cannot be slid free of the locking pin with the bearings in place. Now put the cam on the pivot and stick a small brad through the top of the pivot to hold the assembly together. Or better still, cut the pivot off flush, drill down into it, and push in a big thumbtack, then round off the top of the heart as in *i*.

Let any of your friends try to open that one! It really is easy though. Turn the heart over to start, and slowly move the cam outward until you hear the first ball bearing drop into *x*, then turn the cam a little farther, turn the heart over, and keep turning the cam until the ball bearing drops from *x* into *w*. Turn the cam back into place again, turn the heart over, and get the second ball bearing into *x*. Turn past it enough so the ball will be held in *x*, then turn the heart right-side up, and you'll find the top can be slid off the little locking pin *z* at the point so that the bottom can be swung out to clear the secret compartment. To close, reverse the process. If, when both bearings are out, locking pin *z* will not release the top, move it outward a little or shave off its back. If it releases the top when one bearing is out of the slot, move it inward a little.

[71]

Fig. 71 · *The jigsaw, modern development of the Tanagram. Simple ones with thick sections can be whittled. (Courtesy "Oil Power," Socony-Vacuum Oil Co.)*

Last of the puzzles are the Shinto shrine and the fighting tank, Figs. 72 to 75, both by Hi Sibley in *Popular Mechanics*. Start with a sharp knife. Hard woods, like maple, will be best and last longer. Both are laid out on ¼-in. squares, for handsize puzzles. Make yours larger if you wish.

The roof assembly, *E*, Fig. 72, is made up of four pieces glued together, one for each side of the roof, a ridgepole, and the little locking block below. Uprights *A* must be made one right and one left. Make one piece like *B*, two base blocks like *C*, and eight pieces like *D*. In assembling, first fit *B* between *A* left and *A* right, following with the two base blocks *C*. Next fit three of the pieces *D* together and slide them over and around *A*, then fit on a fourth *D*. Next slide three assembled *D* pieces over the top of the two *A*'s, slide the roof into place, and fit the last *D*.

The tank is somewhat simpler. Make the twenty parts as shown in Fig. 75. The treads are each made up of four pieces.

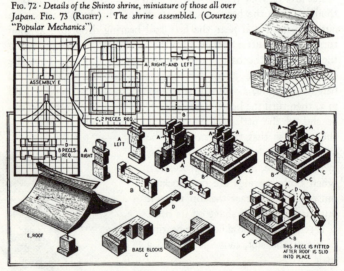

FIG. 72 · *Details of the Shinto shrine, miniature of those all over Japan.* FIG. 73 (RIGHT) · *The shrine assembled.* (*Courtesy "Popular Mechanics"*)

Crossmembers which hold the threads together are alike, except that one is right and the other left. Likewise there are two *D*'s and two *E*'s, each pair including one right and one left. First assemble the treads. Next insert *C* left and *C* right, following with *D* left and *D* right. The *E*'s can now be set in place, permitting *F* to be pushed into the square hole formed by the assembled blocks. When the notch in *F* is exactly between the two *C*'s, crossmember *G* can be pushed into position. *H* and *I* then are put in, finishing the tank.

With these two and the heart puzzle as a basis, you can now design others of your own.

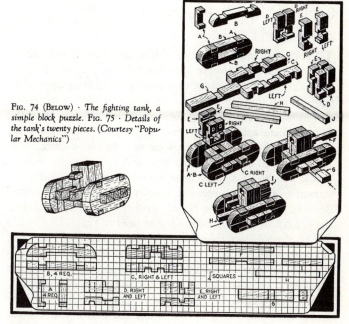

Fig. 74 (Below) · *The fighting tank, a simple block puzzle.* Fig. 75 · *Details of the tank's twenty pieces. (Courtesy "Popular Mechanics")*

Fig. 76 · *Chains entered in a national contest.* (*Courtesy "Popular Mechanics"*)

CHAPTER VII

CHAINS · *Plain and Fancy*

FANS, ball-in-a-cage, pliers, shears, and the chain in all its variations have always been the whittler's standard tricks. Difficult and tricky to make, they usually are of little value when finished, and thus may have helped to give whittling its reputation in most circles of being the loafer's pastime. But when the first chain emerges slowly from a block as you watch pop-eyed, particularly if the knife is in your own hands, it certainly is "the thrill that comes once in a lifetime."

It *is* possible to combine these whittler's tricks into useful and attractive articles of personal jewelry or for wall or mantel decorations—witness the nested spheres of Figs. 101 and 102, the peacock in Fig. 109, or the Indian head in Fig. 108.

The chain is probably the commonest product of whittling, although when finished it usually looks like Fig. 79. It always is a tantalizing problem, because one spoiled link spoils the whole job—and it always seems to be the last link that breaks, probably because the whittler by that time is a little overanxious. The problem is complicated by combining the chain with the fan or the ball-in-a-cage, or both—as did the Chinese, witness Fig. 102.

First you'll need a penknife with a wafer (small and thin) blade and a reasonable amount of patience. Use a straight-grained piece of dry soft wood (white pine or basswood) to start with, about 1½ in. square by 11 in. long. Divide each side into three parts, as at *b*, Fig. 78, and draw parallel lines the length of the block and across the ends. Now crosshatch the two outer thirds on each and the little squares in the four corners of each end. You should now have a ½-in. white stripe down the center of each side and a white cross at each end, Fig. 78 *c*. This white, or unmarked, part is *not* to be cut away; all parts that are cross-hatched *are*.

Fig. 77 · *"The Thrill That Comes Once in a Lifetime,"* by H. T. Webster. *This "whittler's masterpiece" fades into insignificance beside some of the combinations of* Fig. 91, *or the nested spheres of* Fig. 102. *(Courtesy H. T. Webster and the N. Y. Herald Tribune Syndicate)*

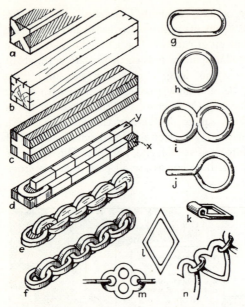

FIG. 78 · *Steps in making a simple chain, b to f. The diagonal cross at a is an alternate start, used especially for endless chains. Eight link shapes are shown in sketches g to n, shapes j and k being shown in the making in Fig. 81 f and g, p. 78*

Whittle away the crosshatched wood, first by cutting off the edges, then by making stop-cuts along dividing lines and cutting away the waste wood until the long cross of Fig. 78 d is left. Look closely at the cross, and you'll see that it looks like two boards cutting across each other at their centers, each board being ½ in. thick, 1½ in. wide and 11 in. long. Mark off every two inches along one of these boards as at x, Fig. 78 d. This will require five marks and will leave 1 in. of waste wood to be crosshatched at the end. Carry each mark all around the piece, until you strike the crossing board.

On the opposite board, measure in 1 in. from the same end, then mark off 2-in. lengths as before, again making five marks all around the board. Crosshatch the 1-in. lengths at the end, then whittle them and the 1-in. pieces off the other end, until the cross looks like d, Fig. 78. By crosshatching your cross as d is marked, you can begin to see where the links will come. Lay out the semicircles that form the outsides of the links, then whittle a V-notch down to the crossing board at each of your 2-in. marks. Round these up until you get a piece like e.

Now it begins to get hard. Take a pencil and rough in the outlines of the insides of the links, as at the left-hand edge of e. Whittle out each little crescent down to the crossing board and smooth up the sides of the links. You may want to thin the links a little while you are doing this, say to ⅜ in. Next begin to cut away the little plug of wood that holds the first two links together. You will have to work from all four sides, making stop-cuts straight down, then cutting toward them at an angle from the edge of the other link. Work slowly and carefully, cutting with the knife as in a, Fig. 81, first cut. Remember that you are cutting across grain and that supporting sections of the wood are not very strong, so keep your knife blade sharp and cut carefully without much force.

After you have cut through the first cut, begin the second, which is between two links in the same plane, therefore somewhat easier to get at. Make a stop-cut in the center, then a V-cut toward it from each side. If links are close together, you may have to use the knife almost like a saw at the center of the blank.

As you cut links free, round and smooth them up, as in f, Fig. 78, and there's your simple chain! If you have broken one or two links in making it, you are much more likely to remember the primary rule—*take it easy!*

There is also another way to form the long cross for a chain, shown at a, Fig. 78, using the diagonals of the piece. You may prefer also to work out only one link at a time, keeping the main

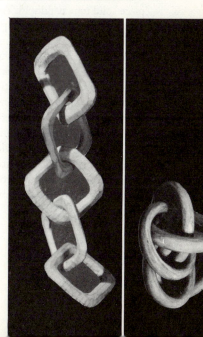

Fig. 79 · *What an ordinary chain looks like.* Fig. 80 (Right) *Quintuple links.* (*Courtesy Remington Arms Co.*)

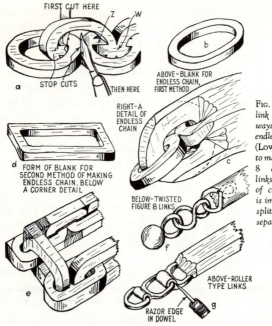

FIRST CUT HERE

STOP CUTS

THEN HERE

a

ABOVE-BLANK FOR
ENDLESS CHAIN,
FIRST METHOD

b

RIGHT-A
DETAIL OF
ENDLESS
CHAIN

d FORM OF BLANK FOR
SECOND METHOD OF MAKING
ENDLESS CHAIN. BELOW
A CORNER DETAIL

BELOW-TWISTED
FIGURE 8 LINKS

c

f

e

ABOVE-ROLLER
TYPE LINKS

RAZOR EDGE
IN DOWEL

g

FIG. 81 · *Details of link separation, two ways of making an endless chain, and* (LOWER RIGHT) *how to make twisted figure 8 and roller-type links. The rotation of cuts in sketch a is important to avoid splitting off links in separating*

piece solid for a handhold. You can do that too, as at right, Fig. 82, which incidentally may help in visualizing the steps.

When you have made one chain, all the variations are easy. Eight link shapes are shown from g to n, Fig. 78. They can be made square, round, or just with rounded corners, and may be combined for special decorative chains. The simple oval link is at g, the round link at h, the figure 8 link at i, the diamond at k, and the cloverleaf at m. The twisted figure 8 at j must be cut out of the solid, as at f, Fig. 81. At g in the same figure is the flat or roller link shown at k, Fig. 78, indicating how it is made from a flat piece of wood. These links are interlocked in a long joint that is a very close fit, so you will have to use the razor edge to separate it.

The heart-and-circle combination at n, Fig. 78, requires a cross

〚 78 〛

with one pair of arms twice as long as the other—in other words, it requires a block $\frac{3}{4}$ by $1\frac{1}{2}$ in. in cross-section. One more pointer on simple chains: To get maximum length with the fewest possible joints, make each link very long and butt it up tightly against the next link in the same plane, making z (Fig. 81 a) as long as possible and w as short as possible.

Next you will probably want to try the interlocked hearts at left, Fig. 82. Again you will need a cross, but this time only long enough for two links. Simply shape the links like hearts instead of round or oval, keeping their pointed ends *out* so you have maximum room in which to work when you separate them. If you plan the interlocked hearts for a present, use some harder and finer wood than pine—mahogany or walnut for example.

Once you have mastered the trick of separating links, chains of any size are merely a matter of time, even down to the matchstick-size necklace of Fig. 84, or the matchstick ball-and-chain of Fig. 39, Chap. III. For these you will have to use a very fine blade, and the cutting edge from a razor blade, perhaps supplemented by a low-power magnifying glass held in a frame.

Now for the endless chain. There are two ways of making them, the first method easier to visualize but the second easier to do because it avoids grain trouble in all but a few links. Since a long chain of this type is quite decorative, you had better use a finer wood, such as oak, mahogany, walnut, or maple, depending on use. And take this tip from me: Make every link as long as possible and keep links in the same plane close, as described before, so that you get the longest possible chain with the fewest joints.

Now for the first method. Cut out a circular plate of wood like b, Fig. 81, about two-thirds the diameter of the chain you want to make. In other words, if you want a chain 12 in. in diameter when you get through, cut out an 8-in. circle. Cut out the center section so that you have a ring that is

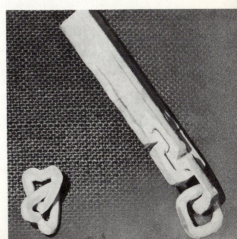

Fig. 82 · At right are the steps in making a chain from the diagonal cross, keeping the piece solid for a handhold. At left are the interlocked hearts in white pine

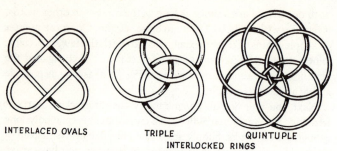

INTERLACED OVALS   TRIPLE   QUINTUPLE
                    INTERLOCKED RINGS

Fig. 83 · *Three types of interlocked rings*

square in cross-section, mark it as at *a*, Fig. 78, and whittle out a
circular diagonal cross. From then on it is just a matter of making
an ordinary chain, except that you must divide the circle evenly
into links before you start so that you do not end with half a link
to join on at the beginning. The procedure is shown at *c*, Fig. 81.

The other method is to whittle out a rectangular box such as
shown at *d*, Fig. 81, again about two-thirds as long as you want
the finished chain to be. To convert the length of a rectangle such
as this to the diameter of a circle which you may be trying to
fit, divide twice the length by 3. (In other words a rectangle
15 in. long is equivalent to a circle 10 in. in diameter, and will
give a chain about 15 in. in diameter, figuring the one-third
enlargement mentioned previously.) Make the sides of this box
into a simple cross meeting carefully at the corners, then lay the
sides out in even links so that the corners work out as at *e*, Fig. 81.
This arrangement requires cutting of only one link across grain
at each end; if you are willing to take a chance on more for greater
space between the two lines of links while you are whittling
them, figure the end piece for three links.

If you want an ornament in the chain, such as the heart
locket of Fig. 84, remember to allow wood for it, preferably
at the end, so that the grain runs vertically in it, and leave
enough wood for a good-sized link to join it to the chain ends,
for *two* links must go through the locket-supporting link.

Combining the principle of the links with several other whittling stunts discussed in succeeding chapters is the "what-is-it" of Fig. 85. This offers a fine test of a whittler's skill, but I warn you is little more than a dust catcher when you get through with it. If you *must* try one, study the photograph carefully so that you get the cranks and hinge joints arranged properly, otherwise the squirrels will not move outward as the hand is rotated.

Another group of trick link combinations that all whittlers like to try is the interlocked rings, Fig. 83, obvious from the drawing. The interlaced ovals require rings that are not quite plane, or flat, otherwise they would not interlace. The triple rings must be made carefully, the left-hand one tilting *up* from center, the two right-hand ones *down*, and also *down* at top and bottom, otherwise the rings cannot be made flat, as they should be. The quintuple links are also interlaced, hence will not be quite flat, although by a slightly different combination and proper tilting of certain links, you can get the effect of Fig. 80.

An outgrowth of these link combinations is the triple-snake or

〚 81 〛

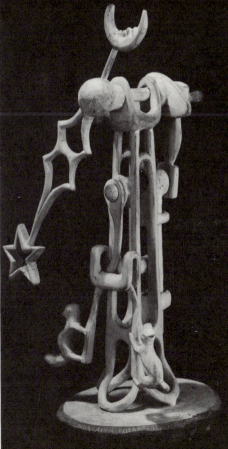

FIG. 84 (TOP) · A necklace, made as an endless chain with links of matchstick diameter, with a match in the middle to prove it. FIG. 85 (BELOW) · The "what-is-it," a difficult combination. (Courtesy Remington Arms Co.)

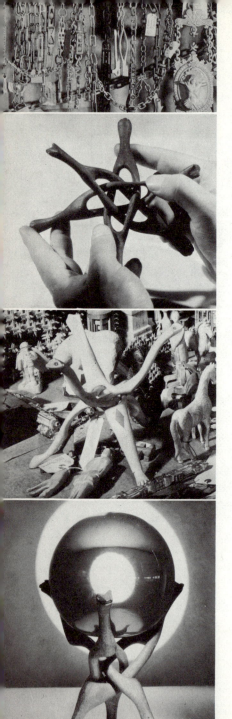

triple-dog tripod, shown finished in Figs. 88 and 89. An old East Indian and Jamaican trick, it is used as a support for a bowl or crystal ball, and is basically only three oval links worked together. Since the greatest strain comes near the ends of the links, these should be left heavier, and the piece should be made in the harder woods, such as walnut, mahogany, etc.

I usually start with a block 1½ by 1¾ in. by 6 in. long. Whittle this into a rough hexagon, which can be laid out thus: Draw a center line down all the long sides of the block. On the two wide sides, measure four-sevenths of the distance from the center line to the edge and draw parallel lines each side of center (for example, on the given block it is 4⁄7 × ⅞ in. = ½ in. over on each side). These two lines mark corners of the hexagon, the remaining corners being the center lines on the narrower sides. (For blocks of other dimensions, have one dimension ⅞ that of the other and the block four times as long as the smaller dimension.)

Now study the drawings, Fig. 90, carefully. Notice that the pairs of snake heads take up alternate corners of the hexagon, and that the paired tails take up the diagonally *opposite* alternate corners at the other end. Begin to rough in the heads and tails, remembering that if the head pair is at one

Fig. 86 (Top) · *A group of prize-winning chains. (Courtesy "Popular Mechanics.")* Fig. 87 · *Top view of the dog tripod, showing triangular center hole for fastening.* Fig. 88 · *A taller tripod. (Courtesy "Popular Mechanics."* Fig. 89 (Bottom) · *The trio of Fig. 87 supporting a crystal ball*

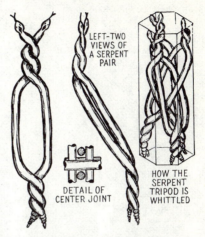

FIG. 90 · *The secret of the tripod. The snake pairs are cut in an erect position from a single hexagonal block of hard wood. Dog tripods are similar—one dog for each two snakes*

LEFT-TWO VIEWS OF A SERPENT PAIR

DETAIL OF CENTER JOINT

HOW THE SERPENT TRIPOD IS WHITTLED

corner, the same corner at the other end of the block is blank and must be cut away. Now cut in at the center section, roughing in the bodies, and working at each face alternately. While the piece looks quite complicated, you will find the same pattern on each face. It may also help if you realize that each body link has one other going through it, and itself goes through the third.

Work very slowly and carefully, for if you cut away too much wood to clear one body pair you will be taking away wood needed for the adjacent one. Work progressively until the links take form, then separate them with the wafer blade of a penknife, shape up the links, head and tails, and you will find that the tripod will open outward and set out flat as does the dog tripod in Fig. 87. From the top it should look like Fig. 87; if it does not, thin the sides of the bodies until it does. The holding screw for bowl or ball can go through the small triangular hole at the center.

Finish by smoothing up, oiling, and waxing, or shellac if you must. If you prefer dogs to snakes, consider each side of a dog's body as a snake, combine the heads to make one dog head and the two tails to make his foot, and there you are!

CHAPTER VIII

BALL-IN-A-CAGE · *Nested Spheres*

T HE query, "How did you get it in there?" always greets the
whittler of a ball-in-a-cage, just as it does the whittler who
puts a ship in a bottle. And the uninformed simply will not
believe that the ball-in-a-cage is whittled from one piece. Yet it is,
and this is how it is done.

Start with a squared-up piece of straight-grained white pine
or basswood about 1½ in. square and 6 in. long. Lay out on each
side pencil lines about ¼ in. in from each edge and ¾ in. from
each end. This gives you the outline of the cage. At its center,
mark a line all around the block. Extend the lines marking diagonally opposite cage bars over one end of the piece or draw two
¼-in. squares on diagonally opposite corners, as at *a*, Fig. 93,
and measure *D*, the maximum diameter of the ball that will turn
inside the cage. (For the 1½-in. block, *D* is 1⁷⁄₁₆ in.) Measure
half of *D* on each side of your center line and carry these lines
all around the block *within the cage lines*. These mark the upper
and lower edges of the block for the ball.

Begin cutting by sinking deep stop-cuts on all outlines of the
piece, then split out wedges of waste wood until you separate the
side bars, as at the top of *b*, Fig. 93. Square and smooth up all cuts.

Now you are ready to start the ball. Be sure you
have stop-cuts along the lines of the side bars, then
cut out long wedges until the side-bar shape stands
out, as at the top of *b*, Fig. 93. Round up the ball by
cutting wedges off the top and bottom as well as the
sides, being careful always not to cut into the side
bars or to split out a wedge before stop-cuts have been
made all around. *Do not thin the side bars any more*

[[85]]

Fɪɢ. 91 · *Four elaborate chains, each
whittled from a single piece, incorporating swivels, sliding joints,
ball-in-a-cage, etc. (Courtesy Remington Arms Co.)*

Fɪɢ. 92 · *A simple
½-in. square ball-in-a-
cage with notched base*

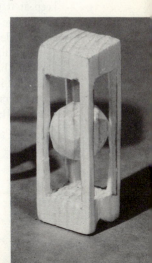

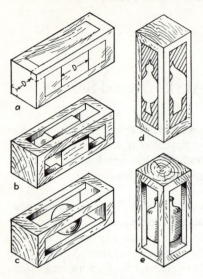

FIG. 93 · *Three steps in making a ball-in-a-cage. a shows block with cage laid out on top and ball blank laid out on side, showing how to obtain blank length D from block end. Blank with waste end wood out at b, finished piece at c. At d is a bird-in-a-cage pattern (which shows shape of body for completed piece) and at e a jug-in-a-cage*

than necessary to smooth them up, or the ball may fall out between them.

That is the simple ball-in-a-cage, Fig. 92. Probably next you will want to make it smaller, say from a ⅝- or ½-in. square block, or combine it with the fan and the chain. It can also be used as a handle decoration for back scratchers (Fig. 98), paper knives, spoons or other wooden cutlery, walking sticks (*e*, Fig. 96), pendant or locket for a chain (*d*, Fig. 96), and so on.

Next try a cage containing two or three balls side by side, and keep at it until you can get two or three nicely rounded balls into a cage so closely that they do not rattle around inside. Also try a single ball in a square cage, working from six sides to round up the ball.

With that preliminary training, you are ready to try the circular ball-in-a-cage, Fig. 100. Cut a circular block from soft, straight-grained wood, squared up like the block in *b*, Fig. 81, Chap. VII, but not so large in cross-section. Lay out curved side bars and ends on it, as in *a*, Fig. 96. You should be able to get four or more ball-in-a-cage units around the circumference, perhaps more if the cross-section of blank is square in proportion to its diameter. Whittle out each ball-in-a-cage individually, working just as you would on a straight one, but being very careful to cut across or with the grain all the time, instead of into it. Round up the balls as before and smooth up the side bars, taking light cuts to keep from splitting them loose, always cutting in the directions indicated by the arrows in *a*, Fig. 96. Notice how you must change the direction of the cut when you move from the outside edge *y* of a side bar to its inside edge *x*.

Some whittlers will prefer to leave the piece in this state; others will want to whittle through the end pieces of the individual cages so that the balls can roll around the complete circle. If you want to do this, be sure before you start that the balls

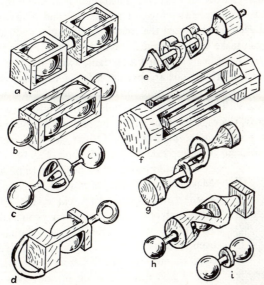

FIG. 94 · *Several swivels and sliding joints, all based on the ball-in-a-cage principle*

are all the same size and the space between crossbars in one compartment is the same as that in the next, otherwise some of the balls will fall out instead of making the circuit. Cut the holes through slowly and carefully to avoid splitting the end pieces, starting by putting a small hole through the center, then enlarging it until it meets the inside corners of the side bars. This should give a hole large enough for the balls to roll through, after it is properly rounded up and smoothed out.

Animals, birds, fish, bottles, jugs—in fact anything that can be made to have a cylindrical or spherical shape somewhere on it—can be put inside a cage. The job is done just as it is with the simple ball, except that the center blank is whittled to the desired shape instead of being rounded up.

Try the bird of *d*, Fig. 93, first. Make the layout as shown, then cut squarely across the block at each end, taking out the crosshatched wood at each end. Then smooth up the bird, being careful to leave plenty of wood at the tail and a rectangular block at each side between the cross bars. This gives you a blank so you can make the bird have fan wings and tail. After the tail and wings have been split down for fans, swing the bird so his head and tail project out at opposite sides of the cage, shaving off on the body and shortening the inner blades of the wing fans as necessary. The bird should fit tightly, otherwise it will not stick across the cage but will fall to the bottom. Fig. 93 *e* shows another possibility, a jug-in-a-cage. Others are pig, elephant, whale, chicken, curled-up cat, fat dog, or rabbit, Fig. 95.

The ball-in-a-cage does not have to be square. Make it as many-sided as you like, simply putting a side bar at each corner. At *c*, Fig. 96, is a hexagonal one, and at *d* is an octagonal one. A. O. Stenwick of Red Wing, Minn., went even further. He took a round 12-inch block of solid walnut and whittled from it a *round* cage with a lion inside, spacing his side bars as he wanted them! Another real test for any whittler

[[88]]

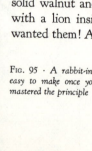

FIG. 95 · *A rabbit-in-a-cage, easy to make once you have mastered the principle*

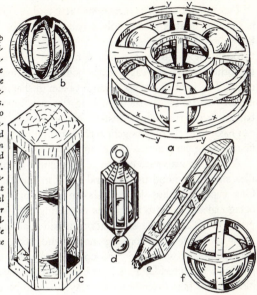

FIG. 96 · A group of ball-in-a-cage variations that are unusual. At a is the circular ball-in-a-cage with four compartments and three balls. At b and f are two designs of ball-in-a-ball, or nested spheres, the design of b being utilized as shown in FIG. 97. A hexagonal ball-in-a-cage is shown at c, and an octagonal one in d, the latter made up as a pendant. At e is a handle decorated with the ball-in-a-cage

is the pair of monkeys which can be picked out of the contest entries in Fig. 126.

The swivels and universal and sliding joints of Fig. 94 are simply other variations, the only difference between them and the standard ball-in-a-cage being that the balls are connected to some outside element by bars. Thus in a the two balls, each in its own cage, are connected by a bar between cages, making the piece practically a dumb-bell with a cage over each end. In b there are two dumb-bells, with the cage going over one ball of each. The trick in both types is to make the ball close to one end of the cage and not to cut it loose from the end. Instead, take a small wafer blade or the razor cutting edge and work through the end from the outside until the connecting bar is cut through to the ball. The bar is then thinned so it slides and turns easily in the hole, and its attachment to the ball rounded up.

〔 89 〕

Two universal joints are shown at *c* and *d*. That shown at *d* is simpler, in that it is simply a ball in a two-bar cage, the ball being held in the cup-shaped endpiece by its bar, which extends through the end to form a link outside. A half ring is formed at the other end of the cage, so the joint can be made as part of a chain. The joint of *c* offers a real problem in shaping the spherical socket for the ball without making the mouth so large that the ball can slide through it. Instead of the shallow cup, the design can have long clasping fingers extending around the ball, but such fingers have parts across the grain, hence are weak.

At *e* is an elaborate edition of the simple dumb-bell and ring idea shown at *i* and used several times in the chains of Fig. 91. One type of sliding joint is shown at *f*, Fig. 94, made in an octagonal block, with four arms extending each way to the end piece, much as do the side bars of a ball-in-a-cage. But at their outer ends, instead of forming another end piece, each set of four bars passes between the bars coming from the other end and joins in a cross inside. This joint can also be made in a hexagonal block, three bars extending each way, and can be varied in many other ways, some shown in Fig. 91. Remember in making it that your block must have an *even* number of sides to start with. One bar is whittled from each alternate corner, bars from adjacent corners going to opposite end pieces.

At *h*, Fig. 94, is a swivel with spiral side bars. Because of the spiral, only three side bars are needed; in fact, if the spiral is made "slow" enough, only *two* bars are needed. Such a piece is cut from a round bar, and the size of the ball inside is figured by subtracting twice the planned bar thickness from the diameter of the blank. (This gives a size corresponding to *D* in the simple unit, Fig. 93.) These

[90]

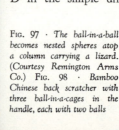

Fig. 97 · *The ball-in-a-ball becomes nested spheres atop a column carrying a lizard. (Courtesy Remington Arms Co.)* Fig. 98 · *Bamboo Chinese back scratcher with three ball-in-a-cages in the handle, each with two balls*

spiral cages can also be made with one, two, or more balls inside, just like the simple ball·in·a·cage. Dozens of other variations will suggest themselves to you as you work.

Now for the ball·within·a·ball·in·a·cage, and after that the nested spheres. Take a simple ball·in·a·cage, and cut into the ball at four or six points, cutting sideways until you have formed a second ball inside the first. You may have to use a flattened and sharpened wire·end or your razor cutting edge for some of the closer cutting. For a variation, whittle out a fairly good·sized sphere, and inside it whittle another ball, cutting through the outer one in holes of varying pattern, Fig. 96, *b* and *f*.

Now try putting *another* ball inside the inside one. Oh yes, it is possible, witness Figs. 97 and 99. And look how the Chinese did it—Figs. 101 and 102. The first is made in walnut and includes four spheres nested one inside the other; the second is in ivory, again with four spheres, each beautifully decorated with relief pierced patterns. And the outer ball is only a bit over 3 in. in diameter! The man who made it must have spent months or years at it with special tools. I have seen nested spheres like this in the bases of chessmen, and "Believe it or not" Ripley has one with 17 others inside. Beside such patience, I think even Job might be a little envious.

[91]

Fig. 99 (Top) · *Two groups of nested spheres*. Fig. 100 (Left center) · *A circular ball·in·a·cage* (Both courtesy "Popular Mechanics.") Fig. 101 and Fig. 102 (Bottom) · *Chinese nested spheres, the lower in ivory*. (Courtesy Metropolitan Museum of Art)

Fig. 103 · *Some typical 1-piece whittling stunts, four of them fans*

CHAPTER IX

FANS · *Plain and Shaped*

Wᴴᴵᵀᵀᴸᴵᴺᴳ fans, usually very ornate, from a single block, has always been considered quite a stunt. Actually, it is very simple, after you have tried it once or twice. As in any other whittling, there are a few little tricks to it, including straight-grained soft wood, thorough soaking after the blank is formed, and interlocking or threading the leaves or blades. Once these are learned, you can go on to elaborate double-swirl fans in any

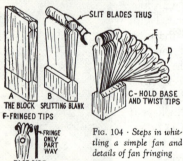

Fig. 104 · *Steps in whittling a simple fan and details of fan fringing*

size from those on the end of a matchstick to those two or three feet in diameter and with blades up to an inch or two wide. I should also like to suggest two new stunts, one using the fan for wings or tail on a bird, or fins on a fish, the other forming or shaping the fan blades.

⟦ 92 ⟧

First, you will need a piece of straight-grained soft wood, say white pine or basswood. Thickness is not really important, as long as the piece is not thicker than your knife blade is long—the thicker the piece, the wider each individual fan blade will be. For your first try, use a piece about ½ in. thick, 1 in. wide, and 6 in. long, similar to block A in Fig. 104. About 1 in. up from the base or butt, notch the block deeply from each face until the remaining part is between $\frac{1}{16}$ and $\frac{1}{8}$ in. thick. Upon this thin part the individual blades will be pivoted. Now shape the longer end of the block to any shape you want—perhaps at first just a notch or two on each flat side will be enough. The block will now look like B, Fig. 104.

This blank is then soaked in water for 12 to 24 hr., depending upon thickness, until the water has worked into it thoroughly. If you are in a hurry to speed up the job, boil the blank for 15 or 20 min. instead. This soaking or boiling softens the wood somewhat and also reduces the tendency to split and crack.

Now take the thoroughly soaked block and begin to split down the side from the long end, as in B, Fig. 104. The thinner you can make each individual blade without cutting through or curling it too much, the greater the number of blades you will have when you get through. At first, probably $\frac{1}{32}$ or $\frac{1}{16}$ in. thick will be about right. When you start at the top of the blank you can be almost careless, but as you approach the deep notch that forms the pivot, take it easy. Split each blade down only to that notch, not beyond it. This is the place where straight grain is absolutely necessary; otherwise your knife blade will run off to one edge or the other and spoil the blank.

When you have split down all the leaves, you are ready to form the fan. Hold the butt of the piece tightly as

FIG. 105 · *An elaborate fan with double circle, interlocked and interlaced blades, and elaborately carved base*

[93]

at *C* and *D*, Fig. 104, and twist the tops of the group of leaves a quarter turn. This will give you a fan-shaped top as at *E*. The tips of the blades can then be interlocked as at *D*, and your fan is complete.

If you will examine the pivot now, you will see that the blades have all bent around it—unless the blank was too dry, in which case the leaves have all broken off or cracked there.

Using this method, you can make any of the fans illustrated in Fig. 111, keeping them spread open until they dry either by inter-locking or by threading. Threading is necessary when the blade shape is so simple that no notches are available to interlock, such as a feather shape, for example. To do this, take a long piece of thread by the center and wind it once around the outer leaf of the fan near the outer edge. Then bring each of the other blades close, in turn, and as you bring them up, weave the two thread ends in and out over them, so that the threads cross between each pair of blades, as in *A*, Fig. 114 (see page 98).

If you have more than enough blades to make a complete circle, or a fan of the width you want, either split them off the base block to make another fan, or make a second fan, on top of the first. It is possible, by taking a wide and fairly thick blank, to make such

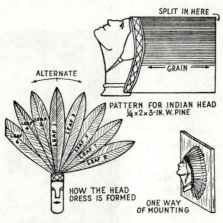

SPLIT IN HERE

GRAIN

ALTERNATE

PATTERN FOR INDIAN HEAD
¼ × 2 × 3-IN. W. PINE

HOW THE HEAD
DRESS IS FORMED

ONE WAY
OF MOUNTING

Fig. 106 · *The Indian head blank, and* (Left) *how the blades are spread alter-nately in forming the head-dress. The first leaf is left centered, the second swung left, the third right, the fourth left, and so on. This requires accurate notching, thorough soaking, and careful spreading*

a fan group as that in Fig. 112, which has a number of fans and part-fans, or "sprays," carved from the same piece of wood. In addition, blade tips are fringed as shown in Fig. 104.

Such multiple fans are easier made if they are spread from two sides, as at top center, Fig. 103. Instead of notching the blank near one end, notch it from both sides near the center, and then notch it again about a half inch or so away, on the other side of the center. Then, after soaking, the blank can be split in from both ends, as long as you are very careful to soak well and split down the blades carefully to the center hub.

With these few tricks mastered, you can produce fans with as elaborate a blade shape as you wish, even to the drilled and ribbon-laced double fan such as that in Fig. 105. Bases, after the fan is completed, may also be shaped to any form you want—for example the center fan of Fig. 111.

The next step is to whittle a bird or flying fish with fan wing, tail or fins, as in Fig. 107. However, instead of forming the fan by twisting and spreading as you did before, in this case it is better to bend one blade to the left, the next to the right, and so on, as in Fig. 106. This will give proper sweep to the bird's wings or the fish's wide fin.

[95]

Fig. 107 · (Top) *Bird and fish with double-spread fans.* (Center) Fig. 108 · *Indian head with head-dress formed of fan.* Fig. 109 · (Bottom) *Both tail and top-knot are fans. Notice special blade shape*

With this mastered, you can go on to formed birds with wings and tails formed of fans. Figure 113 shows the blank for a bird. It is also possible to make such pieces as the Indian head (Fig. 108), the daisy (Fig. 110), and the peacock (Fig. 109). In the Indian head, the deep notch is just above the headband; on the peacock it is at the base of the tail and between head and topknot.

The little French Empire lady of Fig. 113, complete as to skirt, over-skirt, flounces, and tip-tilted fan, to say nothing of the headdress, is formed by the same principle from a single piece of wood. The blank in Fig. 113 shows how she is made. She may be finished by smoothing up the fan blades, using colored threads for interlacing or threading between leaves (see Fig. 114), and painting in oils or with water colors. The impor-tant thing to remember in whittling her, as in whittling the daisy or the peacock, is that fragile or unsupported sections should not be finished until just before you soak the blank. Other-wise the grain across the daisy stem, or the lady's forearm, may cause you to break it off. In splitting the fans on the lady, begin with the big ones on the skirt and finish with the delicate ones that form her fan.

It is essential that the blades of the

[96]

FIG. 110 (TOP) · *Triple-fan daisy. Stem and leaves are danger points.* FIG. 111 · A *group of fans. Note the ornate base on the center one.* FIG. 112 · A *complex fan with "feath-ered" or fringed tips.* (FIGS. 111 & 112 *courtesy* "*Popular Mechanics*")

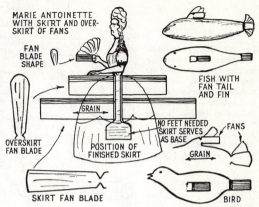

FIG. 113 · *Patterns for French Empire lady, bird, and fish. Notice that fan overskirt is shorter, also that overskirt fan blades are shaped to create the looping effect. Bird wings and tail blanks are set clear of body to avoid sticking at back*

skirt-shaped fan be brought as close together as possible, so that the skirt line may be as unbroken as it can be made. Remember, however, that if you make the hub of the fan too small, it will split as the fan blades are separated

The lady, as well as the Indian head, involves another new trick in fan whittling, that of forming a fan after it is made. The only essentials for forming are patience and a well-soaked blank principally the latter. In fact, after you have split down all the blades, you had better soak the blank again to avoid trouble. Then begin by bringing each blade to the place where you want it, bowing it downward as well as outward and interlacing it with thread to hold it in place. On some pieces, too, special spreading of the fans may be advisable. For example, in the Indian head, where the notch at the top of the headband is curved and something like 1½ in. long, the center blades are pushed out farther, the blades at top and extreme bottom being fairly near the center line of the head.

For the lady, try first with a piece ¾ in. thick by 8 in. wide by about 8 in. long, and follow the blank in Fig. 113. The Indian head requires a piece about ¼ or ⅜ in. thick by 2½ in. wide by 2½ in. long, the daisy a piece ⅜ in. thick by 2 in. wide by

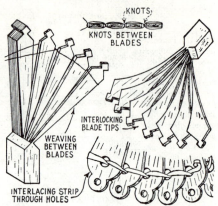

FIG. 114 · *How to thread or interlace fan blades to keep the fan spread open. At left is the simplest method, with the thread simply woven between blades. At top is stiffer support obtained by knotting between blades. At lower right is a decorative lacing with ribbon through holes. At upper right are simple interlocked blades*

4 in. high, all straight-grained, dry white pine or basswood.

With this principle, any number of similar shapes may be made. A few suggestions are: Christmas or other tree, lamp, tepee, umbrella, ballet dancer, Hawaiian belle, Liberty bell, in fact any-thing that has a fan, cone, or bell shape. It is also possible to put birds with fan wings and tail into a ball-in-a-cage, as in Fig. 111, or put as elaborate a fan as you wish into a bottle, as in Fig. 147, Chap. XII. They may also be combined with wooden links, the ball-in-a-cage carved in the butt, or some similar idea, always remembering that the fan is fairly fragile. I personally prefer to form fans on such pieces as the girl and the Indian head which make very attractive mantel or cupboard decorations. I have one Indian head mounted with the head-dress against a panel, thus making it into an interesting wall decoration.

In order to hold the blades of a formed fan in position, it is almost essential to thread or lace them into conical shape, as in the lady's dress, Fig. 113, or the Indian headdress, Fig. 108. The simplest lacing (top left, Fig. 114) is simply a thread tied at its middle near the outer end of the first blade, then woven out and in between blades. Better positioning and greater rigidity, plus more equal spacing, may be obtained by knotting the thread between blades (top center), or drilling a hole through the blades near the outer ends and lacing through that (lower right), Fig. 105. Of course, broad-tipped, narrow-based, flat fans can be formed simply by interlocking blade tips (upper right).

For the fun of it, try to put a fan into a bottle, as in Fig. 147, Chap. XII. Form a fan base that will pass through the bottle neck and lie flat at its bottom (it may be in two sections, glued together). Lace the fan with the simplest lacing, soak it thoroughly, then refold it as a woman's fan is folded. Insert the base, put a drop of glue in the socket, and pass the fan into the bottle, maneuver it into its socket and press it in tightly. Reopen the fan with two L-shaped wires, space it evenly, and press outward on the two outer blades with the wires. Weight or wedge the wires in this position until the fan dries again—and there you are.

Spray or brush fans to be left out on a mantel or bookshelf with varnish, lacquer, or shellac. If natural-wood finish is preferred, without sheen, simply brush the fan with linseed oil. To darken slightly, mix a little crude oil with the oil; for very dark brown, mix in burnt umber; for red-brown, mix in burnt sienna.

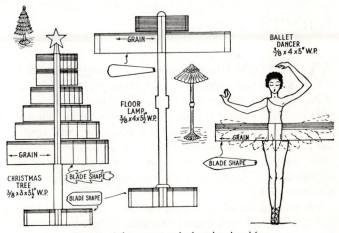

Fig. 115 · *A few suggestions for formed or shaped fans*

CHAPTER X

JOINTS · *Hinge and Pivot*

WHITTLING these pieces from a single block is the stunt here, just as in the three preceding chapters. With the hinge joint, you can make pliers, nippers, shears, and scissors; with the pivot joint, knives, razors, locks, wrenches, reels, rollers, doors that swing, and guns. You will need all the skill you possess, all the patience, a good, sharp, thin-clip blade, and very straight-grained soft wood, such as white pine or basswood. The rewards are exceptionally intriguing and interesting finished pieces.

For practice before you tackle the hinge joint, try the pliers in Fig. 117 *l*. Lay out pattern *i* on a piece ¼ by 1 by 3¾ inches. Whittle out blank *j*, and split through between jaws on line *y-z.* Cut out wedges at top and bottom as shown at 1 and 2 in *j* to create the result sketched at *k*—as though one half of the pliers passes through the other, which is exactly what it eventually will do.

Rock the blade through very carefully parallel with the surface, as shown in cut 4, sketch *l*, cutting until all the wood on top and bottom which joins the two parts is severed. Take care to keep the cuts parallel, or you will weaken the interior jaw. If the grain is straight, you should have no trouble, but if you want to be on the safe side, soak the piece for a while first. Now make cut 5 and the corresponding cut on the other side, both across the grain but made again by rocking and pushing on the knife blade.

Try gingerly now to open your first pair of pliers. If they show no intention of opening, go over all the cuts again and take out a little wood at 5 to create a slot. Now they should open.

FIG. 117 · *Pliers and scissors, and how they are made*

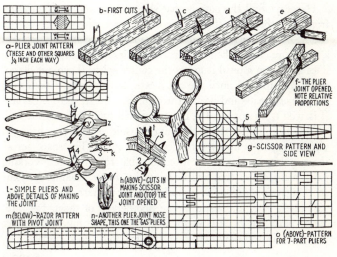

You are ready now to try the hinge joint, better, more flexible, and permitting much wider opening. Lay out a $\frac{1}{4}$ by $\frac{1}{2}$ by 3-in. block as at *a*, Fig. 117. Make the first cuts, as at *b*, rocking the blade in slowly straight down the middle toward, and up to, the place where the joint will be. The simple reason for making these cuts first is that if the wood intends to split anyway, it may as well split before you waste a lot of work on it. Next, rock across grain to make the cuts shown at *c*, going only exactly one-third of the way through the piece from each side and making sure these cuts meet the ends of the lines split in from the ends.

Now comes the careful part—perhaps soaking the piece will make it easier. Rock and push the thin clip blade straight through the piece from side to side along lines *w-w* and *x-x*, being very careful to keep them parallel. Pull the knife blade partly out of the slit thus made, then rock it in wider and wider arcs until you have severed all the wood above the hexagon that forms the joint (which is crosshatched for convenience in the blank layout *a*). Meet previous cuts squarely and cleanly, gaging frequently by measuring with the blade outside the blank.

Hardest of all the cuts is that shown in *e*, and its companion from the other side. If your clip blade has a long point, you can use it, otherwise take a razor edge and sharpen its end to form a miniature chisel, then force it through exactly along the dotted lines shown in *a* until it meets the center splits. Then cut downward and upward until the cut meets *w-w* and *x-x*. If your cuts are properly made and cleanly through, the joint should open as at *f*. If it won't, do not force it, but go over all cuts again until it will.

You will notice that the hinge inside is really a hexagon with two points in the direction of the grain. The space across those points is the smallest permissible for a smooth-working joint in a piece of this width. *It can be greater*, making the joint an elongated hexagon, as indicated in the pattern for the seven-part pliers at *o*, and again in the photograph of them, Fig. 118, *but it must not be less*. Also, if elongated too much, one part will slide up and down on the other, making a poor joint.

Notice one unusual thing here—you have whittled out a pair of pliers with a joint and have not made a single shaving! This joint is peculiar in that it is a splitting or slicing job rather than a cutting one. Its variations are endless. You can make almost any type of pliers with it, from the crude one you have just finished to the familiar gas or electrician's pliers shown in Fig. 117 *n*. It is also the basis of the scissor joint, *h*.

For the scissor, use a piece ¼ by 2 by 5 in., and whittle out the blank from pattern *g*, Fig. 117. Do not shape up either blade or handles until you find out how the wood intends to act. Mark out the joint. If you study the sketch of the open scissors, you will see that the joint is simply the hinge again, except that the lower split extends down only an eighth or a quarter inch, then turns over to make the passing blades of scissors instead of the meeting blades on pliers. Force the knife tip or razor edge through, as at *h* 1, then split up between the blades parallel with the upper surface, as shown in 2. Now if you make diagonal cut *3* through from the top to meet 2, and make another as dotted at 4 in layout *g*, all that remains is to make a simple hinge joint as before. After it is finished, thin down and round up the handle, trim the blades to proper thickness, and your scissors should look like Fig. 119. If

[[103]]

FIG. 118 (TOP) · *Seven pairs of pliers, all in one piece* ½ x ½ x6 in. *Pattern is shown in* FIG. 117 *o.* FIG. 119 · *Finished scissors*

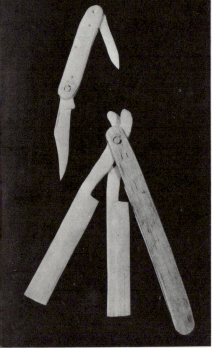

this, or any similar hinge joint does not work properly, thin it slightly at the sides, as shown at 5 and 6, Fig. 117 g. This is similar to using a wider hexagon.

Vary my patterns as you will by using squares of different size. And try to make a pair of pliers in a wooden match. I've done it, and a fifty-year-old scoutmaster did it to win a prize five weeks after he learned to whittle. We both ground chisel points on needles.

Figures 120 and 121 show the pivot joint in use. It is similar to an axle, exactly as if you were to drill a hole through the mating pieces and push a dowel rod through. But, just like the other pieces in Chaps. VI through X, the real trick is to make it of one piece of wood. It can be used in making a wheel that turns inside a fork (as on the old-fashioned bicycle of Fig. 120 and 123), or one-piece wooden razors, pocket knives, or any of the half-dozen pieces in Fig. 124. Only be sure you have straight-grained wood!

Let us assume you are going to make the old-fashioned bike of Fig. 123 and that you have the blank all cut out of a piece of ½-in. white pine. First shape up the frame and forks, cutting through between fork and wheel by taking out thin shavings

[104]

Fig. 120 (Top) · An old-fashioned "bike" with pivots (Courtesy "Popular Mechanics"). Fig. 121 · Whittled one-piece razor and a one-piece knife. Fig. 122 · Chinese sampan carved from a nut; the doors open and close. A second nut forms the base (Courtesy Lorena Wynkoop)

all the way in from the wheel periphery *except where the pivot is to be.* Figure 123*f* shows the steps in forming the pivot itself. Begin by cutting around the pivot with the knife tip, taking out a little V all around it deep enough to go through the fork. Take it easy, and change the direction of your cut to conform to the change in grain direction as you work around. Be sure, too, that the blade tip is razor sharp, or it will tear out or break off the pivot. Gage V depth with the knife tip.

Cut out a V around the pivot on the other side of the fork also, making sure before you start that the pivots on opposite sides are exactly in line. Figure 123 A shows what I mean.

Lay the knife blade flat on the surface of the wheel and gradually rock it in toward the pivot all around, rocking it forward a little, then lifting it a little to cause it to split the wood free. If you cut through deeply enough in forming the pivot, the fork will lift free. Do the same thing on the other side, then clean up the wheel, and put spokes in if you wish.

If you must make the handlebars in the same piece, do it as in Fig. 123 E. This will require a block 1 in. higher.

To make a razor like that in Fig. 121, use the pattern in Fig. 117. I used a blank ⅜ in. thick and so could make something that never happens in real life—a double-bladed razor. After the blank is cut out, follow Fig. 123 H and I. Shape the blade (or blades) and the pivots, then outline the sides of the handle as in H. Using the knife partly as a chisel, and making little crisscross cuts when the cut gets in too deep to permit the knife to be used crosswise of the hollow, whittle out the waste wood inside the handle to form the socket for the blade. Cut through with the knife tip at the butt or tang of the razor blade, and square everything up. You now have just another wheel and fork; treat it the same way. After it comes loose, shape up the tang.

A pocketknife like that in Fig. 121 is a little more difficult because of the back spring which holds a knife blade open. This spring means that you must work only from the front in shaping the blade butt. To simulate the back spring, outline along the

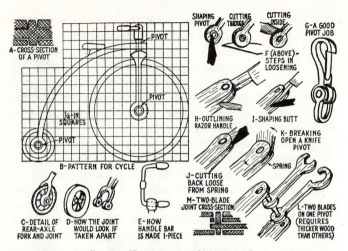

FIG. 123 · *The pivot joint, and how it is made*

back, then rock the blade through as you did before, all around, including as much of the back as you can. Free the blade back from the spring, as in Fig. 123 *J*, by forcing the knife tip between them. No matter how careful you are at this, your knife probably will not reach every little fiber, so the blade will act as if it would not come free. Pressing toward the pivot to avoid breaking it, "break" the joint, as in *K*. Smooth up the tang, then shave and shape until the blade fits properly into the handle.

Figure 123 *L* and *M* show the double-bladed pivot—all that is necessary is to make one side of the pivot long enough to pass through one side of the handle and another blade. Be sure your blank is thick enough, and *saw* between blades to separate them.

Eight other pieces that use the pivot principle are shown in Fig. 124; some of them finished are shown in Fig. 116. The old-style monkey wrench, Fig. 124 *f*, involves a trick. The heads are whittled out close together and the mating faces of the jaws sawed apart. The screw is made just *short* of the lower jaw and rounded up. It has a ball-and-socket joint at its lower end, the hole above the socket being widened out as shown in the dotted lines so that the screw can be swung away from the wrench face. It is swung out in this way, and a nut of suitable size screwed on to make the threads. The lower wrench jaw is drilled, then the bolt (that fits the nut) is screwed into it to tap it.

The one-piece monkey wrench, Fig. 124 a, involves no trick, but exceedingly careful cutting. The really difficult part is to whittle the threads on the barrel. If you can whittle them carefully enough to move the lower jaw at all, you are doing well. The rubber-band gun can be cocked and shoots bands or sticks.

The roller in g may be modified simply to make a reel. The pliers in c involve careful cutting at the pivot to simulate the rivet and figure 8 which makes it adjustable. The gun, e, has three pivots, on trigger, barrel, and a lock for the barrel.

The little door in Fig. 124 d is an easy one so long as you can get at it to sever the ends of the pivots. You may have to cut in as indicated at lower left to do it. But for a real stump look at Fig. 123. This is about twice actual size. The tiny carved doors are actually $\frac{1}{16}$ by $\frac{1}{13}$ in., and they open—to reveal an image carved behind them!

FIG. 124 · *Eight variations of the pivot joint*

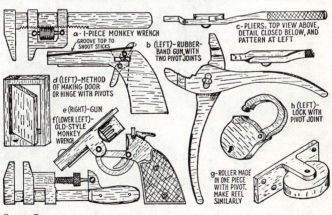

MORE IDEAS FOR
WHITTLERS

FIG. 125 (left), 126
(upper right) and 127
(lower right) · A pro-
fusion of whittling
ideas, all entries in a
national contest, rang-
ing from simple chains
to elaborate figures.
(Courtesy Popular Me-
chanics Magazine)

Fig. 128 · *Seven-masted schooner "Thomas W. Lawson" by Thomas Rosenkvist. Scale ⅛ in. per foot.*

CHAPTER XI

MODELS · *Ships, Planes, Camps*

SEVERAL thousand years before Christ, the Egyptians used models to plan their buildings and their war galleys and to train their youth, as well as to depict historical scenes; for models gave three dimensions, while a picture gave but two. Down through the ages, each civilization has used models for the same purposes, prizing the accurate or the beautiful ones sometimes as much as the full-size reproduction. Today, every speedy yacht, every staid commercial vessel, every warship, every power plant, every large building, dam, bridge, and new commercial product first is a model, for the models reveal things that no drawing, no matter how carefully done, will show, and no eye, no matter how skilled, will catch. We have gone on to make models to be tested, to teach, to explain, even to advertise and to decorate.

The present wave of enthusiasm for whittling ship and airplane models for decoration is really more than that—it is an exact hobby and a chance to make in miniature things that a man may neither make nor own in full size. And it teaches patience and skill. I will never forget how I stood open-mouthed before the famous "Swiss Village"—a complete mechanical town in minia- ture—which once toured the country. More recently I have been impressed by the 30,000-piece miniature theatre whittled by a New Yorker, and the all-wood clock whittled by a European convict that includes 30 miniature dials, each showing time in one of the world's principal cities.

Consider, for example, Mr. Rosenkvist's exact scale model of the seven-masted schooner "Thomas W. Lawson," Fig. 128. It is far beyond the talents of the casual whittler—it takes experi- ence, skill and infinite patience. It also takes special materials and special tools. All I can hope to do in this brief space is to give you preliminary pointers and a simple model or two—if after these your bent is toward models, get plans, materials, and specialized instruction from handicraft magazines and suppliers.

The miniature of the 40-ft. auxiliary yawl "Cavalier," Fig. 129, will give you more than usual training with a knife, for even its sails are whittled. Seven woods in natural finish bring out contrasting colors. Scale is generally $\frac{1}{12}$ in. per ft., modified of course for ultra-small parts like spars, rigging, and masts. Plans are shown in Fig. 131, but you can use other model plans, full-size boat plans scaled down, or even a photograph, simply by using the checkerboard transfer method explained in previous chapters. Enlarge or reduce size by using larger or smaller squares. If the model will be painted, make it of white pine, basswood, or even balsa, for all cut easily; but if it is to be in natural color, use mahogany, walnut, maple, or rare woods like rosewood.

Saw or whittle out the hull blank first. Draw the hull side shape on a piece of fairly stiff paper, then cut along the line and throw the paper hull away. The outline is your first template for the finished hull. Further templates, made as if you were looking

Fig.129·Miniature scale model of the 40-ft. auxiliary yawl "Cavalier," to a scale of $\frac{1}{12}$ in. per foot. Seven woods: walnut, mahogany, teak, spruce, white pine, maple, rosewood, compose it. Even her sails are whittled

at the boat from the front, help to check from the other way. Just below the side view in Fig. 131 is a front view of the hull, showing the outline of five cross sections corresponding to the number on the lines of the blank at lower right, Fig. 131.

Whittle and test, whittle and test, until the hull fits its templates. Don't forget that the deck is higher in front, or at the bow, to ride over waves and fend off spray, while it may be quite near the water at the stern. This sloping, called "sheer," is shown in the blank drawing at lower right, Fig. 131. When the deck is shaped, make a stop cut all around it about $\frac{1}{32}$ in. in from the edge, and slope the deck surface down from the center to the stop cut until the rail stands up about $\frac{1}{32}$ in. Then from the top view in Fig. 131 sketch in the proper location for the cabin and the cockpit (open space just back of the cabin) and cut out the little section forming the cockpit. Cut the center down about $\frac{1}{8}$ in., the sides only $\frac{1}{16}$, thus form a little seat all around inside the cockpit. Also cut in at the after end of the keel for the propeller.

The cabin is a simple little rounded-end piece with the cockpit coaming (raised rail to keep water out) made of paper and glued onto it. If the hull is walnut, use mahogany for the cabin, and simulate portholes with heavy pencil or drawing-ink dots. Glue it in place on the hull, and on it glue two little slivers of teak (or other contrasting-color wood) for the companion-way hatch (cover of the passageway or ladder leading down into the cabin from the cockpit)

FIG. 130 · *Gaar Williams concept of the model builder's exhibition night. (Courtesy "The Chicago Tribune")*

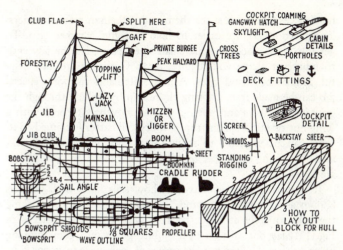

FIG. 131 · *Details of construction of the "Cavalier" model*

and the skylight (windowed opening up further forward). Usually it is easier to glue these pieces in place before they are shaped up. On the hull also glue the hatches for the chain locker (⅛ in. round) and the lazaret (⅛ in. square and at the extreme stern). From a bit of toothpick, whittle a little two-blade propeller and glue it in place, then in a slit above it glue a rudder shaped as shown. Other bits of toothpick can be shaped for the bowsprit and the boomkin, and glued in place, although the rail must first be whittled away in little slots to allow the inner ends of these pieces to lie flat on the deck.

Whittle the masts from kitchen matches, and glue them into holes drilled just forward and just aft of the cabin and cockpit assembly, and slanting just a little to the rear. In the cockpit glue a little round-headed bit of toothpick for a binnacle (compass case) and a little square bit with a ⅛-in. paper disk glued on its front for the gearbox and wheel by which the boat is steered.

In all this work, you will find sharp-nosed tweezers handy to hold pieces while you shape them or put them in place. Jewelers' long-nosed pliers are easier to hold and give a firmer grip. To get into tight places or bend small metal parts, file the jaw ends to whatever shape you require. Small C clamps are also help-ful, as are small hand vises. A makeshift hand vise for a special job can be made from a spring clothespin by drilling through the gripping members and putting a small stovebolt through with a wing-nut or nut from the top of a dry cell battery screwed on it. Jaws can be whittled to shape. Small files and sanding sticks made by gluing sandpaper on bits of sheet metal or $\frac{1}{4}$-in. dowel are also helpful.

It is usually most effective to show sails filled with what is known as a "quartering wind," which means it is not striking the ship squarely at front, back or side. From the patterns in Fig. 131, lay out sails on $\frac{1}{4}$-in. white pine, with grain running up and down. Hollow out the center of each piece from one side, with the deepest part of the "belly" thus formed near the bottom of the sail. Study Fig. 129 and see how each sail except the jib forms a straight line where it is fastened to the booms at top and bottom and to the mast in front, but how the fourth side is curved. Also the upper edge of the sail is pushed around a bit further than the lower, hence must be whittled at an angle. When one side is properly shaped, turn the sail blank over and begin to cut away the edges on the other side. Bring each edge down as thin as possible, thus shaping the sail. For strength, leave the wood about $\frac{1}{16}$ in. thick at the middle, but thin it down to a feather edge all around. Real sails are laced to booms and mast hoops, or have little brass T-shaped sliders which run in tracks. This causes the sail to form a series of little arches away from the boom when the wind fills it, and also to pull at its corners (or "clews"). Make a few shallow grooves radiating from each corner, and scallop the edges on the three sides fastened to spars.

Booms (those at sail tops are called "gaffs") are also made from bits of toothpicks, as is the jib club. Main booms on "Cava-

lier" swing on goosenecks on the mast, thus in the model they are simply glued to mast and sail foot. They extend beyond the sail end about $\frac{1}{16}$ in. The gaffs, however, carry a jaw around the mast so that they may be free to swing, and be hoisted and lowered. Simulate this by gluing the gaff on with about $\frac{1}{8}$ in. sticking out toward the mast, then split it carefully, holding tightly at the sail end, pass the split ends around the mast and glue in place. Of course, before the sail is glued on, each scallop tip should be touched with glue. Set the sail so that it makes about a 30-degree angle with the axis of the boat. Notice that the jib is not glued to the mainmast, but rather to the forestay, which in this model is a thread stretched between the tip of the bowsprit and the mast head and glued there. Its lower end can be carried down and glued to the hull also, to form the bobstay.

Form the cradle of two bits of white pine to fit the keel and set square on a flat surface. Make the base of a fine and well-grained bit of any wood you have available; I used rosewood. To this glue the cradle parts, and into the cradle glue the keel.

Rig with fine cotton thread or, better still, fine wire. We already have the forestay and the bobstay in place.

FIG. 132 (TOP) · *Japanese all-bamboo ship model.* FIG. 133 · *"Sea Witch"* and FIG. 134 · *"Cutty Sark,"* both by *Mr. Rosenkvist, the first to* $\frac{3}{16}$ *in. per foot, the second to* $\frac{5}{32}$ *in. per foot.* FIG. 135 · *"Leviathan,"* and FIG. 136 (BOTTOM) · *"Normandie,"* *simplified by Van Riper*

From the tip of the boomkin to the "fantail" (tail end) is a boomkin shroud (bracing cable), and each mast is braced by two shrouds on each side. One passes from the rail at each side of the mast up to just below the mast tip. The other starts from the rail also, about ⅛ in. ahead of the first, and passes up over the crosstrees (a ⁵⁄₁₆-in. length of toothpick glued ½ in. below the mainmast tip and ⅜ in. below the mizzen tip) to the tip of the mast. Corresponding to the forestay on the mizzen is the mizzen brace, which runs from its foot to its peak and passes over a little bracket just below the crosstrees (all these parts can be seen in Figs. 129 and 131). The bowsprit shrouds, from the tip of the bowsprit back to the hull on each side, complete the "standing" or wire rigging.

Running lines come next. We will not have to show the parts of these lines which run down to the deck. From the peak or extreme upper tip of each gaff, run a thread to the mast tip, then back to the gaff about a third of its length from the tip, then back to mast midway from masthead to crosstrees. These, on the full-size boat, hoist the outer end of the gaff. From the outer tip of each boom, run a line to the tip of the mast for a "topping lift," the one on the side

[[116]]

FIG. 137 (TOP) · *Waco Cabin to scale of* ¾ *in. to* 1 *ft.* FIG. 138 · *Fokker DA, which at* ¾ *in. per foot has* 20-*in. wing spread.* FIG. 139 · *Douglas "Dolphin" model.* FIG. 150 · *Tail parts and fuselage for Howard Racer scale model. All by Robert S. Bartlett.* FIG. 141 · *Models in a chess problem*

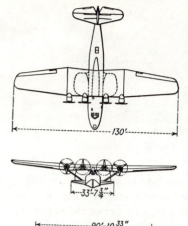

FIG. 142 · *Three-view plans for the "China Clipper," giving full-size dimensions; scale yours as you wish*

—130'—

—33'-7¾"—

—90'-10 33/64"—

—24'-7⅞"—

—84'-6"—

toward which the sail bellies being left slack. On the mainsail, these lines are supplemented by lazy jacks, which help to control the sail when it is raised or lowered. Two lazy jacks meet about two-thirds the way up the sail, then join the topping lift directly above. Also on the mainmast are the backstays, which run from the mast tip to the rail back about halfway between masts and serve to brace the foremast against the forward pull of the sails. The backstay on the lee side (toward which the sail bellies) is slack, but that on the windward (direction from which wind is blowing) is taut. It should have a knot up ½ in. from the rail and another at the rail to simulate the blocks on the full-size stay. From the outer end of each main boom, run to the cockpit a double line for the "sheet" (which controls sail angle).

Now to decorations: At the tip of the foremast, glue on a shaving for a yacht club flag. At the tip of the mizzen, glue on a smaller one for a private flag or burgee. And on the luff (loose edge) of the mainsail just below the peak (outer tip) glue a squared shaving for the Union Jack. These can be colored with oils. On the forward shrouds, glue a thin bit of wood on each side up about ⅜ in. from the rail. Color that on the port side (left side facing forward) red, and that on the starboard green. It is on these screens that night lights are mounted.

With a little nameplate properly lettered, and the whole ship

FIG. 143 · The "China Clipper." (*Courtesy Pan-American Airways*)

linseed-oiled, your model is finished. If you prefer a sailing model, don't make a propeller or rudder or shape the keel. Instead, cut off the hull at the water line ($\frac{3}{16}$ in. below the rail at the stern), remembering the sheer. Then cut off still more on the starboard (right) side, so that the ship tilts that way definitely as she would when sailing. Make a baseboard of white pine, maple, or oak, and on it carve grooves to simulate waves. These should be at right angles to the wind direction, and their slope should be gradual on the side facing the wind and steeper on the other.

On larger models, sails may be made of tracing cloth, good-quality writing paper, or the insides of stiff white collars. Or the ship need not carry sails at all, like the "Sea Witch" in Fig. 133.

Many airplane models are detailed, Figs. 137, 138, and 139, but some little "solid" models are fairly easy to make. White pine, balsa, or basswood are favorite woods. The three-dimension drawing, Fig. 142, tells the whole story. Simply choose your scale—$\frac{1}{16}$ in. per ft. is good in this case, for it gives an 8-in. wing spread. Transfer the drawing to the wood with the checkerboard as before, then shape up the pieces just as you did in the boat model. Assemble with glue, paint it, and you have a "solid" model of the "China Clipper," first commercial plane to fly the Pacific.

Many aircraft models are now made to a scale of $\frac{3}{4}$ in. per ft., as are those in Figs. 137 and 138. A smaller and common scale is $\frac{1}{4}$ in. per ft., better for solid models of ordinary planes.

Before balsa became so popular as a model material, bamboo was quite commonly used, and many model makers still stick to it. If you do, before you glue a bamboo end, burr or roughen it a little, or put knife marks on it so that the glue will have something to stick to. Don't use the pith, or center, of the wood. And when you split a piece into smaller sections, split always in the middle, putting pressure on the knife blade opposite to the direction in which the cut starts away from center. To shape bamboo exactly, boil it ten minutes, then put into a frame of nails or pins over a piece of white wrapping paper. Put this assembly into an oven and bake until the paper begins to turn brown. Then take it out and allow it to cool before taking the bamboo out.

Other types of models are of course legion. The Scout Camp in Fig. 144, for example, is built on a base of 1-in. white pine, about 3 by 4 ft. Whittled blocks form the land surface, covered with plaster of paris held on by tacks. Trees and shrubbery are bits of sponge and coiled pipe cleaners dipped in green paint.

Another fascinating model hobby is to build miniature scenes like the Japanese dish gardens of a few years ago. Make desert scenes, including an oasis, the Sphinx and the Pyramids, an Alpine landscape, a seascape, a Dutch mill, or illustrate a fairy tale thus.

FIG. 144 · *Scale model of Camp Frank S. Betz of Hammond (Ind) Council, B.S.A., one of my first complicated models*

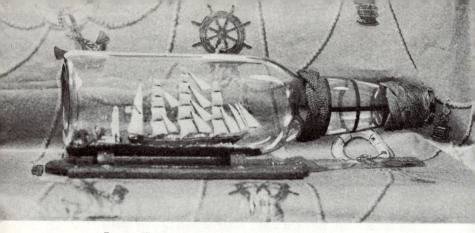

Fig. 145 · The "Great Republic," Donald McKay's largest clipper, under full sail in a giant beer bottle. (Courtesy Seamen's Church Institute)

CHAPTER XII

IN BOTTLES · *Ships, Fans, Etc.*

THE true meaning of the expression "bottle neck" has escaped you until you try to build something on the other side of one. If you live in the East, you've probably seen ships of many types inside bottles of many shapes, and further west it becomes store or tavern scenes, or elaborate frameworks, chairs, fraternal emblems. All these are done the same way. The piece or "picture" is built up and painted *outside* the bottle, then taken apart and reassembled piece by piece inside.

For any bottle work, you will need a series of stiff wires, preferably copper about $\frac{1}{16}$ in. in diameter, bent into the shapes indicated in Fig. 147 *a*. The upper one has a reverse curve for pushing against pieces or threads. Below it at left is a similar piece for pulling, then a close V-notch for catching threads, and a humped and pointed wire for forming putty or sticking into bits to convey them through the bottle neck. At *b* are two good shapes of razor cutting edges, and to their left is a split and forked wire for catching threads and pushing them taut while being glued.

Start bottle work with something fairly simple—say the fan in Fig. 116. Chapter IX explained about fan making, so here your only problem is to make a fan that will fit inside the bottle. Almost any bottle, so long as it is clean and its neck is not too small, will serve. Draw its outline on a sheet of paper, then inside this draw another line to represent the thickness of the bottle. This inner line outlines the space in which your piece must fit.

Select a straight-grained piece for your fan and whittle it down until it will pass through the bottle neck. Make the fan or fans on it and thread them, knotting loosely between leaves so that when the outer leaves are opened the others fan out at even intervals. Draw a bottom pattern of the bottle, allow again for thickness, then make a base block for the fan that is curved to fit the bottle, as at Fig. 147 f. Cut a socket in it for the stem of the fan blank, and try the fan in it to be sure it goes together smoothly and easily. Paint or gild the parts if you wish.

Now split the base into the largest pieces that will slip through the bottle neck, drop them in and arrange them side by side. Coat the mating faces with glue with either a long-handle brush or a wire with flattened end, then press the parts together accurately with still other wires. Be sparing with glue to avoid a "messy" appearance. When the glue has set, drop the fan blank through the bottle neck, touch its end with a little glue, and fit it firmly into its socket. Several straight wires and the long guiding point will help in this. With the reverse-curve wires, spread open the leaves of the fan farthest from the neck. Leave them on it to weight it while it dries, and open other fans above it, weighting each in turn, as in Fig. 147 e. Set the bottle aside to dry (unless you do, moisture from the fan will condense on the bottle interior later). In two or three days, stopper it and seal with wax to keep out moisture.

FIG. 146 · Woodcut by Freda Bone in "Bowsprit Ashore" by Alexander Bone. (Courtesy Doubleday Doran & Co.)

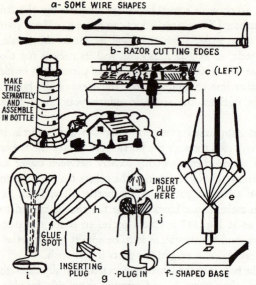

a- SOME WIRE SHAPES

b- RAZOR CUTTING EDGES

c (LEFT)

MAKE
THIS
SEPARATELY
AND
ASSEMBLE
IN BOTTLE

d

INSERT
PLUG
HERE

h

j

e

GLUE
SPOT

INSERTING
PLUG

g

·PLUG IN

f- SHAPED BASE

i

Fig. 147 · Tool shapes for ships in bottles, all of 1/16-in. copper wire, razor cutting edges, and model details. Below left, details of the trick stopper with locking peg, actually pulled in with a thread which is afterward hidden, as indicated in i and j.

The succession of operations is almost the same for any other piece to go in a bottle. Bottle selection is basic, and often suggests what to put inside. Giant beer bottles, wine bottles, and pinch bottles are most commonly used for ships, while flat bottles and flasks handle store scenes and big square bottles chairs and emblems. Normal scenes and ship models are placed in a bottle lying on its side usually, while rockers, chairs, table frameworks and emblems are either supported on the bottom or hang from a stopper. I have seen the three distinguishing balls of the pawn-broker hanging in a bottle, produced by gilding soft rubber balls, then deflating and rolling them up so they could be squeezed through the bottle neck. Once inside, they reinflate and are then tied in place (by strings attached beforehand). Fig. 147 c illustrates the common store in a bottle, the shelves in back being built up tier by tier to fill the back of a flask. The scene is built up outside the bottle as before, then painted carefully. The background of shelves is split into convenient pieces, as is the counter and the stock. Pieces are then slipped through the bottle neck and re-assembled. The human figures should pass through the bottle neck entire, except of course that a projecting arm or leg can be cut off and glued on again inside. Always work on parts farthest from the neck first, working to the neck, and daub up glue spots or cracks with thick paint.

Ships in bottles introduce a number of problems. Most ships are supported in putty pressed against the bottle wall and shaped and painted to simulate waves, and the bottle itself lies on its side in a cradle. If this is true of yours, make up two cradles like that shown in Fig. 150 and glue them to a baseboard.

As before, the model is made *outside* the bottle, then simply brought to shape inside. The hull should be small enough to go through the neck and is cut off sharply at the waterline. Then several tacks are driven in, as at Fig. 150, to hold it in place in the putty. Masts are designed to hinge at the deckline on either a tiny staple, a bent pin, or a miniature paper hinge. Most ships face the bottle neck, so hinges allow masts to fall backward.

The bowsprit or jib-boom is usually a little heavier than scale, because it

[[123]]

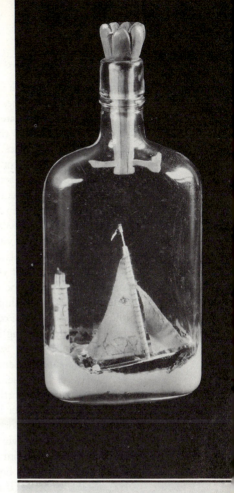

Fig. 148 (Top) · A *sloop*, complete to reefing points, burgee, and tiny skipper, in the bottom of a pint-size flat bottle, with tulip-shape locking-peg stopper. Fig. 149 · An Egyptian or Turkish oared galley in a water bottle

must be drilled for the forestays, as in Fig. 150. These forestays, which are the long lines leading from the mast tips down to the tip of the bowpsrit, are left a foot or two long and the whole model is assembled so that when these are pulled, all the masts rise naturally into place. Use bits of cut-off pins to fasten yards or spars to the mast, or drill the mast and hoist each yard into place after the boat is set up within the bottle. Make sails of bits of paper or cloth, or cut them to shape from the insides of stiff collars, and fasten them to the yards with long lengths of thread hanging from their lower corners. If these lines run down to the boat rail about in line with the particular mast, then they can be shorter and glued in place at the rail.

Try once to see that your plans are all right and that the masts rise naturally into the proper place when the forestays are pulled up, and your ship model is ready. For atmosphere inside the bottle, also whittle out a small boat or two (tug smoke should be white cotton batting) or a countryside panorama. In the latter case particularly, be sure to remember perspective—houses farther away are smaller and nearer the horizon. Paint these and set to dry for later use. Make lighthouses separately if needed.

Take your chosen bottle and clean it, then either paint the inside or the outside green or blue below the putty (which will later form waves and support the ship) or color the putty itself to avoid the unsightly white putty line as in Fig. 148. After the paint has dried, roll putty into long cigars and feed it through a paper tube into the bottle. Be sure not to use too much, and keep it off the bottle. (If it does stain, rub the spot with alcohol.)

When several putty rolls are in place, reach in with a long smooth wire or a spatula and push it carefully against the bottle walls, at the same time smoothing it out. Leave a part higher at the back for the land, and on it put a pebble or two for boulders on the shore line, possibly a twig behind for a gaunt tree. Form waves on the "water," usually at a slight angle to the ship, then paint waves deep blue or green with white tops, and land light gray or yellow, with green for the grass. Oils are best.

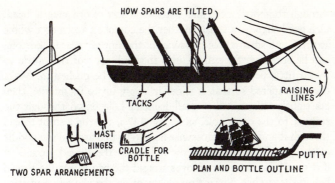

HOW SPARS ARE TILTED

TACKS

RAISING LINES

MAST HINGES

CRADLE FOR BOTTLE

PUTTY

TWO SPAR ARRANGEMENTS

PLAN AND BOTTLE OUTLINE

FIG. 150 · *Details of bottled ship models*

Stick a pointed wire into the end of the little screen or background and put it in the bottle, pushing it into the putty slightly when it is properly positioned against the back of the bottle. If you have a lighthouse, it will probably have to be put in separately, nearer to the shore line than the background and possibly on a slight elevation. Also put in any pieces, such as a tug or small boat, which are to go behind the major piece.

Check the lines on the boat model, making sure none are fouled or knotted and that all hang out as you introduce the ship into the bottle on the end of a pointed wire. When it is placed, push it downward into the putty and at a slight angle so it will look as if it is sailing when the masts are raised. Shape a bow wave at each side of its bow, tip it with white paint, and check the lines again to be sure none are fouled. Then let the putty dry for a day or two. Hoist the masts carefully, pulling each forestay tight, dropping a spot of glue on it and the jib boom, then holding it until the glue sets before cutting it off. Work from the farthest mast forward, straightening or hoisting the yards and setting the sails as you go. Then touch up with paint.

Instead of a cork or twine knot for a stopper, try a trick one like that in Fig. 148. Whittle a stopper long enough to extend

WHITTLING AND WOODCARVING

through the bottle neck and with some sort of ornamental head. One good shape is a tulip, another the cup of an acorn or a whole acorn. Cut a square hole crosswise of the stopper near its bottom, and be sure it is far enough into the wide part of the bottle so that a little peg like that in Fig. 147 h can be pushed in. Make the peg tapered so that it slides in easily up to its middle, then fits tightly. Now drill a small-diameter hole down through the stopper to the cross hole, as in Fig. 147 i, and run a stout thread through it and out the crosswise hole to be tied around the middle of the peg. Try the peg in the hole with the thread around it; if it won't go, cut little grooves around the peg to get the thread below the surface. Put a tiny glue spot on the peg end and stick the thread to it lightly, Fig. 147 h.

As soon as the glue sets, drop the dangling peg into the bottle and follow it with the stopper. Maneuver the bottle and peg around until the peg aligns itself with the hole, as in Fig. 147 g, then pull up on the thread. The plug will go into the crosshole a little way, then the glue spot will release the thread and the resulting "snap" will pull the peg in tightly. Whittle a bit of matchstick or other plug and push it in beside the taut thread, then cut it and the thread off close. Mask the plug by making it look like a lathe center mark, like the point of the acorn, or, as in Fig. 147 j, by gluing in a tight-fitting acorn over it. Touch up again.

Larger boats sometimes have hulls in several parts and must be assembled carefully by dowels inside the bottle. This is very painstaking and tedious work, for all rigging, practically, must be done inside the bottle, but the result is just that much more mystifying. And try putting a ship in the *bottom* of a bottle instead of on its side, or hang a tiny airplane from a knotted cord suspended from the stopper. As before, this is done by knotting the cord around the plane, then passing long ends up through the stopper before the peg is put in. If carefully done it will look as though the knotted loop holding the plane just passes through a crosswise hole in the stopper.

〖 126 〗

Fig. 151 · *"Sift Out Power Dollar Wasters," typical of the use of whittled models in illustration and advertising*

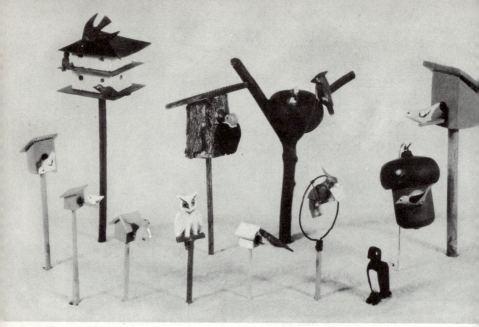

FIG. 152 · *A dozen birds and their houses for dish garden or flower pot*

CHAPTER XIII

CARICATURES · *Birds and Animals*

EXACT proportions in a carved figure impress the observer; careful misproportion amuses him as well. Peculiarly, many of the cuts which lend distinction to the misproportioned figure, or caricature, are unplanned slips of the knife or chisel.

So don't worry if your finished caricature doesn't look like the picture or drawing of mine—yours may be better because of "mistakes." I made dozens of the scotties shown in Fig. 164 before a mistake gave me the basic pattern for those in Fig. 171. And don't resign yourself to the impression that whittling caricatures is not for you—half a dozen people, one an invalid, have written me that they've copied various figures of mine successfully.

One was a butcher's boy, another a high-school girl, several were grownups in various professions. Further, look at Fig. 153— all these elephant caricatures were carved from very hard woods by unlearned and untutored African tribesmen in Kenya, Northern Rhodesia, and Tanganyika!

Before trying such caricatures, let's start out with animal and bird miniatures; they're exceptionally easy. The birds of Fig. 152, though designed for dish-garden ornaments, can be varied in size for garden, flower-pot, curtain-pull or other uses simply by selecting the proper size for the squares in the basic checker-board. Most of them are of ¼-in. white pine taken from bits of old boxes. Use the patterns in Fig. 155, trace your own from a side or front view of a bird in a book or magazine, or make up some new and strange ones. (This applies to any picture in the book— use the checkerboard to vary size.)

Whittle out this silhouette, and you have a bird blank. If you want a simple, conventionalized design, like the penguin, just cut away a little wood at the sides of the head to bring out the shoulders and a little more at the base to separate wings and feet, thin the bill, paint in characteristic colors, and there you

FIG. 153 · *African tribesmen whittled these.* (*Courtesy Capt. George Sherwood*)

are! The effect is exactly the same as if you had taken a thin silhouette of the whole bird and glued small pieces on each side to represent wings. The woodpecker and parrot are similar.

A little more elaborate rounding up gives the bluebird, tanager, and canary that look quite a bit like their real-life contemporaries. Still further shaping of head, bill, wings, and feet, and you have a miniature bird, whittled "in the round," such as the purple martins at upper left or the cedar waxwing at upper center, Fig. 152. A close-up, Fig. 161, shows how the martin house is made. It is simply a block whittled to roof shape at top and with holes bored in at the proper places. Roof and platforms are cardboard, thin wood, or stiff paper, glued in place. The standard is an all-day-sucker stick glued in.

The woodpecker's house, by contrast, is a bit of rough limb, the cedar waxwing's a forked twig, and the parrot's a bit of wire bent into a circle and wired to a matchstick. The parrot's topknot is a glued-on shaving, and a cardboard cracker is glued in his mouth. In every case, much of the effect is gained by painting the bird with oil paints (dull-finish) in his proper colors.

If, instead of caricatured or conventionalized birds, you prefer accurate, true-to-life ones for display or teaching nature study, consult a good bird guide. This will not only give you proper size and proportion, but characteristic colors, poses, and surroundings as well.

Life-size birds are usually easier to make in three parts, one the head and body, the second the bill, and the third the tail. The head

FIG. 154 · *Wooden birds, every one, but very true to life. Whittled by I. K. Scott*

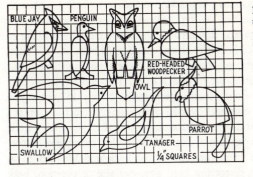

Fig. 155 · *Bird patterns.* Fig. 156 (Below) · *Details of true-to-life birds of* Fig. 154

and body part will be found to be quite similar for most birds, characteristic variations appearing in the size, shape, and position of bill and tail. Your bird guide will show you these. Rough the body to shape, drill a hole at the proper place for the bill, and saw a slot for the tail, which may be grooved to simulate tail feathers. Shape up the bird's body and cut grooves in the back, as in Fig. 156, to simulate wing tips and feathers. Eyes for small birds can be cut-off, black-headed costume pins, pushed into a slight socket to keep them from bulging unnaturally. For larger birds, buy glass eyes from a taxidermist.

Now for legs and pose. Swallows, flycatchers, hummingbirds, and some sparrows usually sit with their legs drawn close under them, so their wooden prototypes can simply be nailed to the proper kind of background. But other birds, like the robin, woodpecker, flicker, and owl, have characteristic legs always prominent, no matter what the pose. It is easiest to make formed-wire legs for these birds, glued into drilled holes in the bird's abdomen, as shown in Fig. 156.

It is amazing how closely birds so made and carefully colored resemble the real birds—witness the kingfisher, wren, cardinal, red-eyed vireo, tufted titmouse, red-winged blackbird, towhee, and Baltimore oriole of Fig. 154. Made of balsa by Scout Executive Scott of Hammond, Ind., they look real enough to sing.

〖 131 〗

Then again, you may want to make an oversize conventional-ized bird like the owl of Fig. 161. A gable-end decoration for an Owl Patrol cabin, this bird is finished purely by soaking in linseed oil. Notice how the characteristic owl eyes and ear tufts have been exaggerated, how the legs have been lengthened, and the wings set out to attain a caricature. The owl is just as easy to make as any of the others; the patterns of Fig. 157 show you front and side views and over-all dimensions. From there on it's just a case of rounding up and accentuating the eyes with a little black paint. The penguin of Fig. 160 is another example of distor-tion for an effect. Here the color is just India ink. You can go on almost endlessly, distorting head size, eye size or position, beak shape, wing shape or position, and pose to get as amusing—and as terrifying—caricatures as you wish.

Next, do you like dogs? Almost everybody does, so Figs. 162 to 172 provide a number of samples. It isn't necessary to make all your dogs of one breed—you can make one look like your own, another like the neighbor's, another like no dog anyone ever saw

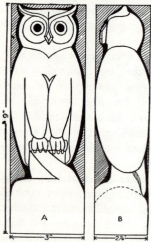

FIG. 157 · *Patterns for the owl*, FIG. 158

before. Figure 168 shows a whippet, dachshund, beagle, spaniel, two tiny scotties, a fox terrier, a larger scottie, and a very conventional terrier. Check-erboard patterns for five of them are drawn in Fig. 167. Simply lay out a pattern, same size or different size, on a checker-board on a suitable piece of wood, whittle or saw it out, and round up or block out just as you did the birds.

Most of these dogs can be made in ½- or ¾-in. wood— white pine, basswood, or harder woods for special purposes—and it is usually easier to let the grain run the long way. This means that sometimes legs will be across grain, and calls for special care to keep from breaking them off. Rough out the body shape first, then shape up ears and legs as you do final finishing. As with the birds, the dogs can be left as rough silhouettes, blocked out to show shoulders, head, and tail (as most of mine are), or carefully rounded up and shaped.

Once you have learned the basic principles of the dogs, you can vary pose, size, and so on almost at will. Figure 164 shows five poses of the same dog, Fig. 162 shows three different sizes, and Fig. 163 a twin arrangement. These dachshunds are in walnut and make use of the same middle ear, forefoot, and hindfoot. Done in polished walnut or mahogany, the twins make an attractive desk ornament. Take care in cutting the long slot between bodies.

Such dogs can be adapted for dozens of uses, for example in the mahogany book ends of Fig. 165. Carve each from a single block, sawing the silhouette out as before. Thin the dog blank proper at each side to proper thickness, and shape it. If you are careful in thinning the blank, you will take off each side another dog blank or two—depending

〖 133 〗

FIG. 158 (TOP) · Heroic-size owl for gable-end decoration. FIG. 159 · A fish in soap. (Courtesy Natl. Soap Sculpture Com.). FIG. 160 · A penguin caricature. FIG. 161 (BOTTOM) · Three purple martens and their house in a dish garden

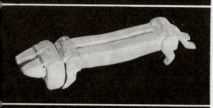

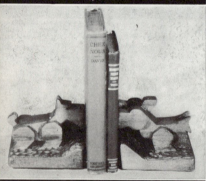

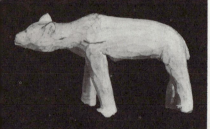

upon width of the block—which can be used elsewhere. Another book-end design caricatures a dachshund's length. His forequarters are depicted emerging from the façade of a kennel forming the book support, while his hindquarters enter a similar façade on the other book end.

Other animals are easy to whittle, too—the polar bear of Fig. 166 is an example. Vary the pose as you wish to meet a decorative scheme; the mahogany elephant of Fig. 173, for example, has been re-posed slightly so that he stands upright with trunk raised atop a circus tub. His tusks and the tub decorations are finished with oil colors, then the whole piece is shellacked.

More elaborate in design and pose are the dogs of Fig. 171. They depend upon knife cuts as well as pose to make them interesting, and exemplify variation of one basic design. Knife cuts show the shoulders, neck, whiskers, and rough coat; and tiny black costume pins (or black beads on short pins) give sparkle to the eyes. These simple shapes are sawed out of ¾-in. soft wood, notched, the head and belly shaped and notched, and the ears and tail shaped last. Grain can run either way, although legs and ears are stronger if the grain is lengthwise of

⟦ 134 ⟧

Fig. 162 (Top) · *Scotties, big and little, but all from the same pattern.* Fig. 163 . *Twin dachshunds in walnut.* Fig. 164 · *Five variations in pose for the same dog* (see Fig. 171). Fig. 165 · *Scotties serve as book ends of mahogany.* Fig. 166 (Bottom) · *Caricatured gaunt polar bear.* (*Courtesy Remington Arms Co., Inc.*)

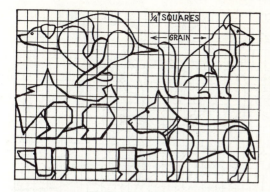

FIG. 167 · *Patterns for five breeds of dogs, on a checkerboard for ease in varying size. Patterns for other breeds can be gotten from profile photographs or sketches and transferred similarly to wood by first drawing the checkerboard over the picture*

them. Before the eyes are pushed in, carefully bore holes for them by pushing in a long straight pin; otherwise you may split the head. Their dull black color is simply India ink. Other arrangements of head and body will of course change pose just as you wish, even to having the dog's head at an angle to his body.

Figure 169 shows similar variations of one basic pattern for a pony. By changing relationship of the head, legs, and tail, you can produce almost any pose you want. The cat is sketched merely to keep the doleful dachshund of Fig. 170 company. Both are sawed from ½-in. or ⅝-in. white pine or basswood, then rounded up only enough to bring out expression, ears, tail, and legs.

An excellent example of animal caricature is Fig. 172, showing two foals carved by George Lang of Oberammergau, Germany. No effort has been made to show the hooves, proper head shape, or

FIG. 168 · *Dogs in variety—whippet, dachshund, beagle, and some odd ones*

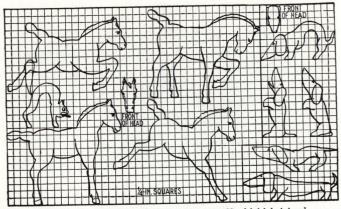

FIG. 169 · *Pony patterns and a cat.*   FIG. 170 · *The doleful dachshund*

shoulders, yet the gawky legginess of the foals is very well brought out. Note particularly how the grain accentuates the angles and long, trembly legs of the animals.

It is probable that the foals were not made with a knife at all, but were carved with woodcarving tools, which we are shortly to learn how to use. They are more convenient for certain kinds of cuts (see Chap. XVII) and can very well be used in making most of the figures in this chapter and the next.

Many modern caricatures are not made in wood at all, but in soap, celluloid, or one of the molded materials commonly called "plastics." The fish of Fig. 159 is an example, for it was carved

FIG. 171 · *Six poses, but all basically the same scottie*

Fig. 172 · "*Two Foals*," *by George Lang.* (*Courtesy German Tourist Inform. Office, N. Y.*).
Fig. 173 (Right) · *Mahogany elephant, and atop a circus tub for the fun of it*

from soap by the Flatbush Boys Club of Brooklyn, N. Y., and won honorable mention in the Eleventh Annual Soap Sculpture Competition. Carving these materials is described in Chap. XV.

Animal caricatures may not necessarily caricature animals, but may represent human traits or actions. "Mickey Mouse," for example, has a mouse face modified to look like a human face, walks on his hind legs, wears clothes, even shows expression. Chapter XIV shows what happens in the human face when emotion is expressed. Making these same changes in an animal face will cause the animal to assume a recognizable expression—a trick commonly used by cartoonists. You can use it, too, to make a horse laughing, a duck crying and wiping its eyes with its wing, an owl with a monocle and mortarboard or a judge's gown and solemn face.

Conversely, it is possible to modify a human shape slightly to give it animal characteristics. Examples are the long ears of a jackass on an otherwise human head, a human head on a wolf's or snake's body, and so on. As you may guess, such caricatures are usually not very complimentary to the subject.

FIG. 174 · "Handworkers," by George Lang. (Courtesy German Tourist Inform. Office, N. Y.)

CHAPTER XIV

CARICATURES · *People*

CARVED caricatures endeavor to do just what caricature sketches do—emphasize characteristic features, expressions, or poses to delineate personality or lampoon the original. Almost any material can be used—I read just recently of a New York sandwich maker who carves his from toast. But primitive and civilized man both use wood for enduring caricatures "in-the-round."

With animal caricatures, the whole body must be characteristic; but with people the face is the dominant element, and the pose of the figure is only supplementary. This has led many cartoonists to use what is called a "stump" figure, in which the head may be half as big as the body, a trick which will work just as successfully in wood. In other cases, the body is overly tall,

〖 138 〗

and the effect is gained by its position. The tailor, shoe-maker, and blacksmith by George Lang in Fig. 174 are examples of this, and, incidentally, three of the finest caricatures I have seen.

It is relatively easy to carve (with either knife or chisel) a grotesque figure representing an idea or a class of people, but it is much more difficult to make that figure a caricature of some particular individual. The tribesmen of Fig. 175, for example, were carved by untutored Africans and represent the identifying dress of their own or neighboring tribes. As such, Captain Sherwood tells me they are readily recognizable. But try to make them represent some particular individual of the tribe!

Let us first consider faces and heads, major element of a caricature. Small differences in whittling or coloring will alter the whole expression, whether or not you want them to. It is thus easy to vary expression on two similar figures—easier to do it than to avoid doing it.

Consider the normal human head as oval, with the eyes in the middle and a little less than an eye-width apart. The face itself takes up the lower three-quarters of the oval, with the nose about one-third its length, or one-fourth the full height of the head. The ears are the same length as the nose and in line with it horizontally. The mouth is a third of the way down from the tip

Fig. 175 · *True caricature by untaught African tribesmen. (Courtesy Capt. Geo. Sherwood)*

of the nose to the chin, and about 1½ eyes wide. Five eye-widths give the normal width of the head.

But the Negro has thicker lips, the Semite heavier brows and a more bulbous nose, the Indian a high Roman nose and prominent cheekbones, the Oriental slanting eyes. These are racial variations; there are also endless variations in people of any given race. It is these variations which determine an individual, and you must learn to recognize them before you can make a recognizable caricature of that individual. Study him: Is his jaw prominent or receding? Is his mouth large or small? Are his eyes close together or wide apart? What is the shape of his nose (Fig. 188)? What are his tricks of expression?

If you could catch all these in a carved head, you would have a portrait, not a caricature, so you must pick those that are particularly unusual and overemphasize them. Cartoonists in your daily newspaper will show you how—the horn-rimmed glasses of Harold Lloyd, the tiny mustache of Charlie Chaplin, and so on. Then, too, certain distortions of facial outline we have come to consider as indicating certain traits—again through the influence of the cartoons. Buck teeth and oversize outstanding ears with mouth hanging open denote the mental defective, while buck teeth and unkempt hair indicate the "hick." A square jaw and rugged features show strength of character, a receding chin and generally soft features show contrasting weakness. Sunken lips and many wrinkles show age; if the face is full it shows complacence, if thin it shows shrewdness.

FIG. 176 · *Simple Italian caricature; two high-relief silhouettes*

FIG. 177 · *Patterns for the figures of* FIG. *176, and a few hat shapes. Above the side view of the woman are two types of glasses commonly used on these figures, both of bent wire, held by sticking the wire ends into holes*

You will learn to recognize other characteristics after you have whittled a few heads. They can be either in-the-round—which means the whole head in three dimensions—as at center, Fig. 176, or in relief, as are the half heads shown at either side. Let's try a simple head in-the-round first—perhaps you've already tried to better the African figures in Figs. 175 and 179. Their eyes and collars are aluminum, the shields painted skin, the loincloths bits of cloth held with beads or a leather thong.

Figure 177 gives the front and side patterns for the lady's head in Fig. 176. Draw her profile on a piece of 1¼ by 1¼ by 4-in. long soft wood (2 in. for a hand-grip to be cut off when the piece is finished), and whittle it out like a thick silhouette. Then cut out a pattern for the front view, lay it on the piece, and trace around it. Whittle to this outline, too. Cut away at each side of the nose, round up the cheeks, the head, and the neck, and shape the collar and dress with a few shallow V-cuts.

Sketch in the shape of the mouth, make a V-cut to represent it, and shape the upper lip to the nostrils, which are just little triangles cut out. Show the line of the cheeks by making a curving stop-cut down from each side of the nose and cutting away the wood, as indicated in the profile view. Shape the lower lip by taking a shallow U-cut just beneath it, and form the point of the chin by cutting away the wood at each side.

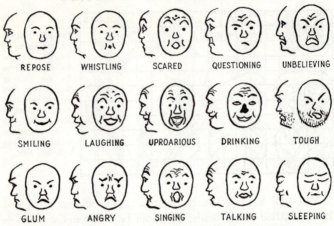

REPOSE · WHISTLING · SCARED · QUESTIONING · UNBELIEVING

SMILING · LAUGHING · UPROARIOUS · DRINKING · TOUGH

GLUM · ANGRY · SINGING · TALKING · SLEEPING

FIG. 178 · *How mouth and eyebrow positions determine expression*

Study the sketch and photograph before you finish the eyes. Notice that the eye sockets are shallow U-cuts sloping outward, backward, and slightly downward. Shape the nose by thinning it slightly at each side, and form the arch of the eyebrows. The eyes will be painted on later—just a curved line with a dot at its center, with a white patch at each side to represent the iris. (More elaborate caricatures have more elaborate eye shapes. The next step is a V-cut for the eye socket with a shallower V-cut above it to show the eyebrow, the pupil itself being shown by a drilled hole or a tiny cut-out triangle. The final step is complete shaping of the eyeball, as in the pipe of Fig. 193, with the pupil shown by a drilled hole and the eyelid outlined above it.)

Shape up the hat and the hair, making a few U-cuts in the hair to represent its texture. Don't try to outline each hair. If, instead of a woman, your caricature is to be a man, cut away more of the hair at the sides, and represent the ears by a rounding V-cut in the general shape of a question mark with a dot at its center. Several men's hat shapes are shown in Fig. 177, as well as glasses formed of wire and held by pushing their ends into tiny

[142]

drilled holes just above the ears or at each side of the nose. If your carica-ture is to be fatter than the Italian one shown, indicate fatness by leaving more wood under the chin and shaping it with circling grooves, leave the cheeks fuller, and possibly put a dimple or two in them. To change expression, see Fig. 178, and sketch on outlines accordingly.

Finish this caricature by painting in appropriate colors, a touch of red on cheeks, lips, and nose tip; flesh color for the face; black or any color for the hat; a different color for the collar; and still another for the dress under it. Such heads are used on bottle stoppers, tie racks, book ends, etc.

The head caricatures in profile are really elaborated silhouettes. Cut out a silhouette of the desired shape, curve down the cheek to form the nose, make a shallow V-cut for the eye socket, and taper off below the nose for the mouth. The mouth is a tapered V-groove with the lips shaped above and below it as you did those of the in-the-round head. The ear is a prominent part of the head from this angle, hence should be shaped more carefully. It should be the highest point on the head, all other surfaces being sloped away from it. Indicate hair as before with a series

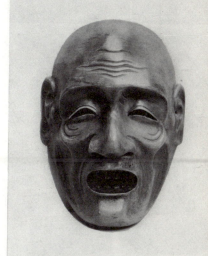

[[143]]

FIG. 179 (TOP) · *Two more simple African caricatures, one a native woman with her baby in a back harness, the other a native officer.* FIG. 180 · *A Japanese mask of an old man.* FIG. 181 · *Another Japanese mask, this one of "Obechima."* (*Masks, courtesy Metropolitan Museum of Art*)

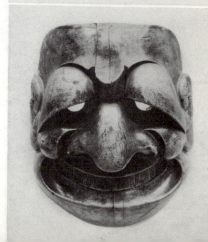

of parallel V-cuts. Changes in the
haircut, addition of a cigar, cigarette,
or pipe, changes in style of dress—
all these help to denote the particular
character. Notice the upstanding collar
and long haircut of the left-hand
head in Fig. 176, elements that are
vaguely reminiscent of Uncle Sam,
while the round face and button nose
of the right-hand head, coupled with
the fringe of hair, meets the car-
toonist's specification for an Irishman.
Such heads are used as decorations
for letter openers, salt spoons, paper
knives, bookmarks, and so on.

Now for a little more on expression.
Figure 178 indicates the variations
and shows how all are accomplished
by simple changes, notably of eyebrows and mouth. The other parts of
the face are merely supplementary;
while they identify individuals they
do not show expression. The three
heads at left give the basic expressions,
an almost straight mouth and arched
eyebrows for the face in repose, an up-
ward-curving mouth for joy, and a
downward-curving one for sadness.
When you smile, wrinkles appear at
the ends of your mouth (and if you are
inclined to stoutness, dimples in your
cheeks), but when you frown the wrinkles become ugly lines leading down
from your nose, and the inner ends of
your eyebrows draw down, too.

[144]

FIG. 182 (TOP) · Chinese caricature in an ivory
snuff-box (Courtesy Metropolitan Museum of
Art). FIG. 183 · Simple Japanese caricature in
slabs of bamboo. FIG. 184 · "Samuel Johnson"
in soap, by Mildred Steinrich; courtesy Natl.
Soap Sculpture Com., as is Fig. 186. FIG. 185 ·
Fiddler and "tooter" of FIG. 191. FIG. 186 ·
"The Toonerville Trolley," by Herman Miller

Fig. 187 · *Patterns for the "tooter" of Fig. 185*

Note that you have muscles that will draw up either end or the middle of your eyebrows, and other muscles that will draw them down or together, but none that will pull them further apart. Thus, as your smile develops into a laugh, your eyebrows rise further from your eyes, even causing wrinkles in your forehead, your mouth opens more, and the wrinkles at the mouth ends grow deeper to make your cheeks more prominent. As you pass from glumness to anger, your eyebrows are drawn downward and closer together, forming wrinkles between them, and the sides of your mouth drop lower and lower. In singing, your mouth opens, but does not widen particularly; in talking it widens but doesn't open so far. Fear causes your eyebrows to rise and your mouth to hang open, and any questioning look pulls down one corner of your mouth only. If you want to appear tough, you pull your eyebrows together and down at the center and twist your mouth so much that it hangs open on one side. Disbelief pulls it open on both sides and widens your upper lip. You will be able readily to place other expressions between these.

Particularly good examples of face expression are given in Figs. 180 and 181, a type of thing you may want to try to whittle. Try these masks small at first—a full-size one is quite a cutting

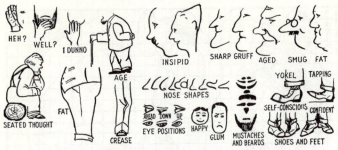

FIG. 188 · *Character in caricature—some of the elements*

job. And study the faces on other figures shown—those of the Italian band in Figs. 185 and 189 particularly.

Before we consider figure caricature, it is probably best to summarize normal figure proportions (more details in Chap. XXII). The unit of measure is the length of the head. Normal figures are seven to eight heads tall, although most caricatures are not over six (in fact, the so-called "stump figure" usually has a body only twice as long as the head). So-called "fashion figures" may be nine or ten heads tall. The body can be divided into three parts—neck to hips, hips to knee, knee to sole of foot. The upper leg and lower leg are about the same length. The foot is about 1 head long, the hand as long as the face (¾ head), the arms about 3 heads to the finger tips, divided in the middle by the elbow. Men's shoulders are about 2 head lengths wide, the hips slightly less. Women are wider in the hips and narrower in the shoulders.

In caricature, all these proportions are varied to suit individual characteristics. Thus the slender man is made even more slender, the fat man even fatter. Generally, fat figures and fat faces are easier to make than thin ones, because the bones all have fat over them, making their exact positions a little indistinct. Cartoons have taught us to suspect the tall, thin figure of meanness or asceticism, the fat figure of jollity or slovenliness, depending upon clothes and pose. You will find that any figure you whittle will be fat anyway at first.

Remember that the figure can be made to accentuate the face expression if properly posed. Don't balance the body on both feet and make the figure symmetrical—it immediately becomes stiff and uninteresting. Cross the legs, the arms, turn the head, let the figure slouch—do anything to avoid a "posed" look. Hand positions are vital in emphasizing expression—watch how many your friends use in talking. A few are sketched in Fig. 188: the hand behind the ear to denote difficulty in hearing, the hand stroking the beard, the finger tips at the chin for "that worried look." As the face ages, it carries more lines; as the body ages, it becomes more stooped, the knees sag, one hand often rests upon a cane. Shoulders are bent, women wear the head shawl, clothes don't fit.

Study and sketch the creases in your own clothes, and check them against those on figures illustrated. Sharp, knife creases denote preciseness and the well-dressed man; baggy, unkempt clothes the hobo or careless man. Notice how prominent a part the set of the clothing plays in Figs. 185 and 189. In Fig. 182, almost no shape is shown by the clothing, and the figure looks a little stiff in consequence. By contrast, notice the sweep of the robes in Fig. 183, formed simply by using the curved outer surfaces of the bamboo pieces to show these shapes. (Incidentally,

FIG. 189 · *The Italian band, complete from director to "oompah." These excellent Tyrolese figures are among the best of modern Italian caricatures. (Courtesy M. W. Perinier)*

MAKE OTHER KING AND QUEEN FATTER AND WITH DIFFERENT DESIGN ON SCEPTRES

FIG. 190 · *Patterns from "Through the Looking-Glass" for a set of interesting and laughable chessmen. If you must concentrate on your game, don't make them*

this figure, a modern Japanese importation, has a simple rounded head with the features painted on.)

Often, clothes can be indicated with just a few well-placed lines, as in Fig. 184. It may, instead, be advisable to show considerable detail (even to the bottle in the fiddler's pocket), as in Fig. 185. This figure, incidentally, emphasizes the differences between fat and thin man so that you can hardly miss them. Also, study the dreamy look of the violinist, the concentrated, puffy look of the horn player. Both are excellent examples of modern commercial Italian caricature. If you want to try to copy the horn player, front, side, and back views of him are sketched in Fig. 187. Note the little touches in the flare of his coat, the bulge of his cheeks, and his oversize feet.

Further details on foot position are shown in the composite picture of the band, Fig. 189, and in the lower right-hand corner of Fig. 188. This figure also shows, at upper left, some of the characteristic gestures and poses we have come to associate with

FIG. 191 · *Caricatures entered in a national whittling contest conducted by "Popular Mechanics" magazine*

FIG. 192 · *Steps in making the typical businessmen of* FIG. 194

certain ideas. You and your friends make dozens more which you can catalogue readily; Figs. 191 and 194 show some of them.

Caricatures of everyday people will find many uses as little statuettes. Those in Fig. 194, for example, were made to illustrate factory executive types in a magazine display. I have made others to accompany machinery models as a scale of size.

The figures in Fig. 194 are copied from full-front sketches or pictures of people in magazines and newspapers. Steps in construction are shown in Fig. 192. The traced outline is transferred to the block by means of carbon paper, and this blank sawed out. The body is roughed out first, then the head and hands, and the whole piece finally shaped up. Little details of pockets, something held in the hand, hair, and so on are put in last. Shape the base as you wish, then either coat the whole figure with linseed oil, or paint it with water colors or oils. Mustaches, cigars, a roll of paper in one hand, etc., can be added with brush or gluepot.

Recently, several New York drugstores have been offering kits including a block of briar, drilled and turned for a pipe-stem. Such a blank is shown in Fig. 193, and with it two examples of heads cut thus. The football hero at right will appeal to collegians,

⟦ 149 ⟧

FIG. 193 · A briar blank, and two pipes. (Courtesy Universal School of Handicrafts, Inc.)

the bowl in the center is a modified head of the Duchess from "Alice in Wonderland." I had to make her headdress smaller in order to keep more wood in the bowl. The Alice chessmen of Fig. 190 are slightly modified from the original sketches of John Tenniel. I have shown the Red Queen; the White Queen was much more portly.)

Briar, of which these pipes are made, is an interesting and hard-to-carve material. Grain runs every which way, and the wood usually breaks ahead of the knife instead of shaving off. Briar is the burl that forms at the roots of the white heather (*bruyère* in French), a bushy shrub growing along the Mediterranean. About a hundred years ago, a French pipe smoker broke his meerschaum in Italy and commissioned a local woodcarver to make him another from the hardest wood available. The woodcarver chose briar. Most briar today comes from Greece. Roots about thirty years old are grubbed out of the ground and buried in a moist trench for a year. (Only a little exposure to sunlight will start a crack and ruin the burl.) The aged wood is trimmed to leave only the close-grained, dense burl, then cut into blocks called *ébauchons*. These are boiled in water to remove the sap, then dried under cover for several months. Pipe makers season them as much as two years more, then cut them into the seventy sizes of roughs needed to make 700 to 900 styles of pipes.

Color your finished pipes, if you like, with aniline dyes, then buff or rub with Tripoli powder, pumice, and beeswax until you get as much polish as you want. But don't lacquer, shellac or varnish them.

〚 150 〛

FIG. 194 · *Eight caricatures of industrial executives. These little figures, 6 in. high, were used to lend interest to a graphic interpretation of some dull statistics*

FIG. 195 · *A familiar soap sculpture by Lester Gaba. (Courtesy Proctor & Gamble Co.)*

CHAPTER XV

OTHER MATERIALS · *Soap, Ivory,*
Bone, Plastics, Celluloid, Leather

THE peach and other fruit pits of Chap. III are not the only materials other than wood that can be whittled successfully. To these must be added soap, ivory, bone, plastics, celluloid, leather, clay, wax, hard rubber, fiber, fiberboard, horn, pearl, and semiprecious stones.

Soap sculpture began in isolated, individual experiments, possibly because some sculptor needed an inexpensive and easily available material for models, possibly because some amateur was intrigued by the ease with which it is worked or the fact that he could always wash his hands of (and with) a spoiled piece. By 1924, soap sculpture was widespread enough that a national competition was sponsored by Proctor & Gamble Co. This contest drew 500 entries, but interest grew so rapidly that the seventh annual contest drew 5,800 entries in a variety of classes. In 1935, there were 4,000.

Consider soap as just another material more easily worked than most, suitable for models, statuettes, figurines, caricatures, low- and high-relief panels. While the soap itself is not very lasting, it can be varnished, colored with water colors, poster colors, or sealing wax dissolved in denatured alcohol. (If you use water colors, use thick paint and daub it on—don't brush it on or you'll have suds. Try for color first on a leftover piece.)

For tools, you will need two knives and a couple of orangewood sticks such as are used for manicuring. You may supplement them with all sorts of others—a hairpin fastened, hump out, over the end of a short dowel and used as a scraper; a comb for scraping multiple lines to simulate hair, to give a rough surface; etc.

Begin by selecting a soap uniform in texture and fairly soft. Usually heavy laundry soaps or specially shaped bath soaps are not sufficiently uniform in texture. To avoid warping and bad cutting, cut off the outer surfaces to get rid of lettering and the hard surface that soap forms on exposure to air.

FIG. 196 · *"Evening," by Richard W. Clark, second-prize winner in senior class, Eleventh Soap Sculpture Competition (1935). (Courtesy Natl. Soap Sculpture Com.). Subsequent photographs from same contest*

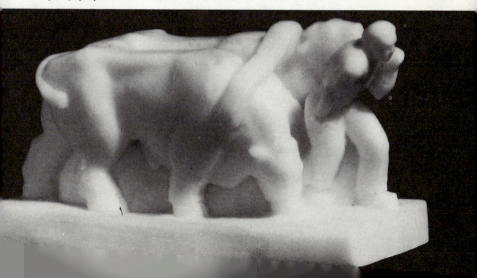

The design—any design so long as it is not delicate and lacy (for soap is much softer but much more brittle and not nearly so sturdy as wood)—is applied by sketching with a sharp-pointed tool directly on the soap or by tracing it lightly (to avoid smearing) from a sketch on paper by means of carbon paper. If it smears, scrape off a thin layer of soap and start again.

Carve soap just as you carve wood. Cut away all waste soap down to within ⅛ in. or so of the outline, then cut away the surplus soap to expose highest and largest points first. You will find the bar of soap small enough so that you can grip the knife in your fingers and make cuts just by closing your hand, using your thumb as a guide—just like peeling potatoes. This is safer than cutting away from yourself, for soap is so soft the knife must be guided carefully. Also, soap will stick to the knife blade and will have to be cleaned off with the back of another knife, otherwise later cuts will be neither smooth nor accurate.

Work first to get the shape correct, then begin finishing by smoothing the rough spots, cutting away sharp corners, and bringing out the details that give expression to the subject. Before you make an intaglio or inset or edge-cut (as in the details of the car in Fig. 186, Chap. XIV) make stop- or outline cuts. They help to prevent overcutting and breaking away of the soap. Details can

FIG. 197. *"Mare and Foal" by Helen L. Young, second-prize winner, advanced amateur class. (Courtesy Natl. Soap Sculpture Com.)*

be brought out best by careful scratching or scraping—here the orangewood sticks come in handy.

If you are carving in relief, you are dealing with a picture in three dimensions (see Chaps. XIX & XX). Subdue extra-high parts and raise very low ones, keeping the high relief to outline the piece against its background. If you are carving a figure, forget pictures entirely. Copy good sculpture or nature until you get the "hang" of it. Find planes, outlines, shapes, by half closing your eyes and looking at the model. Block those in *right* first, or all the details you add will only make the piece worse.

With practice, you will learn to bring out certain things and subdue others to create the effect you want,— for example, follow the sweep of the robe in Fig. 201 to the Infant Jesus held high in his mother's hands, or the elongated face and sweeping lines of the head in Fig. 198. Note how large masses are at the base.

Don't try for detail at all except in exceptional cases—leave that for ivory. Avoid thin, projecting elements if you can, but if you can't, make them thin at the edge but more substantial immediately back of it. Work from all sides, look at the piece from several angles—even change lighting occasionally.

⟦ 155 ⟧

Fig. 198 (Top) · *"Speed,"* by Harry Rappoport, given Lenox Award as best suited for reproduction in pottery. Fig. 199 · *"Skiing,"* by Carolyn Greene, honorable mention, junior class. Fig. 200 (Bottom) · *"Girl with Mandolin,"* by Armando Aroffo . (All courtesy Natl. Soap Sculpture Com.)

When you are satisfied with the carving, set it aside to dry for a day or two, then polish it by rubbing the new harder and drier surface carefully all over with a paper napkin. Finish with your finger tips and the palm of your hand—but be sure your fingernails do not touch the surface, or they will gouge it. Rub carefully, for remember it is not so strong as wood. Constant rubbing should produce a soft finish, smooth enough to reflect some light. This will gradually turn yellow, like ivory.

If you want a finished carving larger than one cake of soap, use two or more joined together. Cut off the outer surfaces as before, then put the cakes in a pan with the edges to be joined under water. Heat slowly until these edges become jellylike, then simply press them together. Pin the joint together with toothpicks outside the lines of any future carving, then set the bars away to cool and dry with a weight on them. When dry, scrape away the soap squeezed out at the joint, then add another bar or go ahead and whittle. Don't try to make two joints at once!

For the delicate lacy effects that soap itself cannot give you, combine other materials with it—ribbon, cloth, paper, lace paper, lace, cellophane, feathers, cotton—anything either

[[156]]

Fig. 201 (Top) · "The Fruit—Jesus," by Edward J. Anthony, first prize, and Fig. 202 · "Aphrodite," by Nik Varkula, third prize, advanced amateur class. (Both courtesy Natl. Soap Sculpture Com.) Fig. 203 (Bottom) · A XIV-century French ivory diptych (about 8 in. wide). (Courtesy Metropolitan Museum of Art)

white or colored, depending upon what you want the finished piece to depict. Lester Gaba, premier soap carver, has secured some very unusual effects in this way. He fastens the other materials on with a solution of sodium silicate—you can get it from any drugstore. This solution can also be used to join bars of soap together or to join them to a base of wood, metal, or plastic.

Ivory, soft jade, soapstone, bone, horn, and cast plastics can also be whittled. They may cut in shavings, or break away from the knife in little bits, depending upon brittleness. Wax and clay cut like soap, leather like very soft wood. Celluloid and some plastics have a tendency to cling and bind the knife blade. Horn also has this tendency, but to a much smaller degree. Bone, ivory, soapstone, soft jade, and hard rubber break away before the knife, the first four particularly resisting cutting. These materials often are cut better with small carving tools (see Chap. XVII).

Ivory takes on a color varying from a light yellow to deep chestnut with age, it becomes woodlike and rots after long contact with the soil, but otherwise it comes down to us unchanged through the centuries. Wood can be burned, marble broken up and

[[157]]

FIG. 204 (TOP) · *Indian ivory bullock and cart.* FIG. 205 · *Mid-nineteenth century Chinese ivory fan.* FIG. 206 · *Nineteenth century Chinese ivory jewel casket.* FIG. 207 (BOTTOM) · *Nineteenth century Chinese ivory vase.* (All courtesy Metropolitan Museum of Art)

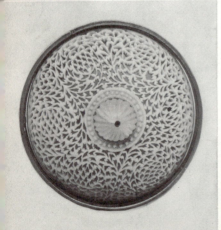

WHITTLING

burned in lime kilns, gold and silver have intrinsic value for coinage, and bronze was once the favored material for cannon; so early statues and carvings in all these materials have been destroyed by later inappreciative peoples. This normally would mean gaps in the traceable history of art, but for ivory, unused for anything else.

The peoples of Asia and Africa have done much of their finest carving in ivory, hence much of it is relatively small—delicate, fragile, but exceedingly beautiful miniatures, statuettes, medallions, plaques, snuffboxes, and jewel caskets. Some of them discovered that ivory brought in contact with metallic salts takes on a brilliant blue color, and their carvings thus colored have occasionally been mistaken for turquoise. Wherever there has been ivory—hippopotamus and elephant tusks in warm countries, walrus tusks in Arctic regions—men have carved it, and in carving left their story. We have knife handles and images of ivory from the days before recorded history; images and figures from Egypt, Greece, and Rome; crucifixes and saints from the early days of Christianity; later carved ivory from the hands of such men as Michelangelo, Cellini, Donatello, and Albrecht Dürer. The Occident had its figures of saints, its crucifixes, and

[158]

FIG. 208 (TOP) · XVII-century Indian jade box. FIG. 209 (LEFT) · XIX-century Chinese ivory paper knife. FIG. 210 · Egyptian carved bone handle. FIG. 211 · Carved stone cup for Charles V of France (c.1530). FIG. 212 (BOTTOM) · Pierced ivory box cover; XVII-century Indian. (All courtesy Metropolitan Museum of Art)

its statues of kings, and the Orient its Buddhas, sacred elephants, many-armed images of Krishnu, even tiny cages for fighting crickets. These were far superior to the ivory carving of the West. See Figs. 102, 206, and 207 and others listed in the Index.

Today, very little ivory is carved; first, because it is relatively hard to get in uncut blocks; and second, because cast plastics and block celluloid have come into common use. These materials are available in all kinds of shapes, colors, textures, and translucences. There are about 300 colors and textures of cast plastics (also called cast resins—do not get the molded plastics, for they are too hard to work), and all can be worked about as easily as hard wood. After you have whittled them to shape, you have the choice of leaving them rough or of polishing. Rough-polish with a buffing wheel, or a wet rag and powdered pumice. When the surface is fairly smooth, wash off and polish with wax.

Cast plastics can be bent or shaped to a limited extent by heating to anything less than about 225 degrees F.—above that you may spoil the color. Pieces of various colors can also be joined together with a special cement supplied by the plastics maker.

FIG. 213 · *Several odd pieces carved from an ivory billiard ball by Edward F. Drake*

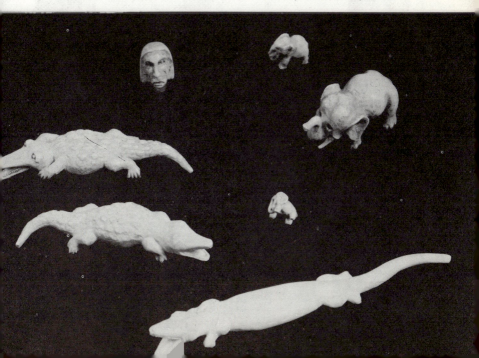

CHAPTER XVI

OTHER TOOLS · Also Chip Carving

NO knife can smooth a large surface as well as a plane, nor can it cut across grain as well as a saw, nor can it do things to a tree as well as an ax (in spite of Fig. 215). Some years ago, I read of a wood caricaturist who did all his figure shaping with a razor-sharp hand ax, using a knife only for details. As a boy, I got the thrill of a lifetime watching a skilled adzman stand atop a butcher's worn chopping block and dress its top down to a surface almost as smooth as a planed one, in a tenth of the time.

Striking examples of skill with crude tools are the totem poles of the American Indian, carved from whole logs with ax and hunting knife, then painted in symbolic colors. Each Indian tribe and family had its "totem," an animal, bird, fish, or plant from which it took name and attributes (the fox for cunning, the eagle for fearlessness, etc.). The totem pole is really a history

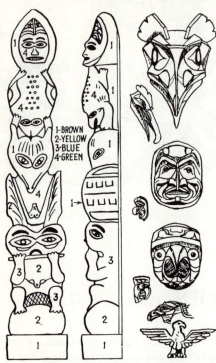

1-BROWN
2-YELLOW
3-BLUE
4-GREEN

Fig. 216 · A totem pole to try, including the color key. Eyes and features are outlined in black. Figures, in order from base, are rabbit, wolf, frog, and thunder god for totem. At right are several examples of ceremonial masks that also use the totem. Side views are shown at lower left of each. That at top has a hinged lower jaw. Masks are all wood, painted in symbolic colors. Often, eyes and jaws move, hair is grass. Sketched at Field Museum of Nat. Hist., Chicago

of the family surmounted by its totem. Most families trace their descent from the mating of a large animal with an ancestor held in captivity, hence the base figure is usually a bear, killer whale, or buffalo. Progressively up the pole are incidents in tribal life, and surmounting all is the totem. That at left, Fig. 214, for example, is the raven, considered a mighty and cunning bird by many Indian tribes. The legend is that the raven learned to use all the forces of nature, so flew away toward the moon. Seeing it at the quarter, he determined to bring it back to earth; so he caught it firmly in his beak and came back with it.

Today, we see totem poles here and there all over the country, for Boy Scouts are carving them to symbolize the achievements of their troops. Some are shown in Fig. 217. Largest in the world is the totem pole dedicated to soldiers of the Confederacy at Gainesville, Ga.

To make a totem, select a pole of straight and enduring wood (see Chap. I). Decide what story you want to tell, or lay out your pole to tell one of the stories pictured here. If your pole is a tree trunk, the stub limbs may be incorporated in your design as ears, wings, arms, or legs, although most Indian totem-pole figures have arms and legs drawn up close to the body.

Lay out the design on the unbarked trunk or clean face of the pole (a discarded section of telephone pole will do very nicely, if it isn't split too much); then, with saw and ultra-sharp hand ax, cut away the wood to the outlines of your sketch. Carpenter's chisels and gouges will help in carving hollows and shaping internal details, feather outlines, teeth, etc. With the chisel and mallet you can make sockets for projecting parts—wings, arm beaks, tails (poles with projections are shown in Fig. 217).

Put in details with knife or wood-carving chisels (see Chap. XVII). Then sandpaper, shellac, or varnish over knots or resinous spots, and paint as you will. Indians depicted things in their natural colors, and

⟦ 163 ⟧

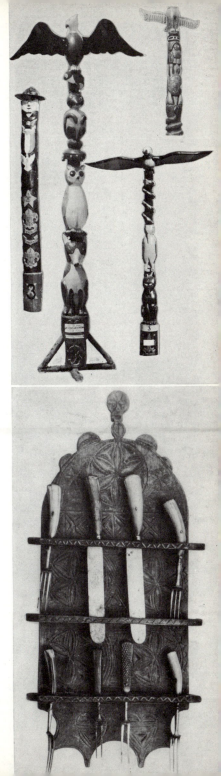

Fig. 217 (Top) · *Several examples of present-day totem poles by Boy Scouts of Troop 3, Hammond, Ind.* Fig. 218 · *Poplar spoon rack with chip-carved daisy design. Made during the eighteenth century in Pennsylvania. (Courtesy Metropolitan Museum of Art)*

also used these color symbolisms: green for growing things and earth (meaning hope, growth); blue for water and sky (meaning sincerity, happiness); white also for sky and snow (meaning peace, death); black for outlining and basic parts (meaning power); red for animal tongues, bird feathers, etc. (meaning war, blood, bravery), yellow for sun and light.

Miniature totem poles can be whittled for ornaments for desk, mantel, bookshelf, knick-knack shelf, or window sill of den or rustic shack. You may want to use a single totem or symbol from the pole as the basis for a grotesque paperweight, desk tray or box, inkwell, book end, letter-opener handle, lamp stand, tie or pipe rack, noggin cup, weather vane, windmill, rural letter box support, garden decoration, or even a war club (from queerly shaped limbs or knots) or walking stick. Boy and Girl Scouts also carve elaborate walking staves with a record of tests passed, etc.

It is also possible to make elaborate totem ceremonial masks. Several examples are shown in Fig. 216. They are painted in vermilion, cobalt blue, and black on the natural wood.

I remember once sitting through a blazing-hot Saturday morning with the lens from a "magic lantern," burning a design on a wood plaque.

〚 164 〛

Fig. 219 (TOP) · *Twenty typical simple chip-carving patterns, any one of which can be worked into a border or a surface decoration. Unless they form squares, a design must be added at border corners.* FIG. 220 · *Simple radial chip design on a box.* (Courtesy Universal School of Handicrafts, Inc.)

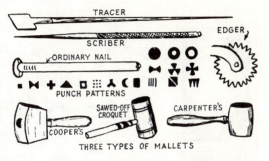

FIG. 221 · *Tools for wood stamping, very similar to leather stamping in execution and results. Stamping is often used to set off carving by giving the background rough regularity and is usually colored darker than the carved piece or the surface*

The smoke got in my nose, and the white focus of the rays was impressed on my eyeballs for hours afterward. If you must burn designs on wood, use heated wires, nails, or an electric burning kit. It is also possible to produce a raised or indented design on wood without cutting it at all. You will need only a handful of good-sized spikes, a triangular file, a hammer or carpenter's wooden mallet (shorten the handle on an old croquet mallet, if you prefer), and a scriber or tracer. The scriber is like that used by machinists, except that its point is rounded off slightly so that it will not tear the wood. The tracer may have a scriber point at one end and a spade edge at the other, or the spade edge only, and is commonly used in leatherwork and metalcraft work.

The process is called wood stamping and is used mainly for roughing backgrounds in surface decoration or for outlining lettering or a design by stamping a continuous design on it or the background. It may also be used to give a dull or rough finish to the ground on a panel carved in relief. In the Middle Ages, it was used to decorate picture frames or to make a gilded pattern.

File flat surfaces on the ends of the spikes, then file in the designs of Fig. 221. These are used just like a center punch or nail set—in fact either of these makes an acceptable punch for this work. Lay out a panel like that at left in Fig. 222, or change its shape so that it will serve as a picture frame or mounting background (see Fig. 1). Trace over the outline with the tracer or scriber against a straightedge, bearing down (or hammering)

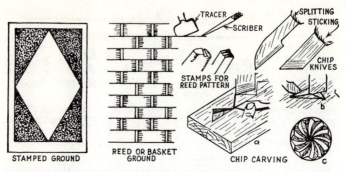

FIG. 222 *Stamping and chip-carving details*

enough to make indentations of $\frac{1}{32}$ or $\frac{1}{16}$ in. If you prefer, use an edger, a toothed or plain wheel like that shown in Fig. 221.

Hold a punch upright just above the surface to be depressed, and hit it with light, sharp blows, moving it to new spots between blows. If you stay carefully within the outlines, the result should be like Fig. 222, left. The background of Fig. 1 was first cut down $\frac{1}{8}$ in., then punched with a rounded and dulled screw driver. With the more elaborate punch shapes, it is possible to make a reed or basket-weave pattern or to produce a continuous background pattern, if punch marks are carefully spaced. Finish by brushing with linseed oil, then rubbing in burnt sienna, dark brown, or black paint. The rough fibers at the edges of the punch marks will hold the color, but it may be wiped off the smooth upper surfaces, and they can then be polished as usual.

South Sea natives hundreds of years ago originated a simple form of surface decoration called chip or notch carving. Peasant peoples, the Frisians, Scandinavians, and our own Pennsylvania Dutch, have kept this form of decoration alive; in fact, it has often been called "Friesland" or "Frisian" carving after the section of Germany where it was most popular. It is basically a simple, small pattern of incised triangles or squares all over a surface, although there are many elaborate variants, some of which appear in Figs. 223 to 226. The sheepfoot blade of your pocketknife will do it, although chip-carving knives are easier to use.

Let us assume that you have the chip-carving knives shown in Fig. 222. (You can make them from old saw blades, or buy them— if you plan to do much chip carving, it will be worth while.) On a waste bit of soft wood mark two lines 90 degrees apart. Put the point of the sticking knife at the point where they join, point it in the direction of one of the lines, *hold it vertical*, and push straight down until the point has gone into the wood about ⅛ in. Withdraw the knife, align it with the other line, and push it down the same distance. Now take the splitting knife, put its point at the outer end of one line, incline the blade at about 30 degrees with the surface of the wood, and push it with your left thumb or index finger along the cut line toward the joining point of the lines, meanwhile keeping the upper edge of the blade in line with the outer end of the other line. This will cause the blade to cut out a little triangle, thicker at its apex, and leave in the wood a sloping triangular hole, as at left, Fig. 222a. Various combinations of this simple triangle will produce border and surface patterns in variety (Fig. 219).

Now draw on wood a ½-in. triangle, and from each apex draw a line to the center. Pose the sticking knife over this center as before and push down ⅛ in. along each of the three lines that meet there. If you consider only two of the cut lines at a time, you have the same triangle as you tried first. Cut the same way as before with the splitting knife, doing each of the three triangles in turn. If you have been careful not to let the point of the splitting knife sink past the sticking-knife line, you will have an incised triangle with its center ⅛ in. below the surface of the wood. This, again, can be repeated in many variations.

The next step is to try combinations of triangles radiating from a single point, as shown in the box of Fig. 220. After each

FIG. 223 (LEFT) · *North German seventeenth-century oak box.* FIG. 224 · *American desk box (1675–1700) covered with "Friesland" carving. (Both courtesy Metropolitan Museum of Art)*

triangle or square is finished, outline it with a V-groove. This box also shows combinations of small flowers with the basic chip-carved pattern. Still another variation, the rosette of curved triangles, is shown in Fig. 222c. Draw a circle, then, with the same radius and a series of points 15 degrees apart on the circumference, draw a series of circular rays from the circumference to the center of the circle. Every second ray will be the bottom of a curved triangle, so follow along the curve with either the sticking or the splitting knife, tapering upward toward the center. Then take out the side as before with the splitting knife, and square up the end. Be particularly careful of grain here—it may be necessary to work from both ends toward the center of the curved triangle, or from its center to the circumference and center of the circle. Also cut very carefully at the center, or you will break out the wood there. It may be better to finish the center last, in fact to make the very center by pressing down the wood with the back of the blade. This motif may be varied by putting a flower in the center of each curved triangle, as shown on the box in Fig. 223, or by using six rays spaced 60 degrees apart, and six more rays meeting them with opposite curvature to form the daisy pattern shown in the box of Fig. 224, or the spoon rack of Fig. 218.

It is also possible to combine chip carving with a design motif—the fighting cocks of Fig. 225 and the Chinaman's head of Fig. 226 are excellent examples by Fred von Hoefer.

Chip carving is usually finished in natural wood or stain. Carefully erase any pencil lines and sand the uncarved surface with fine sandpaper. Then oil or stain and sand again. For a preservative and polish, use floor wax, brushed on so that it does not lump and cake in the triangles.

FIG. 225 (LEFT) · *Fighting cocks*. FIG. 226 · *Chinese mandarin head. Both chip-carving motifs. (Courtesy Universal School of Handicrafts, Inc.)*

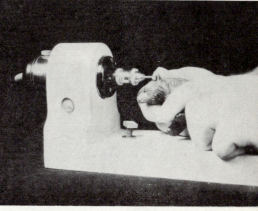

Fig. 227 (Left) · *Sawing grooves with a hand grinder.* Fig. 228 · *Spindle carving with the same machine. (Courtesy Chicago Wheel & Mfg. Co.)*

Spindle or machine carving is the commercial method of carving medium-priced furniture. It can be done fairly easily if you have a lathe, motorized grinder, drill press, or one of the modern hand grinders. If you have any of the first three types of machine, you use milling cutters of various shapes held in an arbor or spindle that projects from the headstock or chuck about 8 in. Cutters as small as $\frac{1}{4}$ in. may run up to 50,000 r.p.m., $\frac{1}{4}$ to $1\frac{1}{2}$ in. 8,000 to 12,000 r.p.m., and larger sizes about 5,000 r.p.m. In a drill press, you may prefer to use routing bits similar to those used by engravers. Plastics may be cut, and bracelets and costume jewelry are being made this way.

The small hand grinder is more versatile although its capacity is lower. Its tools are like dentist's drills (Fig. 227). It is useful in roughing out in-the-round carving or in sinking grounds. Pieces I have made or seen have a mechanical appearance unless hand tools are used at least for the finishing touches. And, frankly, it is not as much fun. If you are one of those impatient people who want to hurry through a carving, you will enjoy machine carving, but remember that these tools are much more dangerous than hand tools. Large-diameter cutters may have a tendency to "run," or pull the work in to them. Alternating grain strata in soft wood cause inaccuracies just as in hand carving, but it happens ever so much faster. If you feed the hand grinder too rapidly, it may stall, and of course there is a startling twist of the wrist as it starts. And the dust will fly, but try it anyhow—you may like it.

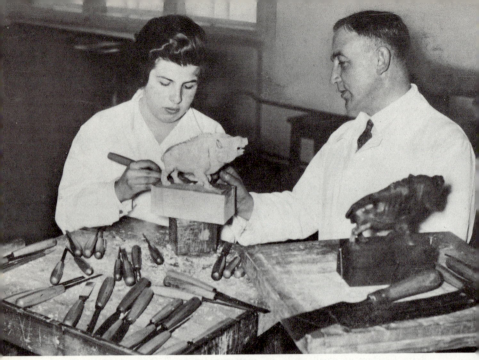

FIG. 229 · *The State Woodcarving School, Oberammergau. (Courtesy German Tourist Inform. Office, N. Y.)*

CHAPTER XVII

CARVING TOOLS · *And Auxiliaries*

THERE comes a time in every whittler's life when he is seeking new fields to conquer, new tools with which to get effects difficult or impossible with the knife alone. Perhaps he plans a large relief with a flat, deeply sunken background, or a statue or decoration too large or too fine for his knife. This is the cue to begin acquiring and using carving tools.

Carving is a matter of heart and perseverance. Anyone fairly adept can develop skill through practice, a knowledge of design through study. The ability to copy the work of others comes easily, but unless the carver's imagination, originality, and heart are in his work, he might just as well be using an ax.

Whittling is vitally important in forming a piece, products are usually small, and the same tool makes and finishes the carving. Woodcarving, on the other hand, is purely decorative, is not limited in size, and plays little part in forming the piece, except in in-the-round carving.

The firmer is like a carpenter's chisel except that it is sharpened from both sides. When the flat side of a chisel is turned down, it digs in; when it is turned up, the chisel runs out of the piece. The firmer does neither, and can be used in either direction without turning over. When the cutting edge is at an angle to the axis of the tool, it becomes a corner or skew firmer, used for squaring up inside corners. Firmers are sized by width of cutting face, from $\frac{1}{16}$ to 2 or $2\frac{1}{2}$ in.

Woodcarving gouges are also like the carpenter's, except that they vary in curvature (called "sweep") and height of sides. Variations are shown in Fig. 230, and again in Fig. 231. Gouges that are almost flat are called flat gouges; those with radii of curvature equal to semicircles, quick or scroll gouges; and U-shaped gouges with high sides, fluters. A very small fluter is called a veiner (for veining leaves, outlining, grooving), and very small quick gouges, eye tools. Size ranges are similar to those of firmers.

FIG. 230 · *Tool shank and edge shapes identified*

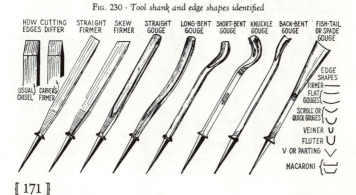

Gouges are the roughing tools for all woodcarving, as well as finishing tools for rounded details.

The parting or V tool has a V-shaped cutting edge square with the axis of the tool. It is used for finishing inside corners, for outlining, and for undercutting. Because it is difficult to sharpen, roughing for V-grooving is usually done with a veiner.

Practically any of these tools may be obtained with a variety of shanks (Fig. 230). The standard tool has the same width of cross-section almost up to the handle. But cross-section may be narrowed rapidly to form fishtail or spade tools, which are easier to handle, conceal less of the work, get into corners and undercuts better, are lighter, and somewhat easier to sharpen. They are not practical in sizes less than ⅛ in.

If a straight tool were used to level off the bottom of a deeply sunken "ground" (short for "background"), it would merely dig in. So tools are made with varying degrees of curvature. If the tool has gradual curvature, it is called long-bent ("grounder" in England); if sharp curvature, short-bent; and if very sharply bent in a sort of hook, a knuckle tool. If a tool has an offset, it is called back-bent, gouges of this group having the cutting edge reversed so that they can be used for undercutting such parts as grapes.

SCRATCH SCRAPER

TOOL BIT (SHAPED) TURNED EDGE

TOOL BIT

ROUTER

SOME MALLET TYPES

11 IN. LONG

10 IN. LONG

7 IN. LONG

8 IN. LONG

PROFESSIONAL 30 OZ. STUDENT 16 OZ. OLD ENGLISH (12 TO 24 OZ.) AMATEUR (7 TO 14 OZ.)

FIG. 231 · *Four carver's mallet shapes, with sizes and weights. Where two weights are given, it indicates the range, the lightest being beech, the heaviest lignum vitae, with hickory midway between. The three tools are useful auxiliaries*

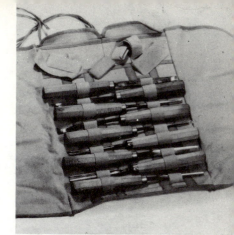

Grounders must not have too much curve or they will not hold an even surface; too little curve causes them to dig in. The quick-bent gouge is useful for deep hollows; otherwise the long-bent is better, because it avoids jamming and sticking.

Formed tools, such as gouges and parting tools, may also be made with a bend to one side or the other (right-and left-hand). The fluter or deep gouge not only can be used for cutting deep U's, but also can be turned over to one side or the other to cut almost any shape of hollow, although ordinary gouges and firmers in combination will do the same thing. With gouges generally, avoid getting the cutting edge in deeply and then lifting the handle, for the cutting edge may snap off. Flat gouges are particularly valuable for grounding and finishing because they do not stick or tear the wood at edges or in slightly hollowed parts.

The commonest special-shape tool is the macaroni, for grounding against upstanding parts. Both sides come up squarely, or at an angle, so that it may be used to either right or left. Other special tools include fluteronis, backeronis, and wing tools.

So, you see, there are several hundred sweeps, sizes, and shapes of tools, not counting supplementary

[173]

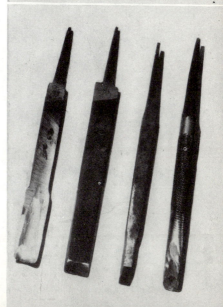

Fig. 232 (Top) · *Kit with nine tools*—½-in. *firmer and corner firmer,* ¼-in. *parting tool,* ½-in. *short-bent scroll gouge,* ¼- *and* ⅜-in. *hollow gouges,* ¾-in. *extra-flat gouge,* ½-in. *scroll and hollow gouges, slips.* Fig. 233 · *A six-tool, low-price kit with* ½-in. *gouge, veiner, parting tool, long bent spade firmer, spade corner firmer,* ⅝-in. *straight firmer.* Fig. 234 · *Tools ground from files*

tools. Which to select? That depends upon what you want to do with them. If you make small carvings or models, probably six short spade tools will do: ⅜-in. straight chisel, ⁵⁄₁₆-in. bent chisel, ¼-in. straight skew chisel, and ⁵⁄₁₆-in. straight gouge, all fishtail tools about 6 in. long over-all, a ³⁄₃₂-in. straight veiner, and a ⅛-in. bent parting tool.

For general use by the beginner, these six tools will prove better: ⅝-in. straight firmer, ½-in. flat gouge (fishtail), ¼-in. straight gouge, ⅜-in. scroll gouge, ⅛-in. quick gouge, ¼-in. parting tool (Fig. 239). Supplement these with: ¼-in. straight firmer, ½-in. scroll gouge, ⅛-in. veiner, ⅜-in. flat gouge, ⅜-in. fluter, ½-in. parting tool (fishtail). These tools are obtainable in sets of six, nine, and twelve tools from suppliers. Get good steel, tempered to straw. If you must put tools away when you are through with them (as most of us must) keep them in a cloth case (Fig. 232) so that their sharp edges are not dulled.

It is possible also to make woodcarving tools of old files, as in Fig. 234, although they probably will not work so satisfactorily as regular tools. Special tools so made may be helpful.

Don't worry too much about tools; worry instead about results. Wood-carving is something like golf—it is

FIG. 235 (TOP) · Arthur Haser, "Ezekiel" in the Oberammergau Passion Play, at work (Courtesy German Tourist Inform. Office, N. Y.) FIG. 236 · Using the gouge. FIG. 237 · Using the firmer to square a vertical edge. FIG. 238 · Using the short-bent gouge. Three ways to hold the tools are also shown

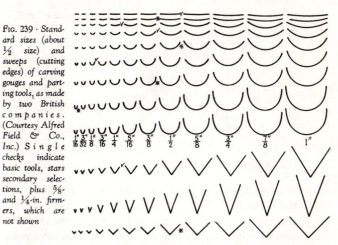

FIG. 239 · Standard sizes (about ½ size) and sweeps (cutting edges) of carving gouges and parting tools, as made by two British companies. (Courtesy Alfred Field & Co., Inc.) S i n g l e checks indicate basic tools, stars secondary selections, plus ⅝- and ¼-in. firmers, which are not shown

nice to have a big bag of matched clubs, but when one gets in a tight spot only the old stand-bys—driver, midiron, mashie, putter —are dependable. I know several professional carvers who have comprehensive kits of tools, but they confess that when "the going gets tough," they use one or two gouges and firmers and forget the rest. They often find it easier to make two cuts with the tool in hand than to make one with a special tool that must be picked up.

It is best to rack the tools or to lay them all on the table or bench with their edges turned toward you, so the proper tool can be selected quickly. But racks are usually out of reach, and, with tools on the bench, first thing you know the bench looks like that in Fig. 229, instead of that in Fig. 243. Another method is to have several sizes and shapes of handles. But your hand will inevitably prefer certain shapes, and you will unconsciously use those tools.

Common commercial handles are round maple or octagonal dogwood tapered toward the cutting edge. The latter, used at Oberammergau, feel more comfortable to me and have less tendency to turn. Brass ferrules, necessary to keep the handle from

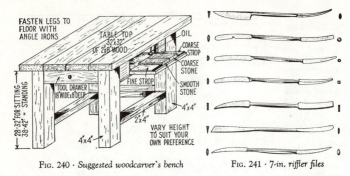

FIG. 240 · *Suggested woodcarver's bench*   FIG. 241 · *7-in. riffler files*

splitting when hammered, should be firmly seated and flush with the surface. Purchased handles are usually about 5 in. long but can be shortened to meet your own needs. Linoleum-carving tools and burins (or solid chisels) for wood engraving often have mushroom-shaped handles that fit into the palm of the hand so that the fingers can guide the stubby tool—permitting carving to be done with one hand.

Sharp tools will cut soft or medium-hard woods easily with hand pressure alone, or at most with a few blows from the palm of the hand when cutting across grain. But if you plan to cut very hard woods (oak, ebony) you will need a mallet. I use a carpenter's mallet like that in Fig. 221, because I am used to it, but you will probably find a regular carving mallet preferable. Figure 231 shows four standard shapes. Lignum vitae is used for heavy mallets, beechwood and hickory for lighter ones. A mallet weighing 7 oz. in beech will weigh 10 oz. in hickory and 14 oz. in lignum vitae. The 14-oz. amateur shape is about right. Or turn your own, if you have a wood lathe, avoiding woods that split.

Your workbench is an individual problem. Figure 9 shows the stand, weighted with a rock, used at Oberammergau. This is small, sturdy, and easy to get around. All students there stand up—in fact most professional carvers do. It allows more freedom, provides a better chance to stand off from the piece and to work at it from many angles. Except on details or small panels, the carver who sits down is likely to produce cramped and poorly proportioned work.

A sturdy woodcarver's table that can also be used as a work-bench is shown in Fig. 240 (a carpenter's bench is all right, if you have one). This has a 32- by 32-in. top, large enough to hold a panel or other piece and leave room for tools. (If you plan to work on panels, cover one end of the bench with a strip of old carpet—it will hold a flat piece without clamping and without scratching, in case a pebble gets under it.) A tool drawer is provided, and a push-in shelf carrying coarse and fine stones and strops so that you can touch up tools conveniently while you plan the next cut.

Sharpness cannot be overemphasized. Many a spoiled piece can be attributed only to dull tools. Sharpen, sharpen, SHARPEN, all the time you are working, and between cuts (see Appendix). A dull tool will show a white line when you look directly at its edge. A sharp tool does not show such a line, seems to stick to your thumbnail if you put it against the edge, and makes a whist-ling sound as it cuts across soft wood. The cut is clean and shiny, not torn or ragged along the edges.

But to get back to tables: Make the top heavy enough to with-stand hammer blows, clamps, or pounding—2 in. thick at least. If all you have to work on is a kitchen table, get a length of 2 by 10-in. plank about 5 ft. long and planed smooth on all sides. Clamp it to the table, and nail or clamp your work to it.

In whittling, you always have one hand free to act as a con-venient clamp, but in woodcarving one hand must guide and steady the tool while the other applies pressure, or one holds the tool and the other the mallet. Even if you can handle the tool with one hand, it is safer to use two, for the odd hand persists in doing its clamping *in front* of the tool edge. That's bad!

Clamping methods need not be elaborate. If you have a car-penter's bench, the regular bench stops will hold a panel securely. Or hold it against a stop with the stand-up vise jaw. (Use a vise in any case to hold a panel to be carved on side or end.) If you just have a table, cut your piece oversize and simply nail it at the

[177]

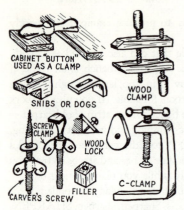

CABINET "BUTTON"
USED AS A CLAMP

SNIBS OR DOGS

WOOD CLAMP

SCREW CLAMP

WOOD LOCK

FILLER

CARVER'S SCREW

C-CLAMP

FIG. 242 · *Clamps and holding means*

edges. But if you have a piece of exact size, or do not want to cut or mar its surface, use one of the clamping methods in Fig. 242. At upper left is a familiar cabinet "button," set to proper height by tightening a long wood screw between work and another block of the same height. The wood clamp is convenient but may get in the way, as may the C-clamp, although the latter can be turned over so that the screw tightens beneath the table.

The wood lock is a little egg-shaped piece held by a screw set into the table at an angle. You must put several of these at various points around the workpiece and tighten all securely, or the piece will work loose. The snibs or dogs of wood or metal are similarly used, except of course that their backs must be the same height as the thickness of the work piece or they must be blocked up. All these permit a piece to be removed easily for inspection. Neat and convenient is the screw clamp in Fig. 242. This is similar to the carver's screw at lower left, for holding very thick pieces or the block for an in-the-round carving. It has a pointed tip with a wood-screw thread on it which is screwed into the bottom of the workpiece by means of the square opposite end and the square holes in the wing nut (which make it a wrench, of course). The screw is then passed through the table and a washer and the wing nut screwed up. It is relatively easy to loosen the wind nut and shift the workpiece as necessary. To keep the wing nut on either the carver's screw or the screw clamp in a readily accessible position, filler blocks may be put on the screw first. These also may be used to block up under a piece to raise it to convenient working height.

In woodcarving, as in whittling, a few extra tools will help. You will need a square, a compass, and a protractor for laying out a design, and a scroll saw, plane, router, scratch, scraper, riffler files, and a rasp or two. The router is a little block plane with a narrow blade or bit set at a desired depth to plane a groove or smooth a ground. The homemade scratch can do the same work.

The scraper will clean up slight irregularities of surface or remove pencil or tracing lines quickly. Riffler files, Fig. 241, have small dead-smooth rasplike teeth and are made in many shapes to fit various curves and get into difficult places. They smooth up details of carving where tools are cutting against grain. Cabinet rasps cut down and shape wood across end grain, where it may be difficult to get results with an edged tool. Get the half-round or half-oval 8- or 10-in. size, "extra-smooth cut."

Lastly, you will need either a pocketknife or two, or a wood-carver's knife. They are convenient for slicing cuts and outlining.

FIG. 243 · *The chief carver at Oberammergau helps a student with her first carving. (Courtesy German Tourist Inform. Office, N. Y.)*

Fig. 244 · *A sixteenth-century courtyard at Abbeville, France. Note carved door, rafters, and low-relief designs. (Courtesy Metropolitan Museum of Art)*

CHAPTER XVIII

SURFACES · *Simple Lines, Woodcuts*

LEGEND has it that a famous English archer once drew his bow in competition and shot an arrow farther and truer than any man had shot before. To commemorate the event, he commissioned a famous woodcarver to decorate his yew bow. The next year, men came from all over England to see him shoot. At last, when all ordinary archers had shot their shafts, he stepped forward, notched a long, long arrow, and drew the bowstring back to his ear. There was a loud crack—the mighty bow had broken! Elaborate decoration had ruined it.

There have always been, and always will be, those who must decorate anything and everything, even to tool handles. A good design, well executed, certainly improves a table top but also usually ruins it for all practical use. The same may be said for the carved chair seat and a host of other misapplied designs. Surface carving, all carving for that matter, is purely decorative, a striving to make something utilitarian attractive to the eye. But it should not make the object useless.

Keep these things in mind as you begin to use carving tools. Figures 236 to 238 (Chap. XVII) will show you how to hold the tools and to make simple cuts. The left hand holds the tool and acts as a fulcrum and stop, while the right guides the tool and applies cutting pressure. After all, a carving tool is just a knife blade with the handle behind it instead of at one end, and the principles that govern knife cutting also govern carving. Read through Chap. III to refresh your memory, then try some of the simple shapes suggested there as knife exercises. Clamp the piece first, and don't cut toward your hand or any other part of your body (a carving tool cuts a small, but very deep, gash when it slips). If you have no bench or clamps, cover an old breadboard or drawing board with carpet, and hold the piece on it on your knees. The carpet helps to avoid slipping.

Fig. 245 · *How to use carving tools; some simple borders*

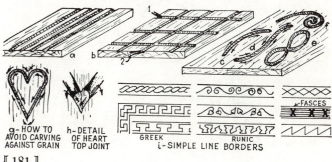

g- HOW TO AVOID CARVING AGAINST GRAIN
h-DETAIL OF HEART TOP JOINT
GREEK
RUNIC
FASCES
i-SIMPLE LINE BORDERS

Try gouges and parting tools not only with the grain, but across it and at diagonals. Then try to make a checkerboard with a veiner or parting tool. Lay out a series of parallel lines in both directions about $\frac{1}{16}$ in. apart, then cut carefully between every second pair. Cut slowly, and keep it up until the grooves do not vary in width and exactly fit their boundary lines (Fig. 245). In making a checkerboard, cut the grooves *across* grain first, then those with the grain, otherwise the cross-grain grooves will break out the corners as they cross the with-grain grooves.

In diagonal cutting, one side of the tool is cutting at an acute angle to the grain, hence cuts smoothly. But the other side is cutting at an obtuse angle, hence may tear as much as cut. To clean up such a cut, make one cut from one direction, and a clean-up cut from the opposite, in each case pressing the tool toward the side of the groove meeting the grain at an acute angle. Do not try to cut to the full depth on the first cut; make a light marking cut down the center first. Or first make a stop cut down the middle of a planned groove with the firmer or knife. For practice with the firmer and parting tool, try the designs of Fig. 246. They show how simple outlining and V-grooving (with one side vertical) can be used to make attractive surface patterns.

Several specialized cuts are quite helpful in carving, the out-lining or stop cut, the sweep, the slide, and the knife cut. The

Fig. 246 · *More types of surface decoration*

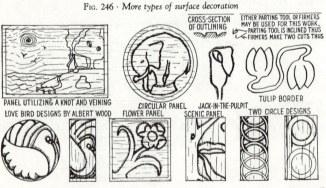

FIG. 247 · *Spot cutting and gouge cutting for decorating an area*

first is familiar to you from whittling—just a knifelike groove perpendicular to the surface that cuts the fibers, avoids splitting past the outline of a shape, or serves as a guiding cut.

The slide cut is a sidewise cut with the gouge to follow a curved outline. For a trial, hold a hollow gouge vertically above the block and rotate the handle, allowing the edge to follow its own path in the wood. It will cut a circle of the same shape as its cutting edge, and this can then be split out. In fact this simple trick is the basis of the spot cutting shown in Fig. 247, a simple method of decorating a surface. All you need is quick gouges of several diameters and you can make a pattern of round holes with either flat or bowl-shaped bottoms. With a flatter gouge, you can follow almost any curved outline to make a stop cut very similar to that obtained with a knife. For this particular cut, it is easiest to hold the gouge like a pencil.

The sweep cut utilizes rotation or swinging of the right hand as the cut progresses, changing the plane of the cut or its shape. With this cut, a firmer can be made to follow the changing contours of a model boat hull, a fluter to change the shape and width of a groove, or a parting tool to shift from a V-groove, with one side perpendicular to the surface of the wood, over to a normal V or a V with the opposite side perpendicular to the surface.

Fluters and parting tools can be used for many shapes and angles, simply by turning them more or less to one side. These tools are hardest to learn to use, for they tend to "run" with the grain and to "fight" against crossing it at an angle. Pronounced strata of summer and winter, or resinous and nonresinous, wood cause alternate "fighting" and "running." First make an outline cut down the middle of the proposed cut, then cut to each side of it at an acute angle to the grain. This may mean cutting from both directions, of course.

〖 183 〗

Carving includes lining in, setting in, grounding out (usually called just "grounding"), bosting, and modeling. Lining in is simply outlining the shape to be carved with a V tool to cut the fibers just outside the design and to preserve major pencil lines that might otherwise be rubbed away. (If the wood is very dark, use Chinese white or a scratched line.) Setting in is cutting down vertically $\frac{1}{16}$ to $\frac{1}{8}$ in. all along the edge of the upstanding elements of a design—similar to a knife stop cut. Grounding is roughing out surplus wood with the gouges, taking the background down to the desired level. This is often combined with wasting away, which is simply cutting away large masses of surplus wood, either by taking crisscross stop cuts and breaking out pieces, or by gouging. Bosting is rough-shaping the design or upstanding elements. Modeling is the final shaping of the design.

First make some of the borders shown in Fig. 245. Any one can be applied around the edge of a picture frame, breadboard, ash tray, or book end, and you use only veiner or parting tool. In fact, a whole surface can be covered with elaborate geometric or runic line designs with only one of these tools.

Another simple form of surface decoration is made with two gouges of varying sweep, in fact can be made with a single gouge. The gouge is simply pressed into the wood vertically to make a crescent-shaped stop cut, then moved back $\frac{1}{4}$ in. or so to groove out a little chip. Several such patterns are shown in Fig. 247. These can be combined with spot cutting or chip carving, and that at left can be used in a single line to represent the ends of books.

FIG. 248 · *Buttons are good pieces for training*

Wooden buttons also offer good training in handling tools, for they are usually too small to hold in any way except by the fingers on a carpeted board. Shapes such as those shown in Fig. 248 can be cut with chisels, knife, or saw out of almost any wood, then be shaped and decorated with firmers and gouges. Various surface decoration motifs from designs to monograms can be put on. An interesting variation is a button cut out of a piece of wood that still has sapwood on it. This will give two tones on one piece of wood. Walnut and red cedar are particularly good. The table in Chap. I gives natural wood colors, and of course any wood can be stained or colored to darken it as desired. Most buttons are finished by linseed oiling and waxing, thus giving an attractive dull finish that brings out the grain. Commercial buttons are usually either shellacked, waxed and buffed, or lacquered. Earrings, bracelets, and costume jewelry can be made thus, including silhouette brooches of various caricatured shapes.

For gouge practice, try a hand bat, simply a ¾-in. mitten-shaped piece, with the contours of the palm of the hand cut out of it, held on the hand with a backstrap or holding peg that passes between the first two fingers.

〚 185 〛

FIG. 249 (TOP) · Buttons, earrings and bracelet of walnut. FIG. 250 · A simple buckle and two buttons of walnut, using sapwood for color variation. Shanks are carved on the backs. FIG. 251 · Two seventeenth-century Swiss chairs, with strapwork (pierced) on backs. (Courtesy Metropolitan Museum of Art)

Wooden sandals for beach or house-hold use can be made the same way by hollowing out where the heel and the ball of the foot rest. Simple straps or thongs will hold them on, or you can put on a whole leather top tacked to the sides of the sole, thus forming the French *sabot*. Real wooden shoes require special long-handled spade gouges for hollowing out the toes, but try them! Other practice pieces for the gouges include bowls, ash trays, fist-shaped door knockers or desk-penholder bases, and molds for sand, clay, butter, or dough.

One of the best ways to learn to handle woodcarving tools is to use them for carving linoleum blocks, or more elaborate wood blocks, and of course the blocks themselves can later be used to make your Christmas cards or to stamp a repeated design on book cover, tablecloth, or wall hang-ing. Linoleum does not split, has no grain, and dulls tools very rapidly. Otherwise cutting it is like cutting wood, but easier. If you have no linoleum, carve a flat surface on a potato—it will print a few pictures just as well and is even easier to cut. Or a paraffin block can be carved and printed, giving a soft, uncontrolled, line edge. Or again, cut a design in a block of rubber, remembering in this particular case to *keep the tool wet*.

[[186]]

Fig. 252 (Top) · *Brayer and ink plate, for inking lino blocks, etc.* Fig. 253 · *Unmounted linoleum that prints the bookplate of* Fig. 256. Fig. 254 · *Mounted lino block with design incised so that it prints the background, as in* Fig. 257. Fig. 255 (Bottom) · *Black or key block (*Left*) and color block for two-color print of* Fig. 258. *Note groov-ing to give lighter sky on color block*

Such blocks last for many impressions and give an attractive soft edge to a cut line. But first a little on the background and technique of linoleum-block cutting:

Back in the T'ang dynasty (A.D. 618–905) the Chinese were already doing block printing, a process of printing designs or pictures on any surface by pressing against it a block carrying an inked raised surface of the desired shape. First blocks were wood. Early in the eighteenth century, the Japanese took up block printing. Early in the nineteenth, Hiroshige and Hokusai began to make color prints by matching several blocks, each printing a different color.

With the development of lithography, printing blocks were made of soft stone, and about 1910 the European process of using thick linoleum was introduced in this country. Now almost every art store sells the linoleum, either unmounted or mounted on type-high plywood blocks (so that it can be put into a printing press), as well as cheap modifications of woodcarving tools for cutting it and necessary material for making prints.

A design for a linoleum block should not have fine lines or elaborate elements. It should be simplified to give fairly large blocks of flat color—a silhouette is ideal to start with.

Draw your design on tracing or other thin paper. Turn the paper over against a window or a sheet of glass with a light under it and copy the design on the back of the paper. This is done to reverse the design, for the block must be carved out backwards or the picture it prints will be backwards. Of course this isn't necessary if the design is symmetrical—both sides are the same, like an upright heart—or if the direction in which it faces is not important. But particularly with lettering, be sure to reverse.

Fill in the areas of the parts that you want to print—they may be the design itself (Fig. 253) or the background (Fig. 254); in the first case the design is to be printed, in the second the background.

Transfer this design to a piece of battleship linoleum (this is the $\frac{1}{4}$-in. thick gray or yellow material) with carbon paper or by rubbing a soft pencil over the backs of the lines, then tracing

FIG. 256 (LEFT) · *Print from block of* FIG. 253. FIG. 257 · *Reversed or background print of block in* FIG. 254. (*Courtesy of Mary C. Tangerman.*) FIG. 258 (RIGHT) · *A simple woodcut. Note blackness.* (*Courtesy Cobb Shinn*)

over the design. Do not use ordinary inlaid linoleum, for it has a glossy surface that will not print, and the body of the material is not deep enough so that large cut-out areas can be grounded enough. Art stores sell linoleum in various shapes and sizes, in some cases already mounted on blocks, and often with a white covering on it upon which a design can be drawn directly—if you remember to draw it backwards.

Now blacken or color all the areas of the block that are to print. These are not cut away, *but everything else is*. Outline the design with a stop cut, but be sure the stop cut slopes away from the design. Thus when the grounding out is completed, the side-walls of a printing surface will slope outward down to the background. This is important because linoleum is so brittle that it must be supported or it will crumble away. Either a knife or a skew chisel can be used for outlining, the skew chisel being held by the blade like a penholder.

With the same tool, cut away a V of linoleum all around the large elements of the design, then around the smaller ones. With a small gouge, waste away the linoleum to be removed, setting in small areas first. This is done so that the larger waste areas can be used as a support or fulcrum for the tool in gouging. When you come to wasting away the large areas, put a piece of cardboard under the back of the tool so that it does not by any chance press directly against elements of the future printing surface. It isn't necessary to "set in" the background all the way down to the burlap backing, except in very large unprinted areas. These must be sunk quite deeply or the print you make later may sink into them and pick up some ink. Finally, round off all edges of the design slightly; this avoids crumbling and raggedness in printing.

To print a linoleum block, you can use printing ink, "soupy" or thick water color, or a thin paste made of rice flour, dry color, and water. Water color or color paste is spread thinly and evenly all over the surface with a brush (be careful not to let any get in blobs along the edges of the design, or it will make a blot on the print). Printing ink is best spread on with a brayer or ink roller of rubber. Squeeze a little of the ink out on a sheet of glass, marble, or iron, then roll the brayer (Fig. 252) over it until it is spread evenly over the surface, just as piecrust is rolled out (in fact, if you haven't a brayer, make one out of a rolling pin covered with several layers of gauze). This spreads the ink thinly and evenly over the brayer, which is then rolled crisscross over the block until all parts of the design are well and evenly inked.

To print, lay a sheet of soft-textured paper over the block. Be careful not to shift it sidewise during application or removal as well as during printing. Print by rubbing all over the back of the paper, first with the palm of your hand, then with a spoon bowl, smooth knife handle, etc. Remove the paper carefully. It should carry the design. If you are not entirely satisfied, go to work on the block again, correcting it where necessary. If smudges or blots appear in areas you want to remain white, ground them out a little deeper. If the design doesn't print dark enough, apply a little more ink; if the print is too inky, use a little less ink, working some off the brayer on an uninked corner of the glass. Mounted blocks can be set up in a hand printing press and printed by any printer, or linoleum and paper together can be run through a loosened wringer. The Japanese print by rubbing the paper first with the palm of the hand, then with a baren, which is a woven red disk about 5 in. in diameter, padded with vegetable fiber and covered with a baren (bamboo leaf) or a bit of cloth. You can make one of wood padded with horsehair and covered with corn husks dampened so that they shrink on tightly.

Linoleum blocks will also print on cloth or leather. The cloth is stretched over a flat surface and the inked block pressed down on it firmly and evenly. A design can be repeated over a surface.

If you want to print several colors, as in the blocks of Fig. 255, you will have to make a separate block for each color. Cut the black or key block first, exactly as before, but be sure to leave the corners on it. Make several prints with this block, and fill in on each a different color, over the areas on which that color is to be printed. Transfer these to the blocks by reversing them as before (or make the prints on oily paper, then "offset" them on color blocks by rubbing with a spoon), the corners of the original black block acting as gauge points. Color the proper areas on each block, then ground out the blocks. Print each in turn, the lightest color first, correcting the proper block when overlaps or other mistakes are printed. It is very important to get each block registered exactly with the others, and this can be done most easily by getting several mounted blocks of the same shape and size. When the colors print together properly, cut off the gauge points on the key block. Outlines on the key block can cover slight irregularities. Several shades and tints of a color can be printed with different blocks, or an effect of tint can be obtained by cutting a series of narrow grooves over the area to be put into a tint. Figure 259 shows a tint thus created. The Japanese produce prints with up to eighteen or twenty colors, by using as many blocks.

Wood blocks carved on the plank or side grain of the wood are made just like linoleum blocks, except that here of course grain must be reckoned with. The grained surface of the wood produces its own little pattern in the flat color, and often will create an effect of clouds or softness in a flat background area. Maple, oak, boxwood, apple, pear, cherry, are used. Grain and relative hardness affect print quality (boxwood, for example, gives a

Fig. 259 (Left) · Two-color print of blocks in Fig. 255. Gray tint repre- sents second color. Fig. 260 (Right) · Design suitable for lino-block or wood- block print. (Court- esy Cobb Shinn)

uniform print, pine and oak show distinct grain). If you carve lettering, remember that it is much easier to incise it (or cut in the letters) than to cut away the background and leave the letters upstanding. Again, remember to cut out letters backwards— if you don't they will print that way. Handy are the sloyd and the Japanese knife, the first a heavy-backboned knife, the second a short-bladed, long-handled knife held like a penholder.

Wood engraving is now almost extinct. Zinc or copper engraving has replaced wood in all commercial work. In wood engraving the design is cut in the *end grain* of the wood instead of on the side or plank face. Woods are usually boxwood or maple, cut to type height (0.918 in.), either in a single piece or several pieces carefully glued together. Boxwood, the preferred wood, is either Turkish (most expensive, but best for fine lines and delicate tints) or American (usually from the West Indies or South America).

Wood engravers use burins or gravers, similar to miniature woodcarving tools but sloped back sharply from the cutting edge and with inner surfaces not hollowed out (Fig. 261). They have ball-shaped handles that fit the palm of the hand, and cutting is done by pushing with the hand, guiding with the finger tips, the thumb resting against the block to restrain the tool. The tool works more like a snowplow than a knife edge, cutting through the fibers, then wedging or lifting them up and out. The block is laid on a leather-covered circular sofa pillow or pad filled with sand, which permits it to be set at any desired angle. Most wood engravers make such fine lines (it is common to make fifty parallel lines to the inch) that they must use a magnifying glass supported in a stand made of two rods, one with a base, stuck through a ball of cork, wood or rubber (Fig. 261). The gouge-shaped tools are used for cutting out blank spaces, the others for putting in details. Gouge width is usually from ⅛ in. down.

Tints on wood engravings are obtained just as they are on lino blocks, by cutting in parallel lines, except that they are thinned out to long points, or cut across with a graver to make them print a broken line. Both methods of shading an edge are shown in Fig. 261. Thomas Bewick (1753–1828) invented this method of putting in gray tones so that the wood engraving became a picture instead of a poster in solid black and white.

In wood engraving, white areas are usually kept to a minimum because of the difficulty of printing without having the paper sink into these hollows. Hence wood engravings are distinguished by their solid blacks and dark grays. To make engravings, transfer your designs as in lino-block printing, or draw directly on a coat of whiting applied to the surface. Or a photograph can be pasted on the surface and cuts made right through it. Mistakes can be corrected by cutting or drilling out an area and gluing in a close-fitting plug. Color blocks are made as previously described. Any library or museum can show you wood-block or chiaroscuro prints that will give you ideas. Store the blocks on edge.

Another "picture-making" technique that may interest you is celluloid etching, really a dry-point engraving process. It offers even greater delicacy of line and attention to detail than wood engraving and a chance to exercise "aesthetic sense." It is more similar to drawing than any of the previous methods, for the *lines that are to print are scratched out*, not left upstanding.

Tools are a sharpened file and a "scratcher," made by heating a triangular harness needle and bending the tip to a right angle. Bend about ¼ in. back from the tip, with the flat side of the needle out. Fasten this into some sort of handle, and it will make V-shaped scratches. The celluloid is 0.02 in. thick or thicker, and can be held on a flat table top, in a photographer's

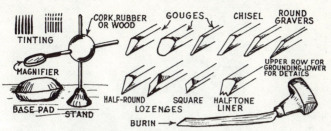

Fig. 261 · *Tools and tool shapes for the wood engraver*

printing frame, or in any other convenient way that gives it proper support. Draw the design directly on the celluloid, or transfer it as before. Where you want darker areas, draw many parallel or crisscrossing lines. Then simply scratch out the lines with the graver, using the sharpened file or knife tip for heavier lines.

To print it, rub ink all over the surface and into the scratches with a dauber made of several layers of cloth tied over a central wad. With dry gauze, rub all ink off the surface of the celluloid, wiping with a circular motion and crossing the scratched lines at right angles as much as possible to keep from wiping the ink out of them. Even when wiped with gauze the background will print as a dark gray owing to the ink left on it. You can use this for gray clouds, etc., by wiping some parts of the plate cleaner than others. If you want a light-gray background, wipe over the surface with the palm of your hand, carefully, wiping your hand often on a bit of clean gauze (or on your apron, as etchers do). If you want an absolutely white background, dust your hand frequently with whiting from a cake or with powder dusted through a cloth bag. Be sure not to get whiting into the grooves.

Now lay a piece of dampened, soft-textured paper (special etching paper, butcher paper, or the back of smooth wallpaper) over the plate, put several damp blotters on top of it, and a felt pad on top of that, then run the whole thing through a wringer, proofing roll, or etching press. Correct between prints as before— each one will be different in tone from every other one anyway.

Fig. 262 · *Amelia Earhart's trophy chest, by Albert Wood & Five Sons*

CHAPTER XIX

LOW RELIEF · *Diapers, Modeling*

PHOTOGRAPHS and surface decoration have one thing in common—only two dimensions. In surface decoration, carving tools do little more than outline a picture or design, just as you would with a pencil. But the carver is not limited to two dimensions—his wood has thickness. When he utilizes that thickness by cutting away the background to make his design stand out and to model the design to give it form, he is carving in relief.

Cutting a linoleum block is simple relief carving, for it involves more than one plane. If the second plane is just below the first and rounded forms are correspondingly flattened, the carving is called low relief, or *bas-relief*. As the ground is sunk more and

[194]

more, additional planes can be introduced to get perspective, forms can be rounded out as in nature, and the carving becomes high relief. There is no definite line of differentiation. Again, as the relief becomes so high that it frees itself from the background, it becomes carving in the round.

If you have modeled clay, you know that you build up from a background or base to get the third dimension—the woodcarver instead must cut the background down. Usually, in low relief, the background is cut down only a little; from ⅛ to ½ in. is the common range, depending upon the subject.

Carving linoleum blocks and the practice carving of Chap. XVIII have taught you the basic principles. Practice in grounding and modeling, as well as an additional, more interesting, and more colorful method of decorating surfaces, is provided by the simple little diaper patterns of Fig. 263. (Diaper comes from *diapré*, an old French word meaning a figured or printed cloth in which the same small pattern was repeated all over the surface. The word probably came originally from *d'Ypres*, for Ypres was once the center for manufacture of such cloth.) The surface is laid out in squares, triangles, diamonds, or some other geometric shape and the pattern repeated in each space or in alternate spaces.

I have chosen the diamond for my geometric pattern. Lay out the diaper pattern full size on paper, then transfer to the space on the wood with carbon paper. In carving the pattern, follow the sequence of operations explained in Chap. XVIII—namely,

Fig. 263 · *Twenty-seven simple diaper patterns, and parts of twenty more*

outlining, lining in, setting in, grounding out, and modeling. I first outline the whole pattern with a knife or a skew firmer held like a fountain pen (the firmer must be very sharp). This cuts the wood fibers and provides a path for the veiner to follow in lining in. The outline cut should be made with the knife or firmer at a slant, to slope the bottom of the cut outward and so create a bank or protecting edge for the upstanding design.

Line in (Fig. 264–1) with a veiner or parting tool, preferably the latter, one side of the cutting edge following the outline cut, the other cutting out a V from the waste wood. When you use the veiner for this work, don't start or end at corners. If you start at an inside corner, the back of the V of the tool may depress and mar the design or the border, and if you end at an inside corner, the cutting edge may go a little too far. After you have had a little practice with the firmer, you may prefer simply to make a second outline cut just outside the first and meet it in a V at the bottom. This avoids changing tools, gets into corners better, and is easier to control because you are drawing the tool toward you. Also, the firmer is easier to sharpen.

Set in (Fig. 264–2, 2a) the pattern with a square firmer and

Fig. 264 · *Steps in carving a simple pattern, and how to compensate for changes in eye level*

gouges. If your block is soft wood, all you do is put the firmer cutting edge in the V of the lining-in cut and push it down into the wood about ⅛ in. If your piece is walnut or mahogany, you may have to pound the handle butt lightly with the palm of your hand, and if it is ebony, you will need a mallet. Use the firmer along straight lines, and shift to gouges for the curves, always choosing a gouge that is a little "quicker" (has a little more sweep or curve) than a concave curve or a little flatter than a convex one so that the blade tips cut into the waste wood, not into the design. Watch grain— the firmer that must be hammered to set a line across grain will sink twice as far (or may split the wood) with

FIG. 265 (TOP) · *A medallion with minimum modeling*

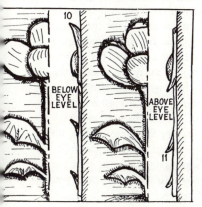

[[197]]

FIG. 266 · *An English wainscot armchair of oak (circa 1600)*. FIG. 267 · *French cupboard door (circa 1400) of St. George and the dragon*. FIG. 268 · *The companion door, Valentine and Orson. Note upper left corner caricatures and "Whirling Cross" at upper center*. (FIGS. 266 to 268 courtesy Metropolitan Museum of Art)

the same force when aligned with the grain. Be sure, too, that each setting-in cut connects with the preceding one, otherwise you will have a series of saw-tooth edges when you ground out. If you plan to sink the ground more than ⅛ in., you will have to do setting-in in two or more steps, wasting away a little of the wood outside the design (Fig. 264–3) in between. Always hold the tool vertical, or you may undercut the design and suddenly have to change the design or to glue in a piece.

Wasting away (Fig. 264–3) is done with quick gouges—the largest you can get into the space. This is just roughing out the wood from the background, and should be done across grain when possible; the cut is easier to control. Waste away large areas with the large gouge, then use progressively smaller and flatter ones. In working into a corner, lift the gouge and swing it at the same time, using the lower tip as a pivot. This enables you to "nibble" away the wood in the corner without fear of splitting.

Grounding (Fig. 264–4) is simply smoothing out the background with a firmer or very flat gouge. Work up against the design or border carefully, making sure your setting-in cuts are deep enough. If they are not, you may have to reset them a little deeper.

〖 198 〗

Fig. 269 (Top) · *Fifteenth-century English oak door, showing modified Flemish* Y (*after the initial* "I" *of Latin* "Iesus" 〖Jesus〗). Fig. 270 · *Sixteenth-century French walnut door, School of Lyons. Note inset buttons.* (*Both courtesy Metropolitan Museum of Art*)

When grounding is complete, your design will look just as if it had been sawed out of thin wood on a jigsaw, then glued onto a background. Many early European and American carved pieces were left just this way—for example, the chest in Fig. 280—although the background might be stamped or otherwise roughened, or painted or stained to make the design stand out. The background itself may be given a pattern with large stamps or with simple knife or chisel cuts, but it should not be smoothed like the surface. The high-relief head of Fig. 1 is mounted on an oval plaque of walnut with simple grounding out and stamping of the grounded surface. In the medallion of Fig. 265, design and border are darkened with stain, and so the ground is lighter. While the ground is normally flat, or nearly so, it need not be. In carving grapevines and grapes, for example, you may find it preferable to sink the ground deeply under the bunches of grapes, but to make it much shallower between. This creates deeper shadows and more depth, thus concentrating attention there. In a border on a table top, where carving should be flush with the surface, sink the ground only immediately under the carving, then taper up to the surface at each side.

⟦ 199 ⟧

Fig. 271 (Top) · A low-relief Indian bust on arrowhead background, by H. Reihl of Streator, Ill. Fig. 272 · Low relief made with a pocketknife. (Courtesy Remington Arms Co., Inc.) Fig. 273 (Bottom) · French sixteenth-century Renaissance door and panel. Note strapwork. (Courtesy Metropolitan Museum of Art)

For variety on simple panels, outline upstanding elements with a veiner to accent them.

The next step is bosting, or rough-shaping the upstanding elements including outlining, lining in, setting in, and wasting away, as indicated in Fig. 264-5, 6, 7. Now model the design—give it its final shape, and clean up any rough spots. In the case of the conventionalized flower of Fig. 264, modeling includes rounding up the edge of the flower center (8) and squaring up the outlines (9), as well as rounding the stems and shaping the leaves. In shaping even these simple leaves, you will find it better to make the final cut with a wide firmer or flat gouge in one cut. This gives a smooth surface and a clean appearance, avoiding sandpapering—which rounds edges and destroys detail while smoothing surfaces. Continuous cuts are vital in very hard woods, for there a clean-cut, shined surface depends upon sure, long, final cutting strokes. You will find the sweep cut particularly valuable for this.

The position a carving is to occupy is a factor often forgotten entirely by modern carvers. But in foliage carving particularly, the piece is likely to look clumsy and heavy if due allowance is not made for position. Assume first the piece is to be at eye level—say in

[200]

Fig. 274 (Top) · French sixteenth-century box-wood mirror back. Fig. 275 · French eight-eenth-century (Louis XVI) oak over-door panel, "Law." Fig. 276 · Companion panel, "Phys-ical Science." Fig. 277 (Bottom) · German sixteenth-century boxwood plaque, "Meeting of Maxmilian and Emperor Frederick." (All courtesy Metropolitan Museum of Art)

FIG. 278 · *Thirty-five patterns for low-relief carving*

a mantelpiece. This means the observer will look at it straight from the front. Curling leaf edges, petals, and other elements standing out from the carving must be thinned at the edges (just as the wooden sails were on the model yacht of Chap. XII) so that they will *look* fragile. But don't thin them very far back, or they will *be* fragile. Only Grinling Gibbons could do that successfully—but he did it usually on pieces safely out of reach. The staircase of Fig. 2 is a pretty solid piece compared with the coat of arms of Fig. 4.

If the carving is to be below eye level—around the frame of a footstool, low table, chair, etc.—the observer will look down on it, so all upper edges of leaves, petals, etc., must be thinned as shown at 10, Fig. 264. This involves undercutting of the upper edge, done by working in carefully with the firmer and nibbling out the wood. Note also that the upper petal of the flower and the upper edge of the leaves stand out farther from the ground— lower edges are squared up.

Assume that the flower becomes a part of a picture frame or

Fig. 279 · *French sixteenth-century plaque from an ivory casket, "Jousting Scene." (Courtesy Metropolitan Museum of Art)*

molding above the eye level, and the whole procedure is reversed, as in Fig. 264-11. Now it is the lower edges that are outstanding and undercut, the upper ones are squared off and at normal level.

There is another factor in this cutting to suit position—a factor very important to the carver—light. A photograph or other flat surface has the same lighting all over it, but a carving is in three dimensions, and so the light hits some parts more prominently than others. Some elements may be shadowed by others. This is an advantage if an element is to be made to stand out, for the background can be deepened behind it or it can be carved in somewhat higher relief. Leaves and other elements can be made to look thin and delicate by thinning their edges—the light gets behind them and creates the illusion. As you carve, stand off regularly and look at your work from several angles to see if the light is causing you to carve a piece so that it looks attractive from your working angle but not so good from other positions. Also, if possible, put the piece in a position and light similar to that which it is finally to occupy to see what the light does to it. You will learn through practice to compensate for any reasonable lighting condition—your eyes will make you do it almost unconsciously by indicating that a particular cut is too shallow or too deep, although by measurement it may be the same as others. (In relief carving, edges of planes must be sharpened to make them more distinct.)

For simple designs like the diaper patterns, you will not need perspective, but for scenes in relief, perspective is vital. Look at the whittled panel of Fig. 272, for example; see how the pier appears to be sticking down into the water and the boats to be drawn up on a vertical bank? Now look at Fig. 277 and see how naturally the figures seem to be standing in a diagonal line from upper left to lower right.

This figure also illustrates several other things—contrast in height and texture of background to create perspective; excellent modeling of the folds of clothes; breaking up of a smooth background with a view of formal gardens, a bracket, and a doorway or fireplace; creation of a pattern in perspective on a flat foreground; sinking of some elements to the ground for clarity.

Perspective really is simple after you have tried it a few times. Remember how the rails of a railroad seem to rise and meet in the center distance? And how the building just in front of you seems to slope downward toward the sides? There are your two basic principles. To make the center appear nearer to the observer, make it larger in proportion, with all side elements becoming progressively smaller toward side vanishing points. To put the center at a distance, make things there smaller, with all other elements becoming progressively larger toward the sides. Gardner and Moyer Wood have made effective use of this principle in carving small bas-relief medallions in the headboard of an explorer's bed, depicting scenes in cities all over the world.

Most successful carvings are usually simple—strong outlines with only essential detail. You should not attempt to make each

FIG. 280 (LEFT) · *Sixteenth-century American oak chest with pine top.* FIG. 281 · *Seventeenth-century Swiss chair back.* (*Both courtesy Metropolitan Museum of Art*)

hair stand out on a head, each leaf on a tree. Such carving has more in common with models made of a million matchsticks than with carving for posterity—you can't see the forest for the trees. Instead, conventionalize, indicating details by a few lines.

Outline your work and cut it free, then detail. Don't start detailing first, because then you will have to sink the surface to desired planes, simply doing all detail over again. After I have not carved a figure for some time, I find myself detailing the head or hands, nibbling the wood away instead of cutting it to the outline in bold strokes. It is probably partly lack of practice, partly the fear all of us have that if we strike out too boldly in cutting we will spoil the piece. But until you conquer the fear of spoiling a piece, your work will lack originality, the vital spark that can make it live.

Perhaps you can combine old elements into something new, perhaps even your elements may be original. Figure 278 gives you thirty-five elements, chosen from sculpture and carving back to the Neolithic, some of the patterns 12,000 years old!

An excellent example of modern low relief is the trophy chest of Fig. 262. From its denticulated upper edge to the wing or feather elements at the upper corners and the scale leading edge of the wing of Miss Earhart's plane, it is modern, yet amazingly simple. The flattened globes at front and sides that depict her flights are separate pieces of teak set into the walls of the chest, the

FIG. 282 · *French eighteenth-century oak panel.* (*Courtesy Metropolitan Museum of Art*)

FIG. 283 (LEFT) · *Modern frame details, designed by F. Marchello*. FIG. 284 · *French fifteenth-century red-pine panel. (Courtesy Metropolitan Museum of Art)*

continents are simple veiner outlining, and the lettering is flush with the surface—the grooving behind it makes it stand out. The buttons and feet are polished rosewood.

Simple scroll patterns form the relief in the chair back of Fig. 266, a conventionalized mask that of Fig. 281. Note the Gothic arch and other identifying elements of Figs. 267, 268, and 284, and the prominent inset buttons of Fig. 270. Strapwork for outlining is used in the door and frame of Fig. 273; the particular strapwork pattern known as the *guilloche* is shown in three forms in Fig. 278. You will find it useful for borders on platters, trays, frames, etc. The straps may be varied by grooving, edging, convexing; the center pearl can be made larger or smaller (if made very large, it is sometimes modified into a tulip or a rose), or the looping can be limited to three or four crosses, the straps running parallel for a foot or two before the looping is repeated. There are dozens of other patterns—figure 8's and knots among them.

See Chap. XXV for low-relief carvings in the "Queen Mary."

CHAPTER XX

HIGH RELIEF · *Pierced Designs*

A S you carved the designs of Fig. 278 in the preceding chapter, you probably wanted constantly to carve just a little deeper in order to make the forms more true to life or more prominent. Let us now indulge that want and carve some pieces in high relief. Steps and methods are but little different from those of low-relief carving, except that upstanding parts are rounded up more, and thin or shaped elements may be undercut to make them stand out better from the ground. Instead of being ⅛ or ½ in. below the surface, the ground now may be as much as 2 or 3 in. below, or may be nonexistent (as in pierced or openwork carving), and parts of the design are often more than half free of the background.

Outlining and lining in are done just as in low-relief carving, but setting in must be considerably deeper. Set in as far as practicable in one "bite," then waste away adjacent ground and set in still farther, alternating the processes until you have the desired depth of ground. If you cut the ground away entirely, the pierced design that results will look (and be) more delicate. Such pieces are commonly used for edge or top elements, delicate borders, framing, or decorative grilles in doorways. They may be used for panels that screen while admitting air, for letting in light through an otherwise solid panel (as in a telephone booth), or for preventing collisions on double-swing connecting doors.

In high-relief carving, grain becomes more of a problem, as does modeling of the design. Bent gouges and firmers are almost a necessity for grounding out and undercutting, and if the design is at all complicated, special-shaped tools will save considerable time. The design is usually more delicate, hence more likely to split, so it is occasionally advisable to "nibble" away wood where a heavy, continuous cut would apparently save time. If the carving is a panel, the edges should be left surface high and shaped into a border or molding that serves the double purpose of framing and protecting the design. Apparently delicate and lacy forms should be solidly backed and protected, for you can never tell when someone will lean or bump against the finished piece.

Motifs for high-relief designs are usually foliage, with flowers, fruit, and leaves conventionalized and tied together with the branches or vines. The background may be flat, but often it is either patterned or covered with low-relief design elements given perspective to make the carving appear deeper than it actually is. Some of these elements may actually be in intaglio, or sunk below the ground.

[207]

Fig. 286 · German sixteenth-century boxwood medallion. (Courtesy Metropolitan Museum of Art)

Other high-relief panels incorporate human or animal figures, including everything from portraits to symbolic, mythical, or legendary figures. Pre-Christian carvers pictured legends of gods and goddesses; later carvers often chose the Nativity, the Crucifixion, or scenes from the life of Jesus. In these panels, too, the background is utilized to give distance or depth to the carving. To avoid the cold and precise outline of a single figure or a group sculptured in very high relief or in the round, the ground will show a scene in perspective, houses, trees, animals, a wall—anything to help create a picture. Note, for example, in Fig. 300, how the deer behind Daphne are only about a third her height to create the illusion of depth, and how the forest atmosphere is created by three gnarled trunks, two leaf clumps, and a roughened background mass suggesting foliage.

In high relief, perspective becomes at once an easier and a more complex thing. Now you have depth as well as surface, so the effect of distance can also be obtained by making objects in the background smaller and in low relief, as well as utilizing either center or side vanishing points.

For example, note in Fig. 296 how the blocks in the back wall are only about two-thirds the size of those at the sides, and the figures at left background are much smaller than those of Mary and Joseph. Joseph is supposed to be standing behind Mary, and so his feet are at a higher level than Mary's knees (thus following the principle of a center vanishing point), the ass and the cow

Fig. 287 · *A modernistic Christmas manger from the dell' Antonio woodcarving school in Bad Warmbrunn, Germany. (Courtesy German Tourist Inform. Office, N. Y.)*

FIG. 288 · *English sixteenth-century oak pediment.* (*Courtesy Metropolitan Museum of Art*)

both appear to be in front of him, and his total height is only slightly more than that of Mary's kneeling figure. Each of the animals in front of him is really in low relief, but your eyes and mine have been trained to consider the width of a cow as a given amount, and that of an ass a slightly smaller amount, so we mentally add these amounts together and place Joseph that much farther back.

Your preliminary sketch of a panel like this will give you proper comparative heights for Joseph and the background figures. It is essential that Joseph's figure be diminished enough to make him appear behind the animals, and that his feet be at a level that makes him appear to be standing on the same floor as that on which Mary is kneeling. This effect is heightened by having lines of the floor radiating outward toward the lower corners of the panel, as indicated in the lines of Mary's robe and of the knees of the cow. The bricks of the side wall and of the arch also have their inside faces sloped along the same lines, and the arch in the background, presumably really the same width as that in the foreground (as indicated by the ceiling design) is carved only half as wide. Supporting columns are also smaller.

This all sounds much more complicated than it actually is, for your eyes have been trained all your life to make these corrections for you and will do it in your sketch and in blocking out the panel if you avoid exact measurements and rigid rules. Remember perspective in scenic panels, but don't worry about it.

Fig. 289 · *Flemish seventeenth-century ivory relief of cupids in a bacchanalian scene.* (*Courtesy Metropolitan Museum of Art*)

Perspective also may be used occasionally to make a panel or surface look wider or narrower. In the second linen fold of Fig. 309, the right-hand edge of the fold is narrower than the left. Such a panel on the side of a cabinet makes it appear deeper, or on the right-hand side of a cabinet front, with the same design tapered to the left on the other side, makes the cabinet appear wider. A tall, slender parchment or linen fold increases the apparent height of a cabinet in the same way. Irrespective of design, dominant vertical lines make an object appear taller; dominant horizontal lines make it appear wider. (The folds of Fig. 309 are late Gothic, and linen fold and parchment fold differ only in that the latter has end rods around which the parchment is rolled, in this being similar to the scroll. The linen fold originally symbolized the muslin cloth over the chalice of the Eucharist.)

In carving such a panel as Fig. 296, it is essential to block out and model in several levels, Mary and the Infant Jesus at the first, Joseph at the second, and the background at the third, for example. This means that your drawing will be cut away as you cut the background down to the first level, unless you are careful to redraw identifying lines on one side of the panel before the other is grounded to the same level. Block out around the side walls and set in down to the elevation for Mary and Jesus. Sketch them, the cow, and the donkey, then set in the panel to the elevation for Joseph and the first background figure. Sketch these in detail, then sink to the third level. Minor errors in sinking in can be corrected in modeling.

A familiar motif from the time of the Tudors in England is the "Tudor rose," Fig. 294. This particular example was removed from Westminster Cathedral in 1896 when some of the early oak carvings were found termite-ridden. The rose was commonly used as a dominant element in panels, as a rosette on borders or molding corners or as an elaborate "pearl" in the guilloche.

Let us try it for our first high-relief piece. The pattern is drawn in Fig. 291: four concentric circles, the inner circle enclosing a "button," and the outer ones enclosing the double row of petals, comprising the design. Between the two outer circles, draw radial lines dividing the space into five equal parts. Divide the space between the inner and third circles similarly, except that the radial lines are spaced halfway between the others. Your layout should look like Fig. 291 *a*. My pattern is $3\frac{1}{2}$ in. in diameter, carved in oak $\frac{3}{4}$ in. thick, of which the lower $\frac{1}{4}$ in. is the base.

Outline the center circle and set in about $\frac{3}{8}$ in., sloping your wasting cuts downward from the second circle, as shown in Fig. 291 *b*. Sketch in the outlines of the petal tops and the little

Fig. 290 · *German XV-century pearwood triptych.* (*Courtesy Metropolitan Museum of Art*)

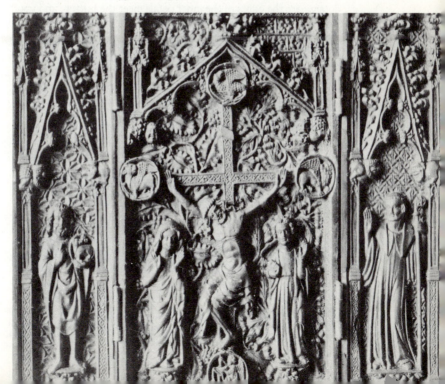

triangular elements between them. Saw or carve the blank out round, and on the round edge mark a line up ¼ in. from the bottom, for the upper limit of the base. In Fig. 291, I have not indicated the base but just the design itself.

Now carve outer elements to shape, outline the outer edges of the inner petals, and waste away the wood toward them downward from the wavy inner outline of the outer petals. Note that the sides of the petals are curved upward and separated by the triangular ridge forming the little decoration between. Shape these ridges, then put in the wavy outlines of the inner edge of the inner petals, and gouge them to shape down to the button. Shape the little ridged triangles between petals as before, and cut a groove down between petals with a veiner. Now round up the button, and with the veiner carve the grooves across it as well as the three little "wrinkle marks" on each inner petal. Your rose should now look like Fig. 291c.

Round up the outer tops of the petals, and undercut the lower edges of the outside petals to make the flower stand out from the base. With a punch or a very small gouge, put in the little round dots where the edges of the inner petals meet the button, and your Tudor rose is finished.

Many carving motifs come from local fauna and flora. Thus, in addition to the Tudor rose, we find the oak leaf a favorite English motif, the pine cone common in cold countries, the water lily and other warm-country plants common in Indian and Japanese or Chinese work. A few common shapes are sketched in

Fig. 291 · *Steps in making the Tudor rose*

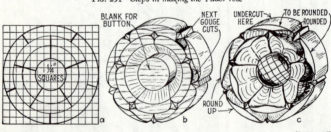

Fig. 298. Step outside your door and you will find dozens of others. Take any one and vary its position or pose slightly, and you have a half-dozen companion motifs for anything from a border to a panel. Not only leaves, but flowers, butterflies, birds, dragonflies and domestic animals will make suitable motifs. They give your pieces a local character that differentiates them from pieces carved anywhere else.

If it is winter, or your chosen subject cannot be held in the pose you want, cut a similar outline from paper, stiff cloth, or some other pliable material, and shape it as you wish. It is particularly easy to design complicated leaf patterns this way, because the pattern is in three dimensions instead of just two. To depict vines, use string or heavy twine.

Comparable help in figure relief can be obtained by modeling first in clay or some similar material. And if you have a detail—hand, foot, eye, ear, mouth, etc.—that you are not quite sure of, model it in clay, or better still, rough it out of a piece of waste wood. This will give you the "feel" of the element, as well as practice, and minimize the risk of spoiling the detail on the major piece. Such details can be kept and referred to again and again in similar work. Several professional carvers I know

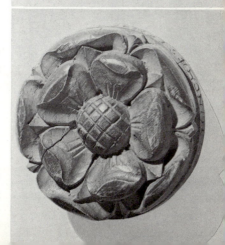

[213]

FIG. 292 (TOP) · Japanese nineteenth-century colored wood panel of peonies. FIG. 293 · French sixteenth-century walnut panel. (Both courtesy Metropolitan Museum of Art.) FIG. 294 · A Tudor rose taken from Westminster Cathedral in 1896. At that time, the dates "1086-1896" were carved on the base. (Courtesy G. W. Stewart)

do exactly that, keeping these trial pieces as models to use in later designs, as in Fig. 322, for example.

If your model is in clay, make a plaster cast of it to keep. Even if you do not expect to make a similar piece later, the detail makes an interesting ornament. And while we are on the subject—never disdain practice. Even if you can make the pieces you want to make, you will be able to make them better and easier with practice on waste wood, for there you need not be quite so careful, so you use bolder, freer, and usually better, strokes.

Also, practice freehand sketching. There are several good books available that will give basic principles; the rest you must get by practice. Most of the sketches in this book are freehand, very poor, to be sure, but my own. They prove one thing conclusively—that I didn't have any formalized sketching training, either. Sketches also have particular advantage if you carve as I do—in spare time and limited quarters. I haven't enough room to keep all my models, but sketches are easily kept. They help particularly in developing new designs, for often a detail in one sketch will suggest a whole design. If you plan to do period carving on furniture, indicate on each sketch its source and period, to save later difficulty in identifying it. It is particularly

Fig. 295 (Top) · *Carved rosewood frame, made by Ernest Weber in 1857.* Fig. 296 · *"The Nativity" in linden wood. German, early sixteenth century.* Fig. 297 · *Flemish seventeenth-century "Domestic Scene," in boxwood.* (All courtesy Metropolitan Museum of Art)

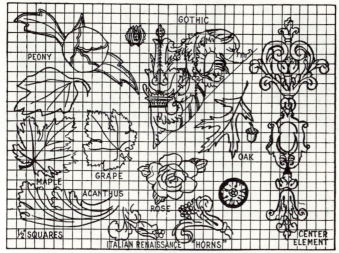

FIG. 298 · *Patterns for flower and leaf motifs*

important that all the elements of a period piece be of that same period.

Several times recently, people familiar with the various periods of furniture making have (from some of my pictures) distinguished between a modern copy and an original piece of that period because some little element was out of character or because the modern carver did too much carving. Normally, don't cover an entire surface with carving, unless it is a plaque or medallion, like Fig. 292. The little cabinet panel of Fig. 293, for example, was originally set off by the blank wood of the whole cabinet. Plain wood has warmth, depth, and beauty in its graining, and the carving should accent, not detract from, the wood itself. Too much carving on a surface only impresses the observer with the amount of work involved. Some carvers will not cover more than a quarter or a third of a given area with carving.

Let us now try a bit of high-relief wood sculpture, choosing as our subject the horse of Fig. 307. This is a familiar subject to everybody; all of us have in our mind's eye the picture of a

Fig. 299 (Left) · *French eighteenth-century cherub.* Fig. 300 · *"Apollo and Daphne,"* a *Flemish seventeenth-century panel.* (*Both courtesy Metropolitan Museum of Art*)

horse that is clear-cut even in details. With such a mental picture, the likelihood of error is much reduced, for you seem to *know* beforehand where the next cut should be made.

The photograph of the horse itself, Fig. 303, and the pattern for the head, Fig. 306, give you all that is necessary to make it. Carve the detail of the harness instead of putting it on later if you prefer, although it will probably be easier at first to work with smooth surfaces. Saw the outline out of a piece of 1½ by 4½ by 4½-in. white pine or mahogany, with the grain running the length of the neck. Round up the neck, leaving the ¼-by-¼-in. mane at the back and showing the heavy line of the throat in front. Shape up the back of the head and rough-cut the ears, then model the face, tapering the block at the nose to about ½ in. thick. The cheekbone and forehead are other rounded forms, and the eye is set in about ⅛ in., then filled with black paint. Model details with the veiner, and use it also for the parallel lines representing the hair of the mane. The harness is thin leather, tacked in place, with fittings of silver wire bent to shape and lacquered to prevent tarnishing.

Such a head can easily be made with a pocketknife, also, except for throat and face wrinkles, hair marks, etc. Notice also, how much character is given by the grain of the wood. It accentuates the swelling lines of the shoulders and neck and gives a surface that looks like hair. Two other head designs are also sketched in Fig. 306, the child's head pattern being that for Fig. 1, and the dog for "Bill," Fig. 308. The child's head, Fig. 1, is carved from white pine with a pocketknife. Note here again how the grain helps out, showing the lines of the shoulders, the cheeks, the chin, and the forehead. The collar is undercut only slightly, to emphasize the thickness due to sewing near its edge, and the shoulders are narrowed to make a more symmetrical shape. Hair is indicated by two meeting lines, and the head is turned slightly to avoid a straight-front view.

In the dog's head, the grain again runs the length of the neck, and the surfaces are not shaped so carefully. This helps to create the rough shape around the jaw that is shown in the photograph of Bill himself, Fig. 304. His collar is a puppy collar cut apart and tacked on, with the brass name plate flattened out, pinned to the background with a brass brad and a screw eye. A length of brass chain connects collar and plate. Background is black walnut, as it is for the others.

These are all examples of applied ornament or appliqué carving, for the high-relief element is carved

〖 217 〗

Fig. 301 (Top) · *"St. Margaret,"* *a German high relief without background. Carved circa 1520 in linden.* Fig. 302 · *Eighteenth - century Chinese screen, Chien Lung (1736–95). (Both courtesy Metropolitan Museum of Art)*

separately. This offers an opportunity to get a contrasting color and grain in the background, as well as to avoid the extensive wasting required to ground out such a panel if made from one piece.

Often this work appears with a special-design background, chip- or spot-carved, with the piece mounted above. In preparing such a background, outline the "seat" for the appliqué, and decorate the rest of the ground outside it as desired. Then glue or screw the ornament to its seat. If in hardwoods, screws are preferable, through drilled and countersunk holes.

Pierced carving, or openwork, may be basically low relief, high relief, or in the round, although it is usually high or low relief. It differs from the normal relief in that it has no background—some examples are shown in the grotesque ornaments atop the pediment of Fig. 288, and in the high-relief rosewood frame of Fig. 295, as well as in most of the later photographs in this chapter. Simplest openwork resembles jigsaw or scroll-saw cutting very closely, in fact may be roughed out with a scroll or jig saw and finished with carving tools. For designs, any geometrical pattern, tracery of connected branches, or figure work can be used. A number of examples are shown. Some of

⟦ 218 ⟧

FIG. 303 (TOP) · Head of "Honey Girl," half-Arab polo pony. See carved head of FIG. 307. FIG. 304 · "Bill," English bulldog. See carved head in FIG. 308. FIG. 305 · Walnut relief of scenes from the life of Christ. Spanish, possibly by Gil de Siloé. (Courtesy Metropolitan Museum of Art)

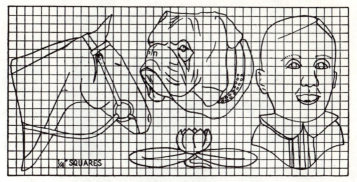

Fig. 306 · Patterns for pieces of Figs. 307 and 308

the designs of Chap. XIX are also suitable for simple openwork.

Ground the carving as before, but before modeling, cut out the ground. (If you plan to do much openwork carving, use a saw table, a U- or V-shaped projecting support bolted or clamped to the workbench or carving table, permitting a saw to be used inside the U.) First drill holes through the ground large enough to allow a saw blade to be passed through each part of the ground. Insert the saw blade with teeth pointing down, and put the handle underneath. Saw out the entire ground, or such parts as you wish, and smooth up the sawed edges with carving tools or (often preferable) a knife. If the panel is so wide that the back of the scroll saw will not clear, use a keyhole saw through a larger hole. Small pierced sections can be drilled out and smoothed up with a knife.

Simple silhouette openwork can be improved in appearance and made to look more delicate by chamfering or beveling the edges of the cut, as in the cusps of Fig. 309. Or, instead, the edge can be made a little concave by thinning with a fairly flat gouge. To do this, chamfer first with firmer or pocketknife, then gouge along the beveled edge. Edges may also be outlined with a veiner, and surface decoration can be added if you wish. The three basic rules are: Under normal circumstances, openings should not

FIG. 307 · Ma-hogany head of "Honey Girl," *mounted on black walnut. Harness is leather, with silver fittings*

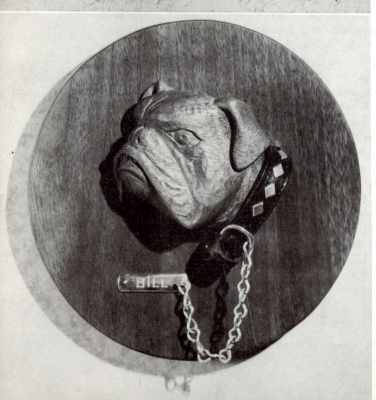

FIG. 308 · Ma-hogany whittled head of "Bill," *mounted on black walnut. Collar is leath-er, with brass name plate and fittings*

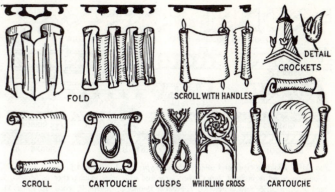

FIG. 309 · *Patterns for Gothic and Renaissance elements. At upper left are two types of linen folds. If handles or rods are provided, they become parchment folds*

remove more than half the wood. Holes should be balanced, i.e., an area should be covered evenly without very large or very small openings. Watch grain; don't cut sections such as stems too thin where they cross grain. Either support them with a leaf or thicken them up.

Now for some general notes regarding high-relief carving:

Many carvers find it difficult to position folds properly in drapery. For figure work, have someone pose in the position you want, then modify the folds as necessary to get the effect you want. For drapery not over figures, throw a cloth loosely over a proper support. I have intentionally selected pieces showing a variety of drapery arrangements.

An interesting variation of high-relief carving may be produced by outlining the elements with a veiner. This produces an additional shadow in the ground to accentuate the figure.

It is essential that you create the impression of delicacy without actually making the piece delicate, and that you do the same with detail. Too much detail again becomes a blurred surface to everyone except the very close observer. Gibbons violated these rules, but it is better for most of the rest of us to remember them. Always provide plenty of support for an upstanding ele-

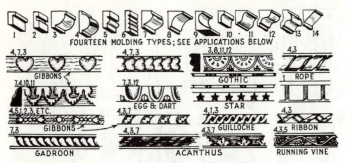

Fig. 310 · *Molding types and some patterns. Types are:* 1, *fillet and fascia;* 2, *sunk fillet,* 3, *quarter-round or ovolo;* 4, *torus (when large and with other moldings) or half-round;* 5; *bead or astragal;* 6, *reed or reeding;* 7, *ovolo or thumb;* 8, *cavetto;* 9, *scotia;* 10, *congé;* 11, *cyma recta;* 12, *cyma reversa;* 13, *beak;* 14, *splay (from Webster's Dictionary)*

ment, and represent detail with a few bold strokes. The Chinese ivory panel, Fig. 302, is a good example of blocking out to create an effect. There is very little detailed carving in it. Faces on the figures are not finished, water is represented by a few patches of wavy lines, mountains by conventional peaked outlines, trees by gnarled artistic shapes with crisscrossed or lined sections to represent leaves, bushes are just clumps of leaves, each leaf at least ten times the normal size. A pattern for the border lilies is included in Fig. 306. For further examples of modern openwork, see Chap. XXV.

Much neglected by modern carvers, the acanthus leaf, Fig. 298 (and Fig. 278, Chap. XIX), was the motif of many pierced designs by Roman carvers, as well as by Grinling Gibbons and others of his time. The staircase of Fig. 2 is a good example. (Most of it is chestnut, while the bold pine-cone finials are lime-wood and the stair treads oak. It is 5 ft. wide by 16 ft. floor-to-floor.) Says *The Art News* of it:

Accented by the massive and boldly worked rectangular newel posts, the acanthus-carved balustrades sweep upward in a majestic rhythm worthy of their role as the dominant architectural feature in a great hall. At the top, the carving is carried across in a short, balcony-like panel.

HIGH RELIEF

Although very solid in conception, the design has both the delicacy and vigor which through their union gave such individuality and style to Gibbons' carving. The openwork acanthus carving has been treated with characteristic freedom. The spirited and exuberant rhythm of the large scrolls displays superbly that imagination and freshness of touch for which Gibbons was famous. The curl of each leaf, the twist of the stems, although blended into an essentially elaborate pattern, have the life of growing things.

The freedom and essential lightness of this wide openwork carving are appropriately emphasized by the compact and solid treatment found in the strings, where oak leaves executed in the grand style are bordered by fillets of guilloche work and other semi-classical bandings. Here a certain sobriety of style that still maintains its crisp individuality is most effectively employed. The design of the square newel posts is equally inspired. The acanthus motif on the four panels echoes the motif of the balustrade, while the molded top and cornice are carved with great restraint, thus leading the eye upward to the pine cones, repeated as finials on four levels. These in themselves are highly characteristic of Gibbons' genius in conceiving his work on a grand architectural scale and yet enlivening it through the use of details revealing his close observation and love of nature. The famous incident of Prince Charlie's hiding place in the Boscobel Oak is recalled by the oak leaves and acorns, which

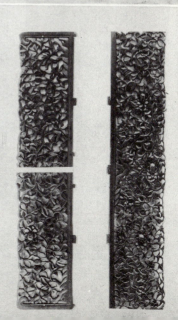

[[223]]

Fig. 311 (Top) · *German six-teenth-century oak medallion.* Fig. 312 · *Volute from a choir stall; late fifteenth-century English.* Fig. 313 · *Top of stand for a screen; Chinese, Chien Lung. (All courtesy Metropolitan Museum of Art)*

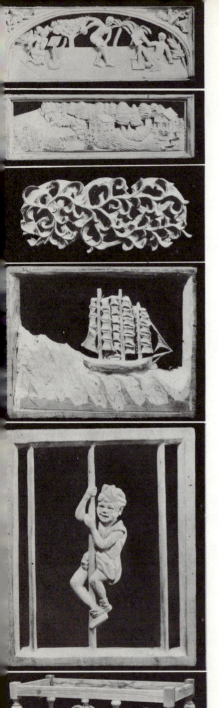

formed the badge of the Royalists after the Restoration.

The staircase is thought to date from 1677 or earlier, for the diarist John Evelyn, Gibbons' friend, mentioned the Cassiobury Park carvings in his diary April 18, 1680. Hugh May was architect of this mansion built for the Earl of Essex.

In carving a serrated-edge leaf like a maple, oak, or grape leaf, set in to a circle enclosing all points. Serrated edges and points can be shaped up later with a skew firmer much more easily. This applies to any design.

In Fig. 310, I have sketched a number of high-relief moldings, some taken from the Gibbons staircase of Fig. 2, others from later illustrations, some original. The top row shows molding types, and the caption gives proper names. At the left of each molding design, several numbers are listed, the numbers of corresponding molding cross sections upon which these particular designs will look well, and about in the order of preference.

Often it is desirable to have a central element in a design to carry a monogram or a date. The scrolls or cartouches of Fig. 309 have been used for centuries for this purpose, particularly in Gothic and Renaissance pieces. Be sure that you modify

〖 224 〗

FIG. 314 · *Openwork whittled panel.* FIG. 315 *Whittled scenic panel with openwork representing sky.* FIG. 316 · *Whittled openwork vine or branch design.* FIG. 317 · *Partially finished panel.* FIG. 318 · *Whittled grille or "squint."* (All courtesy Remington Arms Co., Inc.) FIG. 319 · *Openwork bench frame by F. Marchello*

cartouche design to suit the period—the cartouche at right in Fig. 298 is much more elaborate than those in Fig. 309.

Gothic carvings include a number of characteristic geometric details. A common one is the cusp. Several examples are sketched in Fig. 309, as well as the "whirling cross" in the upper part of a Gothic window. Other identifying Gothic elements are the "crockets," upper right, Fig. 309, which are used to break up the sloping lines of spires. Usually they are placed in rings, one on each corner or peaked edge of the spire. In the sample sketched (from Fig. 305), four crockets appear in each row.

In difficult corners, where there is danger of splitting, you may find it advisable to drill holes to the depth of the ground. They serve as an end point toward which to carve and aid materially in avoiding trouble. Simple undercutting can be done easily with a parting tool or quick gouge held with its axis horizontal so that it cuts a groove just below the top surface of the carving. This will in many cases give enough shadow to show outlines while still preserving the strength of the piece.

When you smooth out a ground, use a square firmer at 45 degrees, or a skew chisel parallel with the grain. This slices across grain and removes gouge marks much more readily.

If your preliminary sketch is faulty, scrape it off with a scraper. This retains a clean, flat surface, while sandpapering introduces tool-dulling grit, and erasing dirties the surface.

Rifflers will help in shaping difficult sections, unless you refuse to use any other tool than the chisel. Rifflers are particularly helpful in leaf details and figure work.

A symmetrical piece is difficult to sketch so that the sides will be duplicates unless you use a half pattern of paper or cardboard. Trace around one side,

⟦ 225 ⟧

FIG. 320 (TOP) · Nineteenth-century Irish black bog-oak plaque. FIG. 321 · French sixteenth-century panel of St. Catherine. (Both courtesy Metropolitan Museum of Art)

FIG. 322 (ABOVE) · Arch and
details for altar paneling by
F. Marchello. Note models in
background for designing furniture in various periods

FIG. 323 (BELOW) · Openwork
altar details by F. Marchello.
Elements on this and the next
page are Italian Renaissance

then turn it over for the other. Cardboard or paper can also be used for templates cut to a shape. They will show exactly where further modeling is needed.

In blocking out and setting in on hard woods, the mallet will come in handy. With a little practice, you will learn to avoid splitting and can chip away areas much more quickly. A wide carpenter's chisel can be used for blocking out and grounding large areas. Razor-sharp firmers will finish the surface without the help of the mallet, and still give sure cuts and good gloss.

Designs should be suited to the wood in which they are cut. Mahogany takes detail well, oak does not. Therefore carving in oak should be rougher, more rugged. White pine takes detail but is likely to leave soft, fuzzy edges. Walnut is about between mahogany and oak but has a tendency to split in small sections. It's grain structure is finer, however, and it takes a better polish. Maple is a hard wood, but contrasts with walnut or mahogany.

The miniature carver should try larger, coarser work occasionally. For the full-scale carver, miniature will teach care in detail.

Occasionally, no matter how careful you are, a piece will be miscut or broken off. Often a detail can be saved by slight re-design; if you look at even well-known carved pieces, you will find that often something happened that necessitated modification of a detail. If a piece is broken off, then glue is the only answer. Very small pieces can be held with commercial glue; larger pieces should be glued with hot glue and clamped until dry. Casein glue, made from a milk base, is also very good and is a cold glue, easy to apply. Lost details can often be replaced with Plastic Wood, or some similar wood plastic. Don't be impatient—give the repair a day to dry before you carve it.

[[227]]

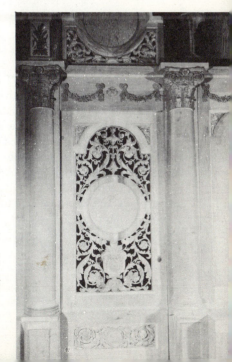

Fig. 324 · Openwork doorway, supporting columns, and portion of altar façade by F. Marchello, showing appliqué carving also

Fig. 325 · *Charles V gives the crown of Spain to his son, Philip II, and his rights as Holy Roman Emperor to his brother Ferdinand. Sixteenth-century German, in boxwood. (Courtesy Metropolitan Museum of Art)*

CHAPTER XXI

IN THE ROUND · Wood *Sculpture*

WOOD sculpture, whether or not known by that name, has always been in favor in the United States, regardless of section of the country. Before the white man came, the Indians had their totem poles. The first ships that came over, as well as the first ones made in this country, carried elaborate figureheads. Inland, the man with an urge for sculpture, with only carpenter's chisels and whatever wood came to hand, produced the once-familiar "cigar-store Indian." Here and there, throughout the country, the pocketknife helped unschooled men and women, boys and girls, to produce all kinds of figures in all kinds of poses. American carpenters also watched and learned from European carvers who came here to decorate fine houses.

From all these backgrounds has come in-the-round wood sculpture as we know it today. The term "in the round" held all sorts of vague terrors for me, until I realized that the chains, ball-in-a-cage, guns, funny little figures and animals, and dozens of other pieces I had been whittling all belonged in this classification. The formally trained woodcarver may feel fearful of anything that is not a panel, but the whittler need have no similar fear—practically everything he has ever made is in-the-round carving.

How does in-the-round differ from relief? Well, the figure has its true thickness instead of being flattened down. There is no ground, hence no support for delicate tracery, nothing but space against which to pose a figure or a group. Almost always, before the carving has progressed very far, all guide lines have been cut away, so one's eye for proportion must be trained. Light getting

FIG. 326 · Josef Mayr, "Nikodemus" of the Passion Play, is also a noted Oberammergau carver. Note blocking out, repair, etc. (Courtesy German Tourist Inform. Office, N. Y.)

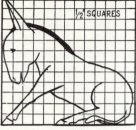

Fig. 327 · *The book-end burro, a simple in-the-round piece*

behind the piece produces effects it could not if the carving were a panel, and so the carver must work and view from all sides. Beyond that, it is really only high relief finished on both sides. If a profile or other sketch is available for the piece, a cardboard template may be made by which accuracy of carving can be checked as it progresses.

For convenience in working, the wood sculptor making anything bigger than a hand-size piece mounts it with a carver's screw on a small, high pedestal (see Fig. 9, Introduction). This pedestal is weighted at its foot or fastened to the floor. Thus the top of the pedestal is clear except for the block, and the carver can work all around it without difficulty.

All this does not mean that you *must* have a pedestal and a large block on which to work. After all, a tall block can be laid on its side and turned over occasionally, then when roughed out, can be clamped by its base to any convenient bench or table. And if your project is little, the block will be little, and often is more conveniently held in your hand. If your piece is very small, it may be advisable to make it on the end of a block. This affords a handgrip that can be cut off when the piece is finished.

One of my friends, president of a pump-manufacturing company, is making a full set of chessmen from maple and mahogany, each very detailed and each carved from a square block with the knife alone. It would be easier to rough it out with the saw—but whittlers are funny that way. One of his kings, for example, has a ⅛-in. staff in his hand that extends unsupported to the base. He admits

FIGS. 328 (LEFT) and 329 · *In-the-round whittling. (Courtesy Remington Arms Co., Inc.)*

he "cheated" on that a little, for after he had it all carved out, he drilled a tiny hole all the way down through it and inserted a steel-rod core to keep it from breaking. The reason? His first king someone dropped and broke off the head of the staff.

This same man has whittled several high-relief walking staffs, using as his motifs the events of the camp where he whittles on them. The most convenient way to hold these pieces, he says, is to put them across your knees, into a couple of spaced forked sticks stuck into the ground, or on an old sawbuck. In any of these supports, the staff can be rotated easily while he is working.

Another figure "whittler" doesn't use a knife at all. Trained early in life as a carpenter, he prefers chisels, so, even though he makes miniatures, all his carving is done with razor-sharp carving tools which he holds by the blade as I hold a knife.

Before you read farther in this chapter, turn back to the totem-pole material in Chap. XVI and that on caricatures in Chaps. XIII and XIV. All these are in-the-round figures, real wood sculpture, whether or not you realized it at the time. At least at first you can follow the same principles here—put side, or side and front, views on a block of the desired

⟦ 231 ⟧

FIG. 330 (Top) · Riemenschneider's handling of a monk's face in the "Blood Altar," Rothenburg. FIG. 331 · Head of Bishop Rudolf von Scherenburg in Würzburger Cathedral, by Riemenschneider. (Both courtesy German Tourist Inform. Office, N. Y. FIG. 332 · German sixteenth-century boxwood tazza cup. (Courtesy Metropolitan Museum of Art)

size by the checkerboard method, rough the block to this outline with knife or saw, then start carving. Any simple figure requires only the profile; the front view will take care of itself as you carve. If the figure is more complicated, requiring two outlines, make your saw cuts in proper rotation, or not quite complete, so that the waste wood is held to the block until all cuts have at least been started. Thus you do not lose guide lines before roughing out is completed. Or if the roughing-out cut is a continuous scroll-saw line, such as would be required in cutting the figurine of Fig. 351 or the ferret of Fig. 338, for example, cut all around the profile outline, then clamp, tack, or tie the waste wood back on the blank, and cut the other outline as well as you can. Rough shaping will give you all the major outlines, so it is almost impossible to go very far wrong except in details. Most of the whittled figures in this chapter were made that way. Three examples are detailed, the figurine, a burro, and a carved black-footed ferret.

First, try to copy the black-footed ferret of Fig. 338, a figure with particularly good lines accentuated by the grain of the wood. Cut its silhouette from mahogany about 2 in. thick, using the pattern of Fig. 337.

FIG. 333 (TOP) · *"St. Jerome and St. Augustine,"* early sixteenth-century German. FIG. 334 · *"Virgin Mourning,"* a French walnut carving, about 1450. FIG. 335 · Sixteenth-century Italian Tuscan School carving of a bishop, polychromed and gilt. (All courtesy Metropolitan Museum of Art.) FIG. 336 · Swiss miniature of the *"Lion of Lucerne."* (Courtesy Annette Navin)

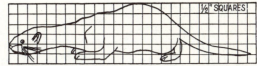

FIG. 337 · *Pattern for black-footed ferret of* FIG. 338

Shape the body first, then the head (remember to leave wood for the ears!), being careful always of the long tail blank and being certain to retain the smooth curves of the muscles over the legs. Shape up the tail, then the legs and feet. The hind legs are particularly delicate, being across grain and free of the body. Shape the ears (the interior is just a veiner cut) and cut a space for the eye, or the eye itself. Cut a V-groove to mark the outline of the mouth and cut little holes or lines for the nostrils. Smooth up and sand all over, then oil and wax to get the shine that resembles the ferret's smooth coat. If you want to be accurate in coloring, put a touch of white on the muzzle and a little black ink or very dark stain on the feet. Insert eyes (any taxidermist has them) and glue on a few short bristles for whiskers or, better still, glue them into holes bored with a needle. Mount the animal on an oval, rough-finished plaque by running brass screws up out of sight between his front legs and between his back legs.

The little burro book end of Fig. 327 is similarly made and finished, except that in his case the black goes on tail and mane. Dozens of other in-the-round animal figures are easy to make, if you have a profile picture, sketch, or model. (See Chap. XIII.) A common subject is the horse, which should have a head half as deep as it is long, a barrel 1 head deep, the top of the body in back and the base of the neck up 2½ heads from the ground, the knee up 1 head from the ground, and the body 2½ heads long.

Smooth-haired animals, and birds or fish, offer little difficulty to the carver; with a little practice you can represent shaggy-

FIG. 338 (LEFT) · *Black-footed ferret, mahogany. (Courtesy Universal School of Handicrafts, Inc.)* FIG. 339 · *Twelfth-century chessman (king), English or Scotch. (Courtesy Metropolitan Museum of Art)*

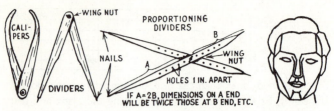

FIG. 340 (LEFT) · *Helpful tools for sculping.* FIG. 341 · *Blocked-out head*

coated animals also. Just don't try to depict each single hair; instead show them in groups or locks—a number of the Oberammergau pictures in this chapter show beard and long-hair arrangements that can readily be adapted to your use. Except in actual wood portraiture, your carving will be better, stronger, if you conventionalize your design, possibly overaccenting the hair, lips, or eyes (Fig. 347), possibly in other ways.

There are also many in-the-round designs (a simple whittled one is shown in Fig. 343—templates will help on these), but you are probably more interested in carving figures of people. General rules of proportion are partially detailed in Chap. XIV. These have the advantage that they are given in multiples of "heads," so that they are applicable to any size or type of carving. First of all, the average human figure is 7½ heads tall (individuals may be 6 to 8), usually roughly figured as a half head each for the neck and foot, 3½ heads for the trunk, 4 for the legs. From the pit of the throat to the tip of the middle finger, with outstretched arms, is half the height of the figure, as is the distance from the ground to the crotch. The distances from the ground to the top of the kneecap, from the kneecap to the point of the iliac,

FIGS. 342 (LEFT and 343 · *More whittling in the round. (Courtesy Remington Arms Co., Inc.)*

and from the pit of the throat to the lower line of the rectus abdominus all are equal. The distance from the top of the head to the pit of the throat goes into the height five and one-half times. From the ground to just below the knee is one-fourth the height. The elbow usually comes just to the top of the hip bone, the finger tips midway between the crotch and the knee. Feet are 1 head long, shoulders 2 heads wide.

The female figure has a longer trunk than the male, the lower limbs being shorter to retain the 7½-head over-all height. The pelvis, or section through the hips, is broader, the shoulders narrower. Children from birth to the end of their first year are only 4 heads tall; from one to four years, 5 heads; from four to nine years, 6 heads; and from nine to fifteen, they are 7 heads.

All these proportions assume that you are *not* making any particular figure; if you *are* making a particular figure, then your carved figure must be in proportion to the subject of the carving, otherwise you will not get a likeness. And each individual will differ in several—or many—respects from these proportions, even as does the fabled Venus de Milo.*

* Exact sizes on the Venus de Milo, famous figure of antiquity, are: height 80½ in., height of plinth, 4½ in., width breast 10½ in., nipple to point left breast 13½ in., nipple to point right breast 11 in., bottom right foot to thigh 41 in., bottom left foot to point of right breast 58½ in., bottom left foot to left

Fig. 344 (Top) · *Swiss crucifixion, showing very gaunt boxwood figure on a walnut cross. (Courtesy Annette Navin.)* Fig. 345 · *"Resurrection," "Tree of Jesse," and figures of Christ and Saints. North Italian, late fifteenth or early sixteenth century. (Courtesy Metropolitan Museum of Art)*

WHITTLING

It is usually helpful to model the figure in wax (best), clay, paste, or plaster of Paris first, then use these dimensions, or proportional dimensions, on the carving—unless you have confidence enough in yourself to start from the block and carve it to shape. With plastic materials, it is possible to start with the body shape, then put clothes on it and arrange folds properly; the carver must, instead, plan for the folds in clothing first, because it is the outer or projecting surfaces that he strikes first as he carves into the block.

Many old-time carvers started with a block of wood or of stone and worked in, with or without a living model. Modern carvers usually make a model figure first, then transfer dimensions through several simple means. Tools are sketched in Fig. 340. The calipers are simply set to a given dimension on the model, then used to measure off the same distance on the piece. The dividers are similarly used (as well as for drawing arcs), except that they are not bowed to pass over or around slight projections. The proportioning dividers make it possible

breast 62 in., around right arm 16½ in., around right shoulder 51½ in., width shoulders in front 19 in., waist 39 in. around, hips 51 in. around, neck 18½ in. around, height of neck 5 in., length of face 7½ in., width of face 6 in., height head from under chin 11½ in., back to front of head 8½ in., knee to bottom right foot 23½ in., length right foot 13 in. (*From Metropolitan Museum of Art*).

〖 236 〗

Fig. 346 (Top) · *Conventionalized horse head by Gardner Wood of Albert Wood & Five Sons.* Fig. 347 · *"Mei Kwei," by Allan Clark, in South American mahogany. Note grain and special outlining. (Courtesy Metropolitan Museum of Art.)* Fig. 348 · *Davy Jones chest, whittled. (Courtesy Remington Arms Co., Inc.)*

to transfer a dimension in proportion from a smaller or larger model to the piece. They may be purchased in several size ranges, or you can make them yourself. The distance between one pair of ends will always be in a given proportion to the distance between the opposite pair, that proportion being determined by the relative lengths of the legs, as indicated on the sketch. Any of these tools can readily be carved out of hardwood.

Almost always, carved figures nowadays are costumed, although you may occasionally want to try a figure in the nude. A pleasing little figurine is sketched in Fig. 349. For this piece you will need a block ¾ by 3 by 5¼

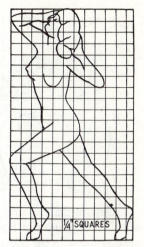

FIG. 349 · A 5-in. figurine of white pine

in. Lay out the profile on it and cut out the blank, then simply round it up. After the more involved caricatures of Chap. XIV, you will probably find this rounded figure easy. The roughed-out block is pictured in Fig. 350, and the finished figurine in Fig. 351. Such a design can readily be modified as you wish; for example, the "Salome" of Fig. 352 is actually the same figure with a different forearm pose (a broken forearm necessitated it).

FIG. 350 (LEFT) · Blocked-out figurine. FIG. 351 · Finished and mounted. FIG. 352 · "Salome"

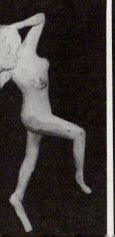

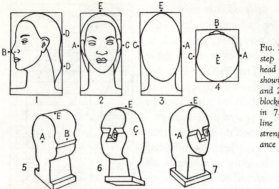

Fig. 353 · Step-by-step carving of a head in the round, showing layout in 1 and 2, blank in 5, blocked-out head in 7. Blocky outline retained to strengthen appearance

Sometimes the eye alone may be fooled in proportioning. I whittled the figurine of Fig. 351 without a pattern of any sort; compare her with the sketch of Fig. 349 and you will note these things: left lower leg too short, hips and right leg too thin, breasts too low. Important, but often forgotten by carvers, is the fact that the chest is not flat, but curved; so the breasts are not parallel, but at an angle to each other. Also, the center line of the neck is in line with the *front* of the shoulders and the *back* of the waistline when the average person stands erect. The waist projects forward about as much as the hips project backward. For details of body structure, consult any art anatomy text.

The head or face often is a bugaboo to the carver, because the proper sequence is not followed in carving it. A class of thirty boys at Cranbrook School, Mich., turned out fifty pieces of sculpture in wood that were so fine they were a request exhibition at the Century of Progress in Chicago. Mr. Cunningham, their instructor, gives these instructions for carving a head like that in Fig. 353:

Plan to have the figure take up the full size of the block . . . First, draw the profiles of the figure on all sides of the block, as in 1, 2, 3, 4. Second, mark the high points that touch the surfaces of the block, A, B, C, D, E. Third, cut out the profile silhouette (1) on the bandsaw.

The block will then look like Sketch 5. If you do not have a bandsaw, a hatchet or gouge will do. Be careful not to disturb the high points. Fourth, cut out the front-face silhouette (2), result as Sketch 6. Fifth, cut away the portions on either side of the nose, as in 6. Sixth, looking down from above on Figure 6, start rounding off the head as shown in 7, working from the top high point (E) down to the four side high points (A, B, C, D). Finish face and neck, rounding off neck from the high points on either side. Round out the figure with a wood rasp and baby plane . . . It is a good idea to close your eyes and carefully go over the carving with your hands—if you find your rhythm obstructed, work out the surface to a perfectly flowing plane. Finish by sanding and bring-ing to a high polish.*

Mr. Cunningham does not advocate slavish copying of natural things but an effort to bring out the "woodeny quality" of the piece by using flat planes and sharp curves of geometrical severity. No effort is made to imitate flesh or hair, and the finished head resembles the block from which it was cut.

Have you ever noticed when you looked at someone in a mirror that his face seemed distorted? Of course, no person's face is similar on both sides, and the mirror reverses this distortion or variation and makes it more apparent. Thus a mirror may be very helpful in aiding you to correct variation or distortion in a carved head—as long as you are not trying to get a likeness.

* Reprinted with permission of Scholastic Corporation, publishers of *Scholastic*, the American High School Weekly.

FIG. 354 (LEFT) · *Modern "Holy Family," by George Lang, unpainted, with lines replacing color.* FIG. 355 · *The more familiar type, depending for its effect upon painting, not carving. Made in Munich by S. Osterreider. (Both courtesy German Tourist Inform. Office, N. Y.)*

Fig. 356 (Left) · Shepherds, Fig. 357 (Right) · "The Three Wise Men," and Fig. 358 · Close-up of the Holy Family of Fig. 354 · All excellent examples of the modern technique in wood sculpture, indicative of the strength in bold lines and planes. By George Lang of Ober-ammergau. (Courtesy German Tourist Inform. Office, N. Y.)

In Fig. 1, I worked particularly to do just that, and found considerable difficulty in making the face appear alive. It was simple enough to carve a child's face, but to make it look like a particular child involved catching one of the child's evanescent expressions. I had a fairly good likeness, but it was not quite right, so I took a thin shaving off at the line joining cheek and upper lip. Immediately that side of the face looked as if it had been turned to stone, and it took half an hour's carving to make it look at all animated again.

Eyes in carvings are often made sightless, the form of the eyeball being carved blank. Ancient Greek statues had the pupil carved as a pit, thus still seemingly sightless. It is possible, however, by leaving a curving triangle of wood extending into the pit to indicate light striking the pupil. Another important factor is ear position (see Chap. XIV). If the ears are placed wrongly, the whole skull will look wrong. The ear is usually enclosed by two horizontal lines, one in line with the eyebrows,

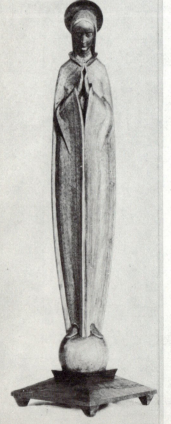

the other with the bottom of the nose. Further, watch the shape and position of the skull, for this element is vital in getting a likeness.

If you are carving in the round from a photograph or sketch, you may want to get the proper length of a given dimension without proportioning dividers. The reducing or enlarging scale of Fig. 361 is very helpful in this. Simply draw two lines at an angle (any angle, so long as lines cross distinctly), measuring on one a given distance, b, on the illustration and along the other the equivalent distance, B, on the carving. Draw a line connecting them. Pin a thin strip of wood along a line so that a triangle set on it will be parallel to the bB line. Then any distance measured on the sketch may be converted to the equivalent dimension on the piece by measuring the sketch distance along the OX line and drawing a line parallel to the Bb line that intersects OY. Thus A is equivalent to a, C to c, etc.

In Fig. 326, note the plugs driven into knotholes in the block. These can be glued in place, then carved to shape. Other faults can be drilled out and similarly plugged.

In Figs. 356, 357, and 358, note the much stronger planes of modern carving which thus use light and shadow to depict character instead of elaborate painting, as did older crèche figures. Beard, hair, and garment treatments are all excellent in these pieces, the garment folds particularly showing how it is essential in carving wood to emphasize a change of plane by making the angle even sharper or more abrupt than it actually is.

[[242]]

Fig. 359 (Top) · St. Peter, oak, fifteenth-century French. (Courtesy Metropolitan Museum of Art.) Fig. 360 · "Madonna," by George Lang. (Courtesy German Tourist Inform. Office, N. Y.)

Hands and feet are blocked out strongly with a few careful cuts, each exact in direction. This probably was done fairly early in the carving, because until hands and feet are clearly delineated it is hard to judge the pose of a figure accurately.

These figures reemphasize the statement made earlier in this chapter—the necessity for suiting the treatment of the technique to the material. If these were clay or wax figures, they would be carefully rounded, with many flowing lines and less distinctive play of light and shadow. But wood in itself suggests angularity and geometrical shapes, so the carver here has accentuated the suggestion. Even with this treatment, each figure is probably a fairly good likeness of one of the carver's neighbors who posed for him. Figure 360 is a striking example of height exaggerated to accentuate the lines of drapery.

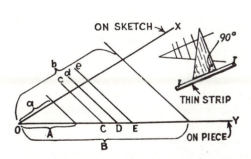

Fig. 361 (Above) Reducing or enlarging scale for working from sketch to piece, using two lines at any angle apart, and parallel lines

Fig. 362 (Right) Parts of the altarpiece, "Dormition of the Virgin," Spanish School—Catalan—sixteenth century. (Courtesy Metropolitan Museum of Art)

Fig. 363 · *English satinwood writing box, inlaid and painted. Late eighteenth century.*
(*Courtesy Metropolitan Museum of Art*)

CHAPTER XXII

INTAGLIO · *Inlay and Marquetry*

INTAGLIO and inlay carving are, like relief carving, ancient arts. Earliest carving was just crude incising; but not long after men began to make relief carvings, they were cutting pictures into a surface. It is easiest to describe intaglio as relief inside out; a mold or impression taken from an intaglio produces a relief. Thus early seals were in intaglio; Egyptian and Assyrian kings 5,000 years ago sealed their orders (written in picture characters in soft clay) with intaglio cylinders. Later they used flat blocks, which eventually became signet rings. Similar blocks were used to coin money—for there were counterfeiters even then, and the true coinage had to be marked.

Intaglio in wood is done almost entirely with gouges, carving first with a veiner, then enlarging the cuts with gouges. Out-lining and lining in are done with the knife and firmer, as in relief. Let us try the medallions of Fig. 364 first. They are easy, but bring out the principles. For the upper one, take a piece of 3-by-3-by-¾-in. white pine and cut it round. Draw a circle ¼ in. inside the edge, outline, line in, and set in ⅛ in. Ground out, and smooth it up. In the center of the ground, draw the cross, outline it, line it in, and set in ⅛ in. Waste away the wood and flatten the ground. It should look in cross section like Fig. 365 a. That's all there is to it! The wolf's head is made similarly from a 3-by-5-by-¾-in. piece, except that his eyes are just meeting curves made with the gouge or knife.

Next try an intaglio design like that on the jewel box of Fig. 368. Lay out the design as you would for relief, but instead of sinking the ground, sink the design. If you want a shallow intaglio, use just gouges, otherwise set in the design a bit first. Check your work by taking an occasional impression with clay, or better, with a bit of dampened and kneaded bread—it is less likely to stick. The finished intaglio can be used as a mold for clay, plasticine, or plaster if it is oiled first, or for molding papier-mâché or forming thin leather. (The leather is dampened, then pressed into the intaglio with a round-point tool. If removed carefully and dried, it will retain the impression.) Intaglios may also be combined with relief carving for contrast.

Inlay, the recessing of contrasting-color materials into a solid background, is at least 4,000 years old. An Egyptian stool in the Metropolitan Museum of Art dating from 2000 B.C. has crossrails and legs with duck heads carved on their ends. Eyes and markings are ivory and ebony inlays. In *The Odyssey*, Ulysses, describing to Penelope the bridal bed he had made, said, ". . . I wrought at the bedstead until I had finished it, and made it fair with inlaid work of gold and of silver and of ivory." Pompeii, too, had its silver and copper inlays.

[[245]]

Fig. 364 · *Two simple intaglio medallions to start with*

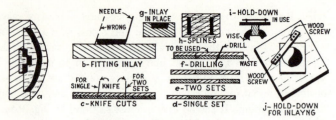

FIG. 365 · *Details of intaglio, inlay, and marquetry*

Ivory, bone, brass, silver, gold, tortoise shell, mother-of-pearl, various-color woods, and other materials may be inlaid. Modern commercial inlay is done with rare figured woods usually from $\frac{1}{28}$ to $\frac{1}{16}$ in. thick (see Chap. I for colors and patterns), the base being routed mechanically. Let us first try an easier inlay, using $\frac{1}{8}$-in. white pine. Turn back to Chap. V to the silhouette of George and Martha Washington. Whittle a $\frac{1}{8}$-in. silhouette of either of them, sloping the sides slightly toward the back. Then place the silhouette over a $\frac{1}{2}$-in. piece of mahogany, walnut, or other dark wood of suitable size, and trace around it with a large needle as in Fig. 365 b. Insert the knife point in this scribed line, and outline. Line in, and set in with the firmer and gouge as nearly vertical and as close to the scribed line as possible. Ground, as in intaglio, being careful not to pry out chips by using the edge of the design for a fulcrum. Breaking down this edge spoils the inlay.

FIG. 366 (BELOW) · *Seventeenth-century Indian pipe case, with ivory inlaid over mica on wood.*
FIG. 367 · *Thirteenth- or fourteenth-century Egypto-Arabic panels inlaid with ivory. (Both courtesy Metropolitan Museum of Art)*

Try the inlay. It should start at all points with moderate pressure. If it does not, trim it carefully until it will. Coat the back with thin glue and press the inlay into place. The bevel will make a tight joint. For convenience in holding while you work, use the hold-down of Fig. 365 *j*. A cross section of the inlay in place should look like *g*. Additional inlays can be set in the original if you give the glue time to dry first. When all are in place and the glue has dried, scrape the surface level (watch the grain!) and sand smooth. Finish with several coats of clear shellac, lacquer, or varnish, the first thinned so that it will soak in. Rub down with steel wool between coats. Any small cracks between inlay and ground can be filled with sawdust and glue.

Now let's try a slightly more elaborate piece, the Abraham Lincoln of Fig. 379, suitable for a book end or panel. Dress a piece of very black walnut to ¾ by 5 by 7 in. Trace the pattern of Fig. 381 in the center, using pencil, scriber, or Chinese white. Make a pattern from Fig. 383 *a* for the oak which surrounds the head, and whittle it from a piece ⅛ in. thick, cutting carefully where it meets the head and shoulders. Other points should extend into the border design. Inlay this piece. Next make a

[247]

Fig. 368 (Top) · *Intaglio coat of arms on a jewel case.* Fig. 369 · *Brass inlay in walnut footstool.* Fig. 370 · *First prize-winning white holly inlay in a walnut table at the National Home-workshop Guild Exhibition, Chicago, 1935. By Robert Zeiner. (Courtesy "Popular Science Monthly.")* Fig. 371 · **Inlaid boxes**

pattern and whittle a piece of ⅛-in. mahogany to form the face and ear, Fig. 383 b (the right eye is an "island" inlay, so can be put in later). Inlay the mahogany, then ⅛-in. maple for the shirt front and border pieces, as in c. Now inlay the right eye from a spare bit of black walnut. Scrape to a level surface (again remember grain!) and scratch in a facsimile of the signature. Fill cracks and the scriber line with a mixture of glue and saw-dust, then sand all over and finish as before.

The Washington inlay (Fig. 378) is similarly made. Inlay oak first, as in Fig. 382 a, then maple to form the head, b. Inlay mahogany for the in-between color shown by the shaded areas, then walnut to form the black areas of the face. Complete by in-laying maple for the shirt front and border. Instead of the maple, you can use basswood, white poplar, magnolia, or holly. Or instead of any of these commoner materials, you can use the rare woods marked on Fig. 381. In that case, your inlay will of course be shallower. Cigar boxes contain woods of several colors, already planed to ⅛ in. thick.

An inlaid piece often tends to warp. Control this by inserting (just a deep inlay) ¼-in. hardwood splines in the back of the piece, above and

[248]

Fig. 372 (Top) · *Marquetry outlining with the saw. This may be done also with the knife.* Fig. 373 · *Late seventeenth-century English cabinet inlaid with ivory. (Courtesy Metropolitan Museum of Art.)* Fig. 374 · *A marquetry tray by Murray Russell, an elaborate piece.* Fig. 375 · *Intaglio initials in a jewel-box top*

FIG. 376 · A Flemish cabinet of ebony with carved and inlaid bone. Made about 1625–1650.
(Courtesy Metropolitan Museum of Art)

below the design, as in Fig. 365 h. If you have a broken corner or two, glue in suitable bits of the proper wood.

Overlays differ from inlays in that they are just shaped veneer glued to a surface. They are usually very thin, hence have a tendency to curl when glued on. Apply hot or casein glue (casein glue stains some woods) sparingly and evenly, keeping it free of lumps and dirt and not too heavy. Coat the seat for the overlay also, then press the overlay down tightly, rubbing carefully all over with the head of an ordinary hammer. Put on a sheet of wax paper (to catch and stop glue that squeezes out), a block to cover the overlay, and clamp in place until it dries. With hot cabinet glue, you can take the clamps off in about an hour; for cold or casein glue, allow two. If the paper sticks to the overlay, dampen it slightly, or scrape it off carefully.

Raised inlays, usually appearing only in borders, are just thicker pieces of inlay set into shallow grooves. Another variation is produced by cutting the inlay a little small, then pressing in a thin strip of contrasting wood or metal or celluloid between inlay and background. Another variation is produced by pressing in or cutting a very shallow inlay in a surface, then filling with thick paint.

〖 250 〗

Fig. 377 (Top) · Thirteen varieties of rare woods form this marquetry panel, much more restrained than Fig. 374. Fig. 378 · George Washington in marquetry. Fig. 379 · Abraham Lincoln in marquetry. All by Murray Russell

FIG. 380 · *Pattern for Washington*

FIG. 381 · *Pattern for Lincoln*

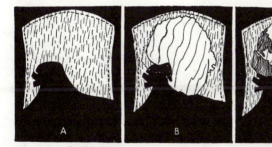

FIG. 382 · *Steps in making the Washington marquetry panel*

FIG. 383 · *Steps in making the Lincoln marquetry panel*

FIG. 384 · *Four borders and five other designs by Murray Russell*

Marquetry (called "tarsia" in Italy) is the forming of elaborate designs or pictures by putting various materials together *without a background*—a glued-together jigsaw puzzle which may be only $\frac{1}{28}$ in. thick. This is glued to a background or held in a frame. When applied in floors, it is $\frac{1}{4}$ to $1\frac{1}{4}$ in. thick and called "parquetry." Marquetry, too, is very old. Jean Macé of Blois was the first French marqueteur, and the greatest was André Charles Boulle, who in 1672 became king's marqueteur. He reduced the amount of ebony in inlay and increased the proportion of color and ornament to give it more life. He also invented the process (which bears his name) of gluing two thin sheets of each of two materials together, cutting the design through all four, then separating and matching up the contrasting pieces to get four complete marquetries. One of his famous pieces is the marriage coffer in the Louvre.

From the Netherlands in the sixteenth and seventeenth centuries, marquetry spread to England during the time of the later

Stuarts, reaching its peak during the reign of William and Mary. During the Georgian period, it was supplanted by carving, but in 1760 the classic revival of the Adam period caused it in turn to supplant carving. In the latter part of the eighteenth century, South German marqueteurs were making elaborate instruments, weapons, and bride chests. Leaders included Roentgen, Riesener, Oeben, and Foulet. While modern marquetry is usually done with a scroll saw, it can also be done with knife cuts. Put the two woods together, then cut the design through both (the pattern may be held in place with rubber cement). If you intend to make only one marquetry, the knife should be slanted as at left, Fig. 365 c, to create a wedge and later tight fit. Otherwise keep it perpendicular, and combine the resulting pieces to get two sets (Fig. 365 e). In difficult corners, it may be necessary to drill through. Do it as at f, running the drill through the waste wood. If the wood is too thin to handle properly, cement on a piece of cardboard to help support it. This is removed just before final mounting. Card-boarding is also usually necessary after several sections have been assembled because the glued joints are so thin that they may not hold well enough to permit handling. In marquetry—in fact, all inlaying—remember always to curb your desire to mix all sorts and colors of woods, or the result will be decidedly rococo.

Some of the inlay and marquetry material in this chapter, as well as Figs. 372, 374, 377–383, 385, and part of Fig. 365, are adapted from material published in *Scouting* and *Everyday Science & Mechanics* by Murray Russell, of Newton, Ia., used with permission of the publishers and supplemented by additional data from Mr. Russell.

FIG. 385 · *Winter scene in marquetry. Note sun effect in sky. By Murray Russell*

Fig. 386 · A lettered 2-in. rosary bead, and Fig. 387 · The interior, showing the "Way of the Cross" and "Crucifixion." (Courtesy Metropolitan Museum of Art)

CHAPTER XXIII

LETTERING · *Alphabets*

OFTEN you will want to incorporate a motto, quotation, monogram, name plate, or just a date in your carving. If you want it to be secret, work it in as part of the design; if it is to be read by others, remember that letters should first be legible.

That does not mean that beauty must be sacrificed entirely to legibility; there is often a happy medium, usually obtained by stressing the elements of a letter that distinguish it from all others—the horizontal stroke of the L, the bottom loop of the B, the roundness of the O. Then arrange the design to support the lettering, remembering that beauty is not obtained by elaboration, but by simplicity, character, and dignity.

First letter forms were simply incised strokes, but the Romans 2,000 years ago were already using an alphabet (Fig. 393) with varying weights of line and with curves and lines at the ends of the basic strokes. These are called *serifs*, and make relief lettering incorporating them more difficult because about half of them must inevitably be across grain. Earliest alphabets were all capitals, but later the lower-case or *miniscule* letters were developed for easier reading, and handwritten "running hand" or "cursive" letters for easier writing. So today we have many kinds of letters, some simple, some elaborate, some with serifs, some without, some with the original vertical lines slanting up, ward to the right (*italic*), some with elaborate tails and loops (*uncials*), some with heavier lines in one direction than the other (the Romans developed shaded lettering, called "rustic"). For the story, read *Alphabets Old & New*, by Lewis F. Day.

In Fig. 388 I have sketched twelve ways of forming the letter I. It is simplest to stamp either the background or the letter (Chap. XVII), or to outline the letter form with a veiner. Lettering is incised with a flat parting tool or firmer, or it may be in intaglio or relief. Occasionally, even in-the-round letters may come in handy to form a handle for a box, or an in-the-round letter of one wood may be pressed and glued into an intaglio letter to form an inlay. Relief letters may be grooved with a flat gouge or tapered to the ground all around with a firmer. Letters flush with a surface can be carved by making a background of a series of V-grooves (very attractive with low-relief or panel carving—see Fig. 262, Chap. XIX), or by "cushioning," which is simply out, lining the letter with a parting tool, so that the letter side is vertical, and grooving the letter surface with a small gouge.

Remember the headline writer's rule when laying out a sentence to be carved—allow a square for each letter except *i, j,* and *l,* which take half a square, and *m* and *w,* which take one and one-half squares. Allow a full square between words, two squares be-

Fig. 388 · *Twelve ways to carve lettering*

OUTLINED   INCISED   INTAGLIO   RELIEF   GROOVED   IN-THE-ROUND

BACKGROUND   LETTER   GROOVED   RAISED   INLAID   CUSHIONED
                STAMPED   GROUND

tween sentences (half a square for the punctuation mark). Unserifed letters limited by vertical lines (like N and H) should be spaced about half a letter apart, but letters can be brought closer to O, Q, P, etc., because they are rounded. L and T can even be overlapped.

To lay out lettering, block out the space where it is to go, then divide up the space among the letters according to the above rule. Whether letters are incised or in relief, you will find it faster to carve all verticals at once, then all the horizontals, finally finishing up the curves. If relief, make it very low—not over $\frac{1}{8}$ in. Roughen or stamp backgrounds, and if you wish, follow the medieval method of gilding or coloring the lettering.

Many mantel mottoes and panel sentences are made in the so-called "ribbon" lettering of Fig. 392, in which whole words are written as if they were formed by laying a ribbon on the surface. This may be varied to look like a twisted vine.

Consider the space to be filled and the letters involved when you plan a monogram—rounded letters like C and G lend themselves to circular or oval designs, while letters like M and H look better in rectangular ones usually. Script or written letters can be modified to fit almost any shape.

〖 256 〗

FIG. 389 (TOP · *Five lettered fraternity paddles, Nos. 1, 2, and 4 incised, No. 3 intaglio, and No. 5 in relief.* FIG. 390 · *A lettered boxwood triptych, early sixteenth-century Flemish.* (*Courtesy Metropolitan Museum of Art.*) FIG. 391 (BOTTOM) · *Unserifed and serifed letters combined on a linoleum block. Note how letters are spaced to make even lines*

Fig. 392 (Right) · Modern capitals in the "ribbon" or "strap" letter typical of the Elizabethan, Jacobean, and Henri II periods. Designed by Lewis F. Day. This and the next five alphabets are from his book "Alphabets Old & New," with permission of Mrs. Day and the publishers

Fig. 393 (Below) · Incised letters from the Forum at Rome

Fig. 394 (Below) · Elizabethan lettering from an incised inscription at North Walsham, Norfolk, England

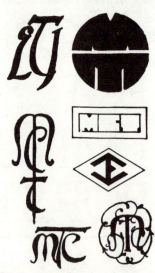

FIG. 395 (TOP LEFT) · Gothic letters in relief. Spanish, fourteenth or fifteenth century. FIG. 396 (ABOVE) · Gothic letters from the tomb of Richard II, Westminster Abbey, and others of the same date, about 1400

FIG. 397 (TOP RIGHT) · French Gothic letters in relief, with foliation of otherwise simple forms. Probably fifteenth century. FIG. 398 (ABOVE) · Monograms, and an initial "M" of the type used to begin a quotation

ABCDEFGHIKLMNP QRSTWY! 1234567890 abcdefghjkmprstuvwxyz

Fig. 399 · *Engraver's Old English*

ABCDEFGHIJKLM NOPQRSTUVWXYZ

Fig. 400 · *Modern initials*

ABCDEFGHIJKLMNOPQR STUVWXYZ& 1234567890$ abcdefghijklmnopqrstuvwxyz

Fig. 401 · *Caslon Old-style alphabet, basis for many modern type faces*

ABCDEFGHIJKLMNOP QRSTUVWXYZ& abcdefghijklmnopqrstuv wxyz 1234567890$

Fig. 402 · *Ultra-Bodoni Italic; note the slant and the extra-fat letters*

ABCDEFGHIJKLMNOPQ RSTUVWXYZ& abcdefghijklmnopqrstuv wxyz 1234567890$

Fig. 403 · *Stymie Bold alphabet; note square serifs*

ABCDEFGHIJKLMNOPQRS TUVWXYZ& 1234567890$ abcdefghijklmnopqrstuvwxyz

Fig. 404 · *San Serif, which must be carefully spaced between letters for ease in reading. All alphabets on this page are present-day type faces made by American Type Founders, Inc. and Monotype Co.*

FIG. 405 · *The French Room at the Metropolitan Museum of Art*

CHAPTER XXIV

DECORATION · *Outdoor, Indoor, Styles*

IN the Gothic period (thirteenth to sixteenth centuries), the *Corporation des Huchiers* (Guild of Cabinetmakers) required a six-year apprenticeship which incorporated four years of training under a member master and two of travel as "journeyman-apprentice" learning what carvers in other countries and other masters taught. Then came an examination before the Guild, after which the novice was locked into his workshop alone (so that he could obtain neither advice nor aid) to make a piece of furniture chosen to incorporate many types of work. This trial piece, if accepted, became his "master piece" (today a much looser term), and he became a "passed master," taking the oath to burn before his shop any inferior pieces.

Today, most of us do not have the advantage of this long period of training, so we may unconsciously or unknowingly combine in a carving elements which individually may be attrac- tive but which weaken each other when combined. This does not mean that you should never combine elements differently or develop new ones, for slavish copying itself is valueless. To give some idea of proper combinations, proportions, and percentage of carving, I have chosen many museum pieces as illustrations.

Each great people developed characteristic carving, and the styles in each country changed in carving as they did in clothes— modern examples are the strongly outlined crèches (Figs. 356, 357, 358, 360) and low-relief ornaments (Figs. 422–429).

Several thousand years ago, Egypt and Greece both had civilizations renowned for their works of art. Rome borrowed from Greece, Constantinople from India and Rome; Renaissance Italy went back seven centuries to Rome again; Russia under Peter the Great took Holland as its model in the eighteenth cen- tury as Spain had taken Flanders for hers 300 years earlier. France

Fig. 406 (Left) · *English late sixteenth-century oak court cupboard, showing guilloche.* Fig. 407 · *French walnut caryatid (1550–1600).* Fig. 408 · *Seventeenth-century English oak baluster.* Fig. 409 · *Same, from Kent, 1693. (All courtesy Metropolitan Museum of Art)*

borrowed from Italy, England from France, Italy, and Flanders, and by the eighteenth century Italy's art, by now decadent, was forced to borrow from France and England again. Korea borrowed from ancient China; and Japan, as a barbarian nation, conquered Korea in 200 A.D. and began a 1,300-year process of absorbing Chinese culture second hand. One result is the gate of Fig. 430.

It is thus that art has lived and developed, each nation teaching another, each period shading into another or reappearing centuries later. Thus there are no real periods—Gothic furniture and architecture, as authentic as the original, is being produced today. Even the word "Gothic," which refers to a style developed through the twelfth to the sixteenth centuries, was originally a term of derision applied to the new "rude and barbarous" art which departed so completely from classical tradition.

Characteristic of the Gothic style are the early pointed arch, the later four-centered or rounded arch, crockets, geometric shapes in general, the parchment and linen folds, the Flemish I, grotesque figures, pierced work—sketched in Figs. 298, 309, 310. Designs in general were limited only by the imaginations of their carvers, although they usually had a religious background. With the exception of the folds and the Flemish I, Gothic furniture was Gothic architecture in miniature—the panel of Fig. 284, for example. Carving was mainly on chair backs, chest sides, doors of credences (church cupboards), in sharply outlined low relief, "windows," fish-net panels or pierced work—the pierced panels probably the most beautiful ornamentation ever developed. Gothic pieces include Figs. 6, 267, 268, 269, 284, 285, 288, 290, 305, 312, 321, 386, 387.

But the stage was set for reversion to the flower and leaf forms of the Italian Renaissance and the return to Roman and Greek motifs which have been used in architecture ever since (except in ecclesiastical buildings, still predominantly Gothic)—the Greek fret (often a continuous swastika), the guilloche or meander, egg and dart, tongue and dart, leaf and tongue, egg and leaf, bead and pearl combinations, running ornament (conventionalized breaking-wave forms), the Greek antefix, and the broad band of bay or laurel leaves, possibly with a ribbon diagonal, Fig. 278.

Gothic and Renaissance were the two great periods of carving as distinct from cabinetmaking. Form was simple, even severe, the carving being the center of interest. Interiors as early as Henry VIII were covered with carved wainscoting, and carved furniture was planned primarily for wall decoration. Among other pieces, this introduced the wainscot chair, straight-backed in England, inclined-backed in America. Its ancestor was the folding Glastonbury chair with · guilloche and bead motives carved on skirt, arms, and top of the back. A fine wainscot chair is pictured in Fig. 266, and several alternate designs sketched in Fig. 412. "Chair" itself comes from the old French "chayère."

As Francis I brought the Renaissance to France and Henry VIII to England, Italian influence came with it. The late Gothic

Fig. 410 · *An excellent American eighteenth-century doorway from the Powel House, Phil-adelphia.* Fig. 411 (Inset) · *Details from paneling in the same house. (Both courtesy Metropolitan Museum of Art)*

four-centered arch became the Tudor Arch in France, with the heraldic salamanders of Francis I replacing the crockets. In England the Tudor Rose (Fig. 294) was finding increasing use, as well as "Romayne work"—low-relief busts in circular medallions that the Italians had learned indirectly from the Saracens. Renaissance pieces through these pages include the French courtyard of Fig. 244, French Figs. 8, 270, 273, 274, 282, 293; Italian Figs. 345 and 322–324, 413, 416 (modern copies); English Figs. 266, 294, 408; Flemish Figs. 289 and 376.

France adapted Renaissance ideas from Italy, combined them with Flemish, added her own. Out of this grew the Louis XIII style, then later the cramped, finicky, "grand style" of Louis XIV, dominated by strong religious feeling. Ideas were mainly Italian, with spirals and bulbs common motifs. These were not lathe-turned spirals, but twisted spirals—hand-carved, of Eastern origin, with concave or hollow parts bigger than the convex ones, and the spiral often very much undercut (Fig. 414). Louis XIV brought scrolls, volutes, floral garlands, and the shell, which was also used so extensively on Queen Anne, Chippendale, and by Savery in Philadelphia. The style developed under Louis XV into rococo, overdecorated pieces. Louis XVI brought the husk pattern, fluting, and the lyre design.

Henry VIII and Elizabethan carving was mostly turned work,

FIG. 412 · *Three examples of oak wainscot chair backs, seventeenth century*

BULKELEY COLLECTION
1650-1675

BOLLES COLLECTION
SCITUATE, MASS. 1650

ESSEX INSTITUTE
SALEM, MASS. 1600

heavy, and showing the cup and cover element often. At the beginning of the seventeenth century, French influence helped to create the Jacobean style, at first in oak, then walnut. The favorite pattern was a triangular bunch of grapes and a triangular leaf grouped into an oblong, other motifs being a row of contiguous half circles, each with a flower motif inside, the guilloche, and foliage scrolls in heavy openwork.

In 1673 came the James II style and introduction of the eagle as a decorative motif, sixteen years later the William and Mary period and introduction of marquetry.

The time of the great English cabinetmakers corresponded roughly with the period of Louis XVI in France, so we find styles of Louis XVI, Sheraton, Hepplewhite, Adam, Directoire, Empire, etc., all being evolved at about the same time. Chippendale, among the whole group, was the great carver—in fact, museum authorities identify his pieces even today by the excellence of their carving. He recognized and adopted the designs of the world's cleverest cabinetmakers, the Chinese. Robert Adam, not a carver himself, used stucco and other subterfuges to avoid woodcarving. His pieces were characterized by wreaths, garlands, and honey-suckle from the Greek, and the anthemion pattern. Hepplewhite, on the contrary, favored the feathers (Prince of Wales), honey-suckle, husk, and concave curves. Sheraton, not a carver apparently, used convex surface curves. Duncan Phyfe, the American, inspired by Sheraton, went on to develop his own style.

American furniture, at first the simple and plain as befits a people wresting a living from a new country, later followed European styles. Good tools were scarce at first, so the colonists lived in crude dwellings with crude furniture—in fact, the Governor's Council of Pennsylvania issued an order in 1685 that the many cave dwellings there be filled up. Early pieces were in native woods, often with simple chip- or gouge-carving motifs, or with adaptations of such Flemish and Dutch designs as the tulip or sunflower, Fig. 280.

When conditions became more settled, pieces of fine furniture

Fig. 413 (Left top) ·
Modern reproduction
of Italian Renaissance
by F. Marchello for
Yale University. Fig.
414 (Above) · English
seventeenth · century
walnut armchair, show-
ing twisted spiral. Fig.
415 (Above right) ·
French walnut table,
1550–1600. (Both pieces
courtesy Metropolitan
Museum of Art.) Fig.
416 (Left) · Italian
Renaissance style table
by F. Marchello. Fig.
417 and 418 (Left
bottom) · Two chests
with low-relief medal-
lions by Albert Wood
& Five Sons

were brought over from Europe, and American cabinetmakers (including Phyfe, Savery, and Goddard) and carpenters copied them. Marquetry, inlay, and elaborate shapes soon replaced carving, except from 1810 to 1820, when plenty of mahogany was available and American carvers used pine-cone finials, carved columns, acanthus leaves, etc. About 1830, undistinguished, mainly inartistic copies began to be produced, and the great cabinetmakers were no more.

Furniture styles in general are so commonly pictured in books and magazines that they are not reproduced here. Many involve more shaping and saw cutting than carving.

Today, the appreciation of original design and workmanship is growing again, and we find carvers here and there producing original work of a high order. Some is illustrated.

⟦ 267 ⟧

Fig. 419 (Top) · Throne chair of Empress Dowager Tzu-Hsi of China, a nineteenth-century piece. (Courtesy Metropolitan Museum of Art.) Fig. 420 · "Der englische Gruss" in Lorenzer Church, Nuremberg, Germany, by Veit Stoss in 1518. Fig. 421 (Bottom) · A small whittled composition. (Courtesy Remington Arms Co., Inc.)

R.M.S. "Queen Mary" contains many fine examples of modern carving, mainly by Bainbridge Copnall and James Woodford, British artists. Across the top of these pages are companion pieces showing conventionalized male and female figures in low relief, and below them are four of a series of fourteen panels depicting a history of shipping from the earliest historic times. These are all by Copnall, while the two casts of panels with piscatorial motifs at left and right are by Woodford. (All courtesy Cunard-White Star Line.) FIG. 422 (UPPER LEFT) · Panel "Air" above a map in main restaurant. FIG. 423 (UPPER

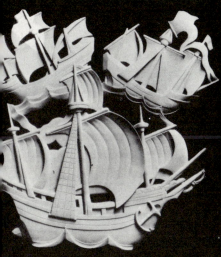

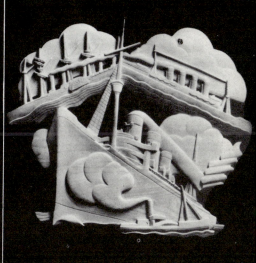

RIGHT) · "Calm," a panel leading up to a mural decoration. FIG. 424 (FACING PAGE, LEFT CENTER · Greek and Viking ninth-century ships. FIG. 425 · Medieval ships of the fourteenth and fifteenth centuries with a royal ship of 1545. FIG. 426 · Cinque port boats, the "Santa Maria," the "Queen of Portugal," etc. FIG. 427 · The "Great Eastern," "Mauretania," and "Queen Mary." FIG. 428 (LOWER LEFT) and FIG. 429 (LOWER RIGHT) · The Woodford panels, carved in soft wood and cast in bronze. They illustrate the possibilities of woodcarving as a means of making patterns for more enduring cast pieces

CHAPTER XXV

FINISHING · *Repairing*

AN old friend walked into the shop of a skilled carver to find him busy under an almost completed table. "I'm cleaning up a bad spot," the carver explained. "But no one will ever know it is there," objected the friend. "*I* will," said the carver.

That is fundamental in finishing anything—to make a workmanlike job. The veriest novice can fill and cover faults and mistakes with pastes and paints, just as he can approximate the appearance of heavily varnished mahogany with half a dozen lesser woods. But real woodcarving is more basic than that; it involves an appreciation and understanding of a clean, sharp cut and of clear, uncovered wood surfaces. This has aways been true—the carver has always wanted to produce a true and honest piece, not something disguised by spurious finishes. Many early pieces about whose *patina* the uninitiated rave were really never finished at all! The carver finished his work with clean, incisive cuts, then did any further finishing by rubbing it with the handle of the tool, a handful of fine shavings, or his own hands. Continual cleaning and service did the rest, aided by spilled grease, soot, butter, milk, candle drippings, and further rubbing with the hands.

Later carvers used raw linseed oil to hasten this result, but the primary reason for the finish was as a preservative, not to add a gloss to a piece already beautiful to them—and beautiful to us even today. Sandpaper was not used—and should not be—for it serves only to take off clean lines and strong edges while covering up the results of inadequate tool work. Of course, if you are carving a ship's figurehead to be painted, anyway, or a piece like the ferret of Fig. 338, Chap. XXI, which is to show a silky fur finish, sanding is advisable, as it usually is for flat, uncarved surfaces and the backgrounds for appliqués.

FIG. 430 · *Yomei-Mon, or "Sunrise-Till-Dark," Gate at Nikko, Japan. Of Chinese design and one of the most magnificent in existence, this portal adorns the Ieyasu Mausoleum. Finished in lacquer, it derives its name from the fact that even the longest day gives hardly enough time to examine its elaborate detail. (Photo copyright by The National Geographic Society. Reproduced from the "National Geographic Magazine" with special permission)*

Many early carvings were polychromed and gilt. Southwest Texas and Mexico have revived the scenic-relief carving of soft wood, painted with oils in many colors; but more formal carving is usually harder woods finished in natural color to show grain and carved lines. It is possible to show grain even on finished outdoor pieces, by soaking the piece in linseed, by using waterproof varnish or clear lacquer.

Professional carvers fill the grain of natural-finished mahogany, teak, and walnut pieces by rubbing in something to show a whitish tinge at the edges of carving, in the grain, and in sharp corners. White lead is commonly used. It may be tinted with colors to give a lighter or darker shade than the wood, with Prussian blue, or grayed with a touch of lampblack. Many paste-type wood fillers also give this result. To get the light-gray "antique wood" finish sometimes effective, use a light-gray acid stain or a silver-gray filler made up of three parts (by weight) of white lead and two parts of fine silica. Thin this with a mixture of half turpentine and half good coach japan. Add a little lampblack or Prussian blue for color. Apply like a paint and let it set for time. Rub it or the others off across grain with a stiff felt block. (Have several, of ½- and 1-in. hard rubbing felt 2 by 3 and 3 by 5 in. or larger).

A piece so prepared can be finished with the medieval carvers' several coats of raw linseed oil at twenty-four-hour intervals (add a little color or pigment to change the wood color if you wish), followed by several coats of good grade wax, well rubbed. Do not use cheap, self-polishing waxes. To make a satisfactory wax, cut or shred beeswax into turpentine until the mixture is butterlike. Heat this before using it, and do not let it lump into corners. "Benzine wax," an alternative, is made by cutting white wax into benzine. Cover it tightly and put in a cool place for twenty-four hours. Take out as needed, thinning with benzine until it can be brushed on. The secret of soft, beautiful, wax finishes is many thin coats, each put on across grain, allowed to dry, and then polished in turn with soft bristle brush, sheepskin or felt, and soft cloth.

An elaborate finish is the French polish, which is a combination of knack and "elbow grease." It is put on over raw linseed
oil (for reddish woods like mahogany or walnut, steep 4 oz.
of Alkanet per pint of oil) without grain filler. Roughness and
open pores are smoothed down somewhat by rubbing the carving
with a handful of shavings. Clean and dust the surface carefully.
The polish is a mixture of ⅜ lb. of pale orange shellac per pint of
alcohol and is applied with a wad or pad of soft, lintless rag. Make
a convenient-sized wad, cover with soft old cotton rag (it must
not be new), smooth out all wrinkles, and pour a little polish on it.
With your finger, put a drop of linseed oil in the center of the pad
and immediately begin to polish over a small area, moving the wad
in circles or figure eights. The oil helps to start. Rub constantly—
if you stop, the wad will stick to the surface and ruin the finish.
Continue in small areas, overlapping each one, and be sure to
get plenty on undercut parts of the piece. Don't press too hard,
and keep adding polish—don't let the pad get dry. Let the surface
dry for several hours, then rub down with fine (No. 5/0) garnet
paper or sandpaper. Apply another coat. Repeat until the grain
is filled up, then rub in well a final coat of alcohol alone.

To repolish such a surface, use a mixture of turpentine, strong
vinegar, alcohol, and raw linseed in equal parts, put in a bottle
in that order, with thorough shaking between additions.

For sanding, garnet paper is better than flint paper or sandpaper and lasts about three times as long. Get the fine grades,
½, 0, 3/0, 5/0, and 8/0, using them over a flat 3- by 5-in.,
rounded-corner, hardwood sanding block (some authorities
recommend a piece of linoleum over the block to give a slightly
more pliable surface). On finishes, use only 3/0, 5/0, and 8/0,
discarding them for a new piece as soon as they load up with
particles of the finish—otherwise they will scratch the surface.
For final sanding, use pliable, worn pieces previously used for
sanding clean wood.

If you want to finish a piece with varnish, shellac, or lacquer,
sand flat surfaces in straight lines with the grain, beginning

with No. 0 paper. When surfaces are smooth, dampen them with a soft cloth or sponge wrung nearly dry. This lifts unsanded wood fibers. Allow to dry, then sand over the surface with 3/0. Dampen again, and follow with No. 5/0. Always sand with the block, and if loaded spots appear on the paper, brush them out with a scrub brush before continuing. Round off outside sharp edges just a little, so that they later do not "wear white."

Bleach out surface spots with laundry bleaching solutions or oxalic acid (½ lb. oxalic acid crystals to 2 qt. warm water) brushed on freely and allowed to dry. Rinse off with several washes of clear water, then a wash containing a little white vinegar or acetic acid. (Such a bleach is also good for cleaning up old pieces before refinishing.) Sand afterward as before.

The wood can now be brought to any desired color by staining. Use water stains, for they are most permanent (even cloth dyes diluted in water work very well and can readily be mixed with more water or with each other to get a desired tint of a color). Put stain on evenly and thinly with a good medium-soft brush. Put on several thin coats rather than one thick, heavy (and consequently streaky) one. Stain at the same time a similarly prepared piece of waste wood, then go on to varnish and rub it to be sure your stain color is right. Walnut, particularly, darkens several shades when varnish or shellac is put on top of the stain—it may be best to use special clear-brushing wood lacquer (it seals end grain too).

Fillers go on next (if you must use them and lose the open grain), after the surface has been carefully dusted. Thin the filler with turpentine, and apply in several thin coats if necessary. Brush on with the grain in small areas, wiping off across grain with a cloth as soon as it turns gray (before it sets hard). Let the piece dry between coats for twelve to twenty-four hours. After the final coat, allow the piece to dry for a day; then put on one or two thin coats of shellac. Finishing coats of shellac, varnish, or lacquer go on top of this, and should preferably be waterproof and stainproof, particularly where white rings ruin appearance.

On walnut use three coats of varnish, first a good interior varnish, dried and sanded with 5/0 or 8/0 garnet paper to remove gloss and reduce varnish thickness. Dust carefully and cover with an even coat of good clear rubbing varnish. Allow this to dry, then rub with fine powdered pumice in water. Follow the grain; use even pressure; cover the whole surface without skipping or staying too long in one spot. Sprinkle enough pumice for the whole job on the surface before rubbing, and use water freely. Pumice the ends carefully to avoid wearing them through.

This is washed off carefully with a sheep's-wool sponge and dried with chamois or clean soft cheesecloth. Next is the finishing coat of rubbing varnish. Give it plenty of time to dry, then rub with pumice stone and crude oil. This cuts the gloss more slowly than pumice and water and gives a dull silky finish.

If you finish instead with shellac, rub between coats with pumice and paraffin oil, thinned for very hard finishes with a little benzine. After the final coat, rub the surface, then wipe clean and dry with soft cheesecloth.

After the preliminary coats of shellac, if color is too light, darken with careful application of alcohol-soluble aniline dyes. Make a weak solution of the proper dye, strain it through cheesecloth, add a little white shellac (two tablespoonfuls per pint of color) as a binder, and apply with a pad in a series of thin coats until the desired color is obtained. Thick application will cause streaks. Follow the grain as usual.

White pine can be reddened with raw sienna, browned with burnt umber, yellowed with linseed or a mixture of linseed and crude oil. Grayish or overly dark walnut can be improved with a little orange. Overly red mahogany can be mellowed with gamboge or browned with a very little of a thin solution of malachite green. Dull brown mahogany is brightened with Bismarck brown containing a little orange. Too heavy or streaky color can be corrected by rubbing with fine steel wool.

Any good furniture polish will protect a finish. Waxed pieces can be washed and rewaxed occasionally, and oiled pieces reoiled.

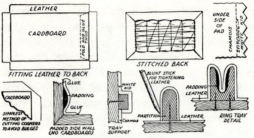

FIG. 431 · Details of lining jewel cases with leather. Padding is cotton batting, thinned at edges and glued lightly in place

A good polish for building up surfaces consists of 12 oz. of raw linseed oil and 6 oz. of acetic acid shaken together, then mixed with 6 oz. of alcohol and an ounce of butter of antimony.

Now for repairs: You'll need a quart bottle of 2/3 crude oil and 1/3 benzene, furniture glue, fine steel wool (3/0), 0000 pumice powder, 00000 sandpaper or 5/0 garnet paper, sticks of transparent shellac in proper colors, an alcohol lamp (don't use candle or gas flames because they deposit carbon that makes a black mark—make the lamp by cutting off an oilcan spout and inserting a wick), and a scalpel (make one from a grapefruit knife or by rounding off the end of an old paring knife).

Either you (no matter how careful you are) or someone else will occasionally break one of your pieces. All you can do is glue them together carefully with furniture glue and—*please*—give them a day to dry thoroughly. Scrape or sand off any glue showing outside mating edges, and rub in a little tinted linseed oil to hide the joint.

Pieces will suffer from rubbed edges, scratches, dents, and press marks. Rubbed edges result from wear. Rub over them with a piece of felt soaked in alcohol colored with walnut, oak, or mahogany stain to match the piece. Rub down surface scratches carefully with the crude-oil and benzene mixture. Then rub over the whole surface, first with a rag soaked in crude oil and dipped in the pumice powder, then with a dry rag. Press marks (from careless packing or bruises) are removed the same way.

Deep scratches must first be filled. Heat the scalpel over the alcohol lamp until it will melt off a little of the waxlike transparent shellac from the stick. "Putty" this into the gouge or scratch until it is filled. Be sure the scalpel doesn't get too hot, or it will burn surrounding finish, and don't let it get dirty! Then sand the built-up part flush with the surface and refinish as before. Dents can be treated similarly, although some can be swelled back flush with the surface by applying hot water or steam carefully (don't try this on veneer—it peels).

Details of finishing such pieces as the horse and dog heads of Chap. XX, etc., are given with the details of carving them. Other finishing elements are similarly given, except lining a jewel box. Lining a carved jewel box is a specialized finishing operation with wide application. Two typical boxes are shown in Figs. 433 and 434.

The box of Fig. 433 has chamois glued directly on the wood. Pieces should be slightly smaller than the space they are to cover for they are stretched into position by smoothing with a rounded stick, a spoon handle, etc. The ring slot at left is made by slotting a block as in Fig. 431, padding the edges with cotton, and gluing a piece of chamois over it.

〖 277 〗

FIG. 432 (TOP) · *Dull-finish carved surfaces framing oil paintings. Gothic-Renaissance style. (Courtesy F. Marchello.)* FIG. 433 · *A simple lining of glued-in chamois.* FIG. 434 · *More elaborate chamois and white sheepskin padded lining*

The box of Fig. 434 is lined with chamois and white sheepskin, the removable tray being built up on a cardboard frame. Ring tray, covering pads, and side walls are all padded with cotton batting, and the tops of the pads are sheepskin, notched and sewn to a chamois bottom. For side and bottom pads, cut cardboard pieces to fit, glue padding (thinner at the edges) to them, then cover with chamois as shown in Fig. 431. Notch the skin at the corners to prevent bulging, then glue the cardboard in place in the box. Adjacent pieces help to hold each other, but the padded top should be held by corner screws. Partitions can be made of thin wood, leather-covered as shown.

Always plan and lay out a piece in advance; don't rely on finishing to correct your mistakes, either in planning or in carving. This story will illustrate my point:

". . . In 1920, the Prince of Wales, now Edward VIII, touring the world, reached Rotorva, New Zealand, there to dedicate a public park in the presence of 5,000 Maori. In order to suitably frame the handsomely illustrated vellum recording the event, rare and valuable totora wood was cut from the oldest and finest war canoe extant and turned over to the greatest woodcarver in New Zealand for conversion into a work of art, priceless and beyond duplication. The woodworker on his own initiative fashioned a frame that measured four inches less across the top than the bottom. A howl went up, and he was instructed to make it over into a perfect rectangle. 'Can do,' said he, and did. Everything seemed O.K. until a stickler broke into lamentations. 'This will not do,' he declared. 'We cannot allow the great grandson of Her Beloved Majesty, Queen Victoria, to be the recipient of a second-hand article. Another frame must be fashioned and made right the first time.' Sound and fury ensued, but the alarmist had made his point.

"Another chunk of timber was cut from the war canoe, another frame was carved to specifications, and presented to the Prince with elaborate ceremony. In no particular did it compare with the original creation either in material or artistry. But it did not come under the second-hand classification, nor was the Prince ever made aware of the error."—From "Bob Davis Reveals:" in an interview with Prof. Peter Buck, Director of The Bishop Museum, Honolulu, Hawaii, and published in *The New York Sun* for Oct. 3, 1936.

SHARPENING · *Stones, Slips, Strops*

SHARPENING does not waste time, but saves it, for sharp tools cut far faster and easier (thus more accurately) than dull ones. The stone itself, coarse or fine, must be composed of sharp-edged grits—coarseness alone does not mean fast cutting.

Sharpening a tool comprises four operations: grinding, whetting, honing, and stropping. Grinding produces a fine saw-tooth cutting edge, usually with a feathery end of turned metal (Fig. 441 b), the wire edge, clinging to it. This must be removed and the size of the saw teeth reduced as much as possible. Whetting gives finer saw teeth, honing still finer ones, but still the wire edge— much finer now to be sure—persists. Stropping straightens out or breaks off these last saw teeth and removes the final wire edge. Once very fine saw teeth are produced, all four operations need not be gone through continually. Frequent stropping and less frequent honing will retain the edge until it is too blunt to cut well.

Either the old-fashioned, large-diameter, slow-speed, water-dipped grindstone, or the newer, smaller, faster emery wheel can be used for grinding, which is required only on new tools, broken edges, or those that have had a long period of service. The emery wheel shapes a tool faster, but will burn it if it is not dipped into water often. It is far better in this instance to be safe than sorry, for too much water never ruined a tool, and too much grinding heat *will*. It draws the temper, giving a soft tool end.

Tools should always be ground on the wheel periphery, with the wheel turning *toward* the cutting edge. If an emery wheel, it should not be too coarse. The periphery should be clean and square and kept that way by regular dressing with an emery stick, a bit of broken wheel, or a diamond dresser. Otherwise the wheel

How to sharpen and test a knife: Fig. 435 · *Whetting.* Fig. 436 · *Stropping.* Fig. 437 · *Hand stropping.* Fig. 438 · *Whetting a sloyd blade.* Fig. 439 · *Thumbnail test.* Fig. 440 · *Paper and tip tests for sharpness*

will load with bits of ground-off steel, will glaze and burn the tool. A crooked surface produces a crooked cutting edge, too. If the wheel has a tool rest, use it, and while sharpening, move the tool across the face of the wheel, thus wearing it evenly.

A broken or poorly shaped cutting edge should first be fed perpendicularly to the wheel to square it up. Then grind the bevel, which properly should vary with the hardness of the wood you plan to cut. A thinner cutting edge—one with a smaller included angle—cuts through wood more easily, but hard woods dull it so rapidly that a thicker edge is advisable. About 15 to 20 degrees included angle (Fig. 444 *a*) is suitable for tools to cut soft woods; 20 to 25 degrees gives the edge more support in hard woods.

When you grind an edge, hold the tool carefully at the proper angle and move it perpendicularly to the wheel (Fig. 441). Done properly, this will hollow-grind the edge slightly (Fig. 444 *b*), giving a little relief just back of the cutting edge that will make the tool hold its edge longer. Chisels and other single-ground tools are ground from the bevel side only, firmers and axes from both sides—in the latter case very evenly to be sure the cutting edge remains at the center of tool thickness.

Gouges must be rotated evenly from side to side (by a wrist-twisting motion) during grinding, so that the whole curved face is cut away evenly. Work carefully, or the corners will be ground away, putting them behind the bottom of the U, and the tool will have a tendency to stick. One gouge, say a ⅜-in. one, may be ground this way intentionally for use in cleaning up a ground close to a corner—but don't do it with the others.

Whetting and honing should really be considered together, for

How to sharpen and test firmers: FIG. 441 · *Grinding, showing resulting wire edge.* FIG. 442 · *Whetting.* FIG. 443 · *Stropping.* FIG. 444 · *Cutting edge angles.* FIG. 445 · *Hand stropping.* FIG. 446 · *Nail and chamfered-corner tests*

the processes are exactly alike, the difference being in the coarseness of the stone. The natural or quarried whetstone is Washita, yellowish, or grayish, and slow-cutting. The natural hone is Arkansas, a white, extremely hard, fine-grit stone that produces an exceptionally fine edge. If preferred, the two may be obtained together, with Washita on one side and Arkansas on the other. Manufactured stones of silicon carbide or aluminum oxide grits, such as Carborundum, are similar in appearance and cutting effect.

Good machine oil, or a fifty-fifty mixture of machine oil and kerosene, is used as a lubricant to prevent loading of the stone. Move tools in straight lines parallel with the axis of the stone. Only in this way can you keep the surface flat and square. If it gets out of square, grind it on the side of a grindstone, or rub down with sandstone or an emery brick. Cover stones when not in use, and keep them clean and moist with a few drops of oil. Clean natural stones by periodic washing with benzine, kerosene, or gasoline, or boil in water containing a little soda. Clean manufactured stones by putting them in a tin pan and heating in an oven. (This causes the old oil to be exuded.) Then wipe it off hot.

Gouges, parting tools, etc., must be finished inside with a "slip" or shaped stone. This is laid inside the curve or V and rubbed *outward* to remove wire edge. Some carvers lift the back end a little to produce a very slight bevel. Rest the tool on the bench with the edge projecting an inch or two for the stoning (Fig. 449).

Stropping is done on smooth leather, just as for a razor, except that many carvers use two strops, the coarser covered with a paste of crocus powder in oil, the second with a little oil only. Here is the second exception to the rule of sharpening against

How to sharpen and test a gouge: Fig. 447 · *Grinding, showing wrist-twist direction.* Fig. 448 · *Whetting or honing.* Fig. 449 · *Removing wire edge.* Fig. 450 · *Stropping, and proper edge shape.* Fig. 451 · *Stropping.* Fig. 452 · *Various shapes of slips*

the cutting edge—always trail the edge on the strop (Fig. 443).

Now to specific tools: Unless nicked or broken, the knife blade is never put on the grinding wheel. Its wedge shape provides proper clearance and support for the cutting edge without shaping. The blade is always sharpened on a flat stone (Fig. 435), being held at an oblique angle. Its side is not laid flat on the stone, for this produces too fine a cutting edge. Instead a further bevel is whetted on by lifting the back of the blade slightly, say 15 to 20 degrees (Fig. 436 *a*), before it is drawn down the stone. If very dull, use the Washita first. The Arkansas, providing the last stroke or two on each side is taken lightly and smoothly, will leave a light wire edge, easily removed by stropping (Fig. 436 *b*). Finally, strop the knife carefully once or twice against the palm of your hand (Fig. 437)—remember to keep the cutting edge *trailing!* Sloyd-bladed knives (Fig. 25, Chap. II) have a pronounced bevel from the edge halfway to the back and are sharpened by laying this bevel flat on the stone (Fig. 438). Whet and strop all the way back to the heel on both sides, and give the tip a bit extra.

To test for sharpness, draw the edge across your thumbnail (Fig. 439). It should catch, not slide. Or hold a piece of paper lightly between left thumb and forefinger and draw the edge across it (Fig. 440 *a*). It should cut cleanly and easily, not drag or bend. Test the blade end by swinging it obliquely across a piece of cardboard or soft wood (Fig. 440 *b*). It should cut in easily, without pulling. Stainless-steel blades are harder to sharpen, but hold an edge longer.

Firmers and chisels are sharpened similarly, except that the edge is pushed the length of the stone instead of being held from

Parting tools and scrapers: FIG. 453 · *Grinding.* FIG. 454 · *Edge detail.* FIG. 455 · *Stropping.*
FIG. 456 · *Stropping inside.* FIG. 457 · *Grinding scraper.* FIG. 458 · *Turning scraper edge*

the side. Hold the blade at an angle of 20 to 25 degrees with the
surface of the stone (Fig. 442 *b*), thus forming an end bevel relieved
by the hollow grinding. Sharpen the edge of a skew firmer similarly. Be sure each has a straight-line, uniformly sharp cutting
edge (Fig. 442 *a*), otherwise it will tear the wood instead of cutting.

Usually any woodcarving tool can be kept sharp for a long time
if you habitually strop, or hone and strop, it while you plan
the next cut. A little practice will teach you how. Whet a chisel
on the bevel face, finishing with a light stroke or two on the
flat face to remove wire edge. It is best to fasten the stones and
strops down, as in Fig. 240, Chap. XVII, so that both hands can
be used in sharpening. Test the stropped edge by the thumbnail
(Fig. 446 *a*), or chamfer the corner off a soft-wood block with a
single push (Fig. 446 *b*). Then inspect the cut face to see if it is
clean-cut. A final strop or two on your palm will help (Fig. 445).

Sharpen gouges similarly, except that you must remember
the wrist twist that insures even cutting over the whole edge
(Figs. 447 and 448). Stone the wire edge out with a slip (Fig. 449),
then whet and hone the blade. Slip a bit of strop bent to the proper
concavity off the edge to remove wire edge (Fig. 451). A sharp tool
"whistles" as it cuts across soft-wood grain.

The point of the V on a parting tool complicates the problem
of sharpening. Preliminary steps in sharpening are similar to
those for the chisel, except that both sides must be sharpened
squarely and evenly to avoid an edge like that of Fig. 453 *b*. A
V-shaped slip takes off wire edge if rubbed on each side in turn,
but it also has the tendency of rounding the bottom of the V
slightly, which accentuates the thick point (Fig. 454 *a*). Thin it,
by using the slip outside as in Fig. 454 *c*, until the edge, greatly

FIG. 459 · *Grinding an axe.* FIG. 460 · *Whetting or honing.* FIG. 461 · *Sharpening a point.* FIG. 462 · *Alternate method using a groove.* FIG. 463 · *Whetting or honing burin.* FIG. 464 · *Shaping burin cutting edge*

enlarged, would look like Fig. 454 b. This also removes the sharp meeting of the bevels just back of the cutting edge, which has a tendency to dig in and cause the tool to drag at the bottom.

Strop the parting tool like a firmer, or cut a V-groove on one edge of the strop, and draw the edge through that (Fig. 455). Strop inside against a square strop edge (Fig. 456).

Sharpen macaroni tools similarly.

A carving hatchet must have a knife edge. Grind it to have a slightly curving edge (Fig. 459), then whet, hone, and strop like a wide chisel, except that you will find it easier to draw the stone across it instead of drawing it across the stone (Fig. 460). Sharpen pointed scribers or other points by rotating them between the palms of your hands while you move them along the stone, (Fig. 461). Or rub them into a special groove (Fig. 462).

Burins are whetted outside originally just like a woodcarving tool (Fig. 464), but afterwards are usually kept sharp by whetting the solid end flat against the face of the stone or hone (Fig. 463).

Scrapers are sharpened quite differently from any other tool, because *they depend for their action on a wire edge or burr.* In regrinding a scraper, grind the end face square and the side face flat (Fig. 457), then rub a hardened steel bar along the edge with considerable pressure (Fig. 458 b) to create a burr. Rub across perhaps three times, first at about a 5-degree angle (Fig. 458 a1), then at 10 degrees (a2), finally at 15 degrees (a3).

Once you have edged a tool, protect it against nicking. Don't throw tools together haphazardly—keep them in a rack or in cloth pockets when not in use. A knife protects its own cutting edge when closed, but needs frequent cleaning and oiling.

INDEX

A

Acanthus, as carving motif, 222
African carving (see Carving)
Airplanes, models of, 116
Alphabets, 254–259
American carving (see Carving)
Animal, in a cage, 86
    expression in human caricatures, 137
    silhouettes of, 50
Antique finish, to get, 272
Appliqué carving, 217
Avodire, characteristics of, 18
Ax, carving with, 161
    to sharpen, 284

B

Backeroni, 173
Backgrounds, for appliqué, 218
    decorating by stamping, 165
    in low relief, 195
Back scratchers, ball-in-a-cage as ornament on, 86, 90
Baits, plug, for fishing, 43
Ball-in-a-cage, circular, 86, 89, 91
    general data on, 85–91
    as ornament on utensils, 86
    simple, how to make, 85
Balsa, used for life-size birds, 130
Bamboo, 115, 144
    as a model material, 119
Baren, how to make and use, 189–190
Bas-relief, definition of, 194
Basket pattern, stamped, 166
Basswood, characteristics of, 16
Beard, to carve, 242
Bed, decorated with panels, 203

Beech, characteristics of, 16
Bench, for carving, 176
Bending strength of wood, 22
Bezaleel, 4
Bible, references to carving in, 3, 4
    woods used in time of, 4
Birdhouse, from coconut, 48
    from hollowed log, 49
Bicycle, old-fashioned, to make from 1 piece, 104
Billiard ball, pieces carved from, 159
Bird, in a cage, 86, 88
    with fan wings and tail, 95
Birds, conventionalized, 128, 132
    heroic size, 133
    life-size, 130
    miniature, for dish gardens, 128, 129
    patterns for, 131
    pose of, 131
Blades, fan, interlacing, 93
Bleaching, for wood, 274
Block, linoleum, 186
    designs for, 187
    history of, 187
    to make, 188
    in more than one color, 190
    to print, 189
    printing on wood or leather, 190
    paraffin, carved for printing, 186
    rubber, carved, 186
    wood, to make, 190
    woods used for printing, 191
"Blood Altar," 6
Boat, model of, 111
Bone, carving, 157
"Bones," to make, 63
Book ends, dog motif on, 134
Boomerang, to make, 61

C

Dover Books on Art

A HANDBOOK OF ANATOMY FOR ART STUDENTS, Arthur Thomson. This long-popular text teaches any student, regardless of level of technical competence, all the subtleties of human anatomy. Clear photographs, numerous line sketches and diagrams of bones, joints, etc. Use it as a text for home study, as a supplement to life class work, or as a lifelong sourcebook and reference volume. Author's prefaces. 67 plates, containing 40 line drawings, 86 photographs—mostly full page. 211 figures. Appendix. Index. xx + 459pp. 5⅜ x 8⅜. 21163-0 Paperbound $3.00

WHITTLING AND WOODCARVING, E. J. Tangerman. With this book, a beginner who is moderately handy can whittle or carve scores of useful objects, toys for children, gifts, or simply pass hours creatively and enjoyably. "Easy as well as instructive reading," N. Y. Herald Tribune Books. 464 illustrations, with appendix and index. x + 293pp. 5½ x 8⅛.
20965-2 Paperbound $2.00

ONE HUNDRED AND ONE PATCHWORK PATTERNS, Ruby Short McKim. Whether you have made a hundred quilts or none at all, you will find this the single most useful book on quiltmaking. There are 101 full patterns (all exact size) with full instructions for cutting and sewing. In addition there is some really choice folklore about the origin of the ingenious pattern names: "Monkey Wrench," "Road to California," "Drunkard's Path," "Crossed Canoes," to name a few. Over 500 illustrations. 124 pp. 7⅞ x 10¾. 20773-0 Paperbound $2.00

ART AND GEOMETRY, W. M. Ivins, Jr. Challenges the idea that the foundations of modern thought were laid in ancient Greece. Pitting Greek tactile-muscular intuitions of space against modern visual intuitions, the author, for 30 years curator of prints, Metropolitan Museum of Art, analyzes the differences between ancient and Renaissance painting and sculpture and tells of the first fruitful investigations of perspective. x + 113pp. 5⅜ x 8⅜. 20941-5 Paperbound $1.50

TEACH YOURSELF TO STUDY SCULPTURE, Wm. Gaunt. Useful details on the sculptor's art and craft, tools, carving and modeling; its relation to other arts; ways to look at sculpture; sculpture of the East and West; etc. "Useful both to the student and layman and a good refresher for the professional sculptor," Prof. J. Skeaping, Royal College of Art. 32 plates, 24 figures. Index. xii + 155pp. 7 x 4¼. 20976-3 Clothbound $2.00

Dover Books on Art

STYLES IN PAINTING, Paul Zucker. By comparing paintings of similar subject matter, the author shows the characteristics of various painting styles. You are shown at a glance the differences between reclining nudes by Giorgione, Velasquez, Goya, Modigliani; how a Byzantine portrait is unlike a portrait by Van Eyck, da Vinci, Dürer, or Marc Chagall; how the painting of landscapes has changed gradually from ancient Pompeii to Lyonel Feininger in our own century. 241 beautiful, sharp photographs illustrate the text. xiv + 338 pp. 5⅝ x 8¼.
20760-9 Paperbound $2.25

THE PRACTICE OF TEMPERA PAINTING, D. V. Thompson, Jr. Used in Egyptian and Minoan wall paintings and in much of the fine work of Giotto, Botticelli, Titian, and many others, tempera has long been regarded as one of the finest painting methods known. This is the definitive work on the subject by the world's outstanding authority. He covers the uses and limitations of tempera, designing, drawing with the brush, incising outlines, applying to metal, mixing and preserving tempera, varnishing and guilding, etc. Appendix, "Tempera Practice in Yale Art School" by Prof. L. E. York. 4 full page plates. 85 illustrations. x + 141pp. 5⅜ x 8½.
20343-3 Paperbound $1.75

GRAPHIC WORLDS OF PETER BRUEGEL THE ELDER, H. A. Klein. 64 of the finest etchings and engravings made from the drawings of the Flemish master Peter Bruegel. Every aspect of the artist's diversified style and subject matter is represented, with notes providing biographical and other background information. Excellent reproductions on opaque stock with nothing on reverse side. 63 engravings, 1 woodcut. Bibliography. xviii + 289pp. 11⅜ x 8¼.
21132-0 Paperbound $3.50

A HISTORY OF ENGRAVING AND ETCHING, A. M. Hind. Beginning with the anonymous masters of 15th century engraving, this highly regarded and thorough survey carries you through Italy, Holland, and Germany to the great engravers and beginnings of etching in the 16th century, through the portrait engravers, master etchers, practicioners of mezzotint, crayon manner and stipple, aquatint, color prints, to modern etching in the period just prior to World War I. Beautifully illustrated —sharp clear prints on heavy opaque paper. Author's preface. 3 appendixes. 111 illustrations. xviii + 487 pp. 5⅜ x 8½.
20954-7 Paperbound $3.00

Dover Books on Art

THE COMPLETE BOOK OF SILK SCREEN PRINTING PRO-DUCTION, J. I. Biegeleisen. Here is a clear and complete picture of every aspect of silk screen technique and press operation—from individually operated manual presses to modern automatic ones. Unsurpassed as a guidebook for setting up shop, making shop operation more efficient, finding out about latest methods and equipment; or as a textbook for use in teaching, studying, or learning all aspects of the profession. 124 figures. Index. Bibliography. List of Supply Sources. xi + 253pp. 5⅜ x 8½.

21100-2 Paperbound $2.75

A HISTORY OF COSTUME, Carl Köhler. The most reliable and authentic account of the development of dress from ancient times through the 19th century. Based on actual pieces of clothing that have survived, using paintings, statues and other reproductions only where originals no longer exist. Hundreds of illustrations, including detailed patterns for many articles. Highly useful for theatre and movie directors, fashion designers, illustrators, teachers. Edited and augmented by Emma von Sichart. Translated by Alexander K. Dallas. 594 illustrations. 464pp. 5⅛ x 7⅛.

21030-8 Paperbound $3.00

CHINESE HOUSEHOLD FURNITURE, G. N. Kates. A summary of virtually everything that is known about authentic Chinese furniture before it was contaminated by the influence of the West. The text covers history of styles, materials used, principles of design and craftsmanship, and furniture arrangement—all fully illustrated. xiii + 190pp. 5⅝ x 8½.

20958-X Paperbound $1.75

THE COMPLETE WOODCUTS OF ALBRECHT DÜRER, edited by Dr. Willi Kurth. Albrecht Dürer was a master in various media, but it was in woodcut design that his creative genius reached its highest expression. Here are all of his extant woodcuts, a collection of over 300 great works, many of which are not available elsewhere. An indispensable work for the art historian and critic and all art lovers. 346 plates. Index. 285pp. 8½ x 12¼.

21097-9 Paperbound $3.00

Dover publishes books on commercial art, art history, crafts, design, art classics; also books on music, literature, science, mathematics, puzzles and entertainments, chess, engineering, biology, philosophy, psychology, languages, history, and other fields. For free circulars write to Dept. DA, Dover Publications, Inc., 180 Varick St., New York, N.Y. 10014.